Graphic
Encounters

Graphic Encounters

Comics and the Sponsorship of Multimodal Literacy

DALE JACOBS

B L O O M S B U R Y

NEW YORK • LONDON • NEW DELHI • SYDNEY

Bloomsbury Academic

An imprint of Bloomsbury Publishing Plc

1385 Broadway	50 Bedford Square
New York	London
NY 10018	WC1B 3DP
USA	UK

www.bloomsbury.com

First published 2013

Library of Congress Cataloging-in-Publication Data
Jacobs, Dale, 1966- author.
Graphic encounters : comics and the sponsorship of
multimodal literacy / Dale Jacobs.
pages cm
Includes bibliographical references and index.
ISBN 978-1-4411-2641-2 (pbk.) – ISBN 978-1-4411-2956-7 (hardcover)
1. Comic books, strips, etc., in education. 2. Comic books and
children. 3. Literacy. I. Title.
LB1044.9.C59J33 2013
371.33–dc23
2013007762

ISBN:	HB:	978-1-4411-2956-7
	PB:	978-1-4411-2641-2
	ePDF:	978-0-8264-4424-0
	ePub:	978-1-4411-3204-8

Typeset by Newgen Imaging Systems Pvt Ltd, Chennai, India
Printed and bound in the United States of America

CONTENTS

ACKNOWLEDGMENTS

I first began thinking about the ideas that have become *Graphic Encounters* in the fall of 2005; in the intervening years, many people have helped to bring this book to fruition. I am grateful to all of them and would like to take this opportunity to acknowledge their assistance and encouragement.

By the end of the 1980s, I had almost completely stopped reading comics. Then about ten years ago, one of my students, Michael Wheeler, began to loan me collections of comics and encourage me to see the possibilities inherent in the medium, and for that he has my deepest gratitude. Without that push, I doubt I would ever have come to teach classes on comics or do any writing about them. As well, I want to thank the students in my comics classes for their insights and enthusiasm, and for helping me think through some of the ideas in this book.

When I began to write *Graphic Encounters*, I was on sabbatical from the University of Windsor, just as I am as I write these Acknowledgements. This time to think and to write has been invaluable and I want to acknowledge the University of Windsor for granting it to me. I would also like to thank the English Department at the University of Windsor for their continuing support.

The ideas that led to this book and that form the bulk of Chapter 1 were first published in *College Composition and Communication* and *English Journal*. I would like to thank Deborah Holdstein at CCC for publishing "Marveling at *The Man Called Nova*: Comics as Sponsors of Multimodal Literacy" (original version of this article © 2007 by the National Council of Teachers of English). At *English Journal*, I would like to thank Louann Reid for publishing "More Than Words: Comics as a Means of Teaching Multiple Literacies" (original version of this article © 2007 by the National Council of Teachers of English). Both of these editors and the external reviewers were extremely encouraging at this early stage.

While doing the research for *Graphic Encounters*, I have had the occasion to consult a number of special collections libraries, including the Michigan State University Comic Art Collection, the Library of Congress, and the Cornell University Library Division of Rare and Manuscript Collections. A very big thank you to all the librarians and staff at these institutions, especially Randy Duncan at Michigan State for his guidance, encouragement, extensive knowledge, and good humor.

In terms of research, I also want to thank Dayna Cornwall for her excellent work in creating bibliographies on education and comics, as well as libraries and comics. Her work was tremendously helpful in shaping my thinking about Chapter One and in giving me the foundation for writing Chapter Seven.

I have also been blessed with feedback along the way from two of the best readers any author could hope to have. Greg Paziuk read early versions of most of the chapters in the book and his careful response helped to make the book stronger at every turn. For that I am extremely grateful. Heidi Jacobs gave me important and insightful feedback to early versions of several chapters, especially the chapter on libraries, and proofread the entire manuscript at a later stage. Getting feedback from the perspective of a practicing librarian transformed the libraries chapter in valuable ways and her comments later in the process helped to strengthen the prose throughout the book. As well, I want to thank Heidi for supporting and encouraging me during the whole project. Thanks for listening and being there to discuss ideas.

I would also be remiss if I didn't mention my local comic book stores and their owners: Tim Girard at Border City Comics and Shawn Cousineau at Rogues Gallery. To both of you, thanks for being there to talk about comics and for your support of my teaching and writing.

Finally, I want to thank David Barker at Bloomsbury Academic for his ongoing support of this project and everyone at the press for all their help along the way. I could not have asked for a better home for *Graphic Encounters*.

CHAPTER ONE

Introduction

Opening the door to the drugstore, I knew exactly where I was headed. In my pocket was my weekly dollar allowance, given to me by my father before we left our house that morning. We had driven 40 miles from Amisk, the very small town in which we lived, for our weekly trip to Wainwright, a town of about five thousand. In Wainwright, there were two large grocery stores, a department store, two hardware stores, both men's and women's clothing stores, a fabric store, a small bookstore, several restaurants, and a movie theatre. More importantly from the perspective of a 10-year-old boy, there were two drugstores, both of which carried comic books. It was 1976 and my dollar would buy me three comics, leaving me a dime for candy later in the week.

The comic books were nestled at the back of the store between the magazines and the paperback westerns and romances. I scanned the selection, giving them a quick once over before I began to make my decisions. Among the brightly colored covers were familiar titles like *The Amazing Spider-Man*, *The Fantastic Four*, *Superman*, *Detective Comics* (starring Batman), *Archie*, and *Casper the Friendly Ghost*, which I, at 10, had recently deemed a little kids' comic. (Archie was still acceptable because it was about the world of teenagers which, at 10, fascinated me.) I had read and even purchased all of these titles since I began reading comics a few years before, their words and images blending together to tell the stories in which I immersed myself.

Along the racks of familiar and often read titles, there were other titles I had seen many times before, but never read because they seemed to be for older kids, though I couldn't have put my finger on exactly why—*Ghost Rider* ("The Most Supernatural Hero of All!"), *Dr. Strange* ("Master of the Mystic Arts"), and *Howard the Duck* ("Trapped in a World He Never Made!"). These were, I was sure, the Marvel titles that I would soon be reading when I was old enough. I was, after all, a Marvelite, a True Believer who looked forward to Stan Lee's Soapbox and his pronouncements about the Marvel Universe as much almost as much as the comics themselves. Sure I read *Superman, Detective Comics,* and *Archie,* but only at my friends' houses, when there were no Marvel comics I hadn't read. At ten years of age, I only bought Marvel superhero comics, my horded allowance going only for what were, in my eyes, clearly superior comics. Like it said in every one of those comics I bought and read that year, Make Mine Marvel!

Gazing at the brightly colored comics in front of me, my search quickly narrowed to the Marvel titles. As I was reaching for my monthly copy of Spider-Man, I noticed a new title—*The Man Called Nova.* He had a great costume, the cover showed him fighting an enormous alien, it featured "The Human Rocket's Power-Packed Origin!" and, most importantly, it promised to be "In The Marvelous Tradition of Spider-Man!" I was hooked without even opening it. When my mother came to get me a few minutes later, I had a new title to buy every month along with *Spider-Man, The Fantastic Four,* and *The Avengers.* I handed over my thirty cents and on the way home immersed myself in the world of Rich Rider and his alter-ego Nova.

*   *   *

Over the past 30 years, comics have become an ever more visible and well-regarded part of mainstream culture. Graphic novels are now reviewed in major newspapers and featured on the shelves of both independent and chain bookstores. Major publishing houses such as Pantheon now publish work in the comics medium, including books such as Marjane Satrapi's *Persepolis,* David B.'s *Epileptic,* David Mazzucchelli's *Asterios Polyp,* and Alison Bechdel's *Fun Home.* Educational publishers such as Scholastic are also getting in on the act; in 2005, Scholastic launched its own graphic novels imprint, Graphix, with the color reissue of the first volume of Jeff Smith's highly acclaimed *Bone* series of graphic novels. At the book fairs of the National Council of Teachers of English (NCTE) and American Library Association (ALA) conferences, graphic novels and comic books are seen in ever greater numbers every year. School, public, and academic libraries are building graphics novels collections. Comics have, indeed, come out of hiding and into the mainstream.[1]

With all this activity and discussion surrounding comics, it seems timely to examine how we might think about the multiple ways comics are and can be encountered by readers and how these practices fit into ongoing debates about both comics and literacy. In examining these practices and the theory that might inform them, I wish to move beyond seeing the reading of comics as a debased or simplified word-based literacy. Instead, I want to advance two ideas: one, that reading comics involves a complex, multimodal literacy and, two, that by thinking about the complex ways comics are used to sponsor multimodal literacy, we can engage more deeply with the ways people encounter, process, and use these and other multimodal texts.

Given my own literate history, such an approach makes sense to me as a way to think about both comics and other multimodal texts. When I was growing up, comics were a major source of entertainment for me and many others of my generation and one of our main access points to imaginative worlds. Whether we read Marvel, DC, Archie, Harvey, or Gold Key, comic books were an important site of literate practice where we learned and practiced not only print literacy, but also, and perhaps more importantly, multimodal literacy—the ability to create meaning with and from texts that operate not only in alphabetic form, but also in some combination of visual, audio, and spatial forms as well. Comics were where I and many others first encountered multimodal texts and literacy, learning how to make meaning from the convergence of text and image; reading comics offered an alternative to the limited versions of literate practice offered in my experience of school during that time. Comic book publishers worked to enable a certain kind of literacy because it was to their advantage to do so; the relationship was reciprocal in that I developed the multimodal literacy needed to read the comics and the comic book companies received the money that I invested in the purchase of their products. In other words, the comic book companies acted as major sponsors of multimodal literacy for me and many other children in the 1970s, just as they had since the advent of comic books in North America in the mid-1930s.

My experience is fairly typical of many people (especially men) who grew up in North America from the 1930s on, especially through the end of the 1970s.[2] In the mid-1970s, comics were readily available to everyone since the distribution of comic books was primarily through newsagents and drugstores; direct distribution through specialty comic stores would not happen until the 1980s. As well, the price of comic books was not yet prohibitive for children and there was much less competition from other media (such as video games, the internet, and a proliferation of television channels) for the time, money, and attention of children. Today there are certainly greater opportunities for children (and adults) to engage in a variety of multimodal literacies and, in fact, we all do so everyday. In their resurgence, comics represent part of that landscape and, in the way they can act as analogs to other kinds of multimodal texts, comics open up a number of possibilities for thinking about multimodal literacy.

Over the years, comics have been used by many types of institutions, including for-profit companies, not-for-profit educational groups, churches, schools, parents' groups, and libraries to sponsor particular kinds of multimodal literacies. By examining the multiple ways these sponsorships have operated and the variety of purposes the expected multimodal literacies have served, it is possible to begin to understand the complexities of literacy sponsorship over the history of the comic book. Looking at this history will help us to think more deeply about multimodality and literacy in relation to comics, while also providing a new lens through which the medium of comics can be examined. As well, by focusing specifically on comics and the sponsorship of multimodal literacy, I seek to show the complexities of these concepts in a way that can be applied to other multimodal texts as well. Before I get to specific instances of multimodal literacy sponsorship in the coming chapters, however, I first need to explain some basic ideas about comics, the concepts of multimodal literacy and literacy sponsorship, and how these concepts can be combined to think about the sponsorship of multimodal literacy in comics.

Comics as multimodal texts/reading comics as multimodal literacy

Defining exactly what we mean when we use the term comics is notoriously difficult, especially since, as Charles Hatfield notes, "definitions [of comics] are not merely analytic but also tactical" ("Defining" 19). That is, these definitions are often tacit forms of argumentation. However, whether you subscribe to Scott McCloud's definition of comics ("Juxtaposed pictorial and other images in deliberate sequence, intended to convey information and/ or to produce an aesthetic response in the viewer" (9)) or to an expanded definition such as the one proposed by Dylan Horrocks (Comics are: a cultural idiom; a publishing genre; a set of narrative conventions; a kind of writing that uses words and pictures; a literary genre; and texts (34)), the visual is clearly an important part of comics and should not be seen as subservient to the written word. As Robert C. Harvey argues, comics are "a blending of visual and verbal content," a definition that begins to get at the importance of the presence of both of these semiotic systems (76). To this I would add, comics are a rhetorical genre, comics are multimodal texts, and comics are both an order of discourse and discrete discursive events. As cultural artifacts, sites of literacy, means of communication, discursive events and practices, sites of imaginative interplay, and tools for literacy sponsorship, comics are far more than simply "sequential art." In other words, comics—comic books, comic strips, and graphic novels—are media that use a combination of sequential art and text in order to create narrative meaning for the audience. This combination of words and images—multimodality— works to create meaning in very particular and distinctive ways; in a multimodal text, meaning is created through words, visuals, and the combination of the two in order to achieve effects and meanings that would not be possible in either a strictly alphabetic or strictly visual text.

If we think about comics as multimodal texts that involve multiple kinds of meaning making, we do not abandon the concept of word-based literacy, but strengthen it through the inclusion of visual and other literacies. This complex view of literacy is one that has begun to be embraced by many educators, including a number who have written about the use of comics in education such as

Rocco Versaci in "How Comic Books Can Change the Way Our Students See Literature" (2001), Gretchen Schwarz in "Graphic Novels for Multiple Literacies" (2002) and "Expanding Literacies through Graphic Novels" (2006), and Bonny Norton in "The Motivating Power of Comic Books: Insights from Archie Comic Readers" (2003). While Schwarz is the most specific of the three with regard to literacy, calling comics "a new medium for literacy that acknowledges the impact of visuals" and encouraging teachers "to explore and use the graphic novel to build multiple literacies," none of these articles go very far in fleshing out what is meant by a more complex view of literacy or how comics might be useful in teaching such literacies ("Graphic Novels" 262; "Expanding Literacies" 58). Meanwhile, texts such as William Kist's *New Literacies in Action: Teaching and Learning in Multiple Media* (2005) fully embrace broader definitions of literacy that are consistent with ideas of multimodal literacy, but apply these ideas to a much larger range of media than comics alone. Other texts, such as Stephen Cary's *Going Graphic: Comics at Work in the Multilingual Classroom* (2004) and Michael Bitz's *When Commas Meet Kryptonite: Classroom Lessons from the Comic Book Project* (2010), are informed to some degree by the idea of multimodal literacy, though this concept is certainly not the focus of either book. Although they agree on the importance of the interaction between words and images in comics and spend a great deal of time on how to use that interaction with students, in the end both see comics as a scaffold for alphabetic reading and writing and a bridge to more conventional literature. Multimodal literacy is certainly acknowledged, but traditional alphabetic literacy is finally still given primacy.

On the other hand, James Bucky Carter, in the introduction to his edited collection *Building Literacy Connections with Graphic Novels: Pages by Page, Panel by Panel* (2007), explicitly references the NCTE position statement on multimodal literacies, and this concept informs not only his ideas, but his choice of essays in the collection. As can be surmised by the collection title, *Teaching Visual Literacy: Using Comic Books, Graphic Novels, Anime, Cartoons, and More to Develop Comprehension and Thinking Skills* (2008), editors Nancy Frey and Douglas Fisher go even further in their exploration of visual and multimodal literacy in relation to comics. In the introduction, they write, "We think of visual literacy as describing the complex act of meaning making using still or moving images. . . . Further, these visual literacies are interwoven with textual ones, so that their interaction forms the basis for a more complete understanding" (1). This combination of visual and textual (what I would call alphabetic) literacies comes close to what I will shortly describe as multimodal literacy, a concept that also heavily influences the work of Katie Monnin, especially as seen in her book *Teaching Graphic Novels: Practical Strategies for the Secondary ELA Classroom* (2010). In a vivid metaphor for this conception of literacy, Monnin asks teachers to visualize two actors, "Print-text," who "voice[s] his lines in words," and "Image-text," who "act[s] out his image visually" (xvi). She continues the metaphor, writing, "Both will communicate meaning, yet they will do so in their own unique formats, sometimes standing alone, sometimes standing together" (xvi). Despite the excellent work by Monnin and the others cited here, the way we think about multimodal literacies in relation to comics still needs to be more fully articulated. By situating our thinking about comics, multimodality, and literacy within a framework that views literacy as occurring in multiple modes, comics can be used to greater effectiveness in teaching at all levels as a way to arm students with the critical literacy skills they need to negotiate diverse systems of meaning making.

Such a shift to regarding comics as multimodal texts, rather than debased written texts, means that it is important to examine the reading of comics as a form of multimodal literacy, rather than as a debased form of print literacy.[3] In making this kind of radical shift in our thinking, I draw on ideas from Gunther Kress and the rest of the New London Group and their groundbreaking and influential attempts to reconceive how we approach texts, literacies, and the pedagogies related to both.[4] Why is such a shift important? In "Design and Transformation: New Theories of Meaning," a key chapter in the New London Group's *Multiliteracies: Literacy Learning and the Design of Social Futures*, Kress sets out our contemporary communicative situation:

> The semiotic changes which characterise the present and which are likely to characterise the near future cannot be adequately described and understood with currently existing theories of meaning and communication. These are based on language, and so, quite obviously, if language is no longer the only or even the central semiotic mode, then theories of language can at best offer

explanations for one part of the communicational landscape only. Theories of language will simply not serve to explain the other semiotic modes, unless one assumes, counterfactually, that they are in every significant way like language. (153)

Kress clearly believes that other semiotic modes do not operate in exactly the same way that language does and that we need to develop "an adequate theory for contemporary multimodal textual forms . . . so as to permit the description both of the specific characteristics of a particular mode *and* of its more general semiotic properties which allow it to be related plausibly to other semiotic modes" (153–4). The ways in which we communicate have changed, as Kress and the rest of the New London Group see it. Teachers should engage this change in thinking about texts and literacies, rather than to see other modes as either hindrances or intermediate steps to the mastery of print literacy. Such a shift in thinking would acknowledge the multiple sites of literate practice of students, quite the opposite of my school experience in the 1970s when literacy was seen as only alphabetic, a situation that still reflects the experience of many current students at all levels of study.

This changed concept of communication, or "multiliteracies" as it has been christened by the New London Group, "engages with the multiplicity of communications channels and media" and with "the increasing salience of cultural and linguistic diversity" (Cope and Kalantzis 5). Speaking for the rest of the New London Group in the introduction to the collection, *Multiliteracies: Literacy Learning and the Design of Social Futures*, Bill Cope and Mary Kalantzis further explain, "Multiliteracies also creates a different kind of pedagogy: one in which language and other modes of meaning are dynamic representational resources, constantly being remade by their users as they work to achieve their various cultural purposes" (5). As we function in the world, our literacies operate not only in the alphabetic realm, but in the visual, audio, gestural, and spatial realms as well. We are all both consumers and producers of multimodal texts, navigating the world around us in complex ways that go well beyond functional print literacy or even an expanded, social constructivist version of print literacy. As Cope and Kalantzis explain, it is important to examine "the multimodal ways in which meanings are made on the World Wide Web, or in video captioning, or in interactive multimedia, or in desktop publishing, or in the use of written texts in a shopping mall" (5–6). I would add that multimodal meanings are also made in newspapers, in speeches by political candidates or government officials, in music videos, in sporting events, in visual art, and in many other instances of communication. Finally, and most importantly in terms of this book, multimodal meanings are made as people engage with comics, a type of multimodal text almost always left out of such expanded discussions of literacy or even the more restricted domain of visual rhetoric.[5] By examining comics as multimodal texts and reading comics as an exercise of multiliteracies or multimodal literacies, we can shed light not only on the literate practices that surround comics in particular, but on the literate practices that surround all multimodal texts and the ways in which engagement with such texts can and should affect our thinking about them.

As texts, comics provide a complex environment for the negotiation of meaning, beginning with the layout of the page itself. The comics page is separated into multiple panels, divided from each other by gutters, physical or conceptual spaces through which connections are made and meanings are negotiated; readers must fill in the blanks within these gutters and make connections between panels. Images of people, objects, animals, and settings, word balloons, lettering, sound effects, and gutters all come together to form page layouts that work to create meaning in distinctive ways and in multiple realms of meaning making. In these multiple realms of meaning making, comics are inherently multimodal, a way of thinking that moves beyond a focus on strictly word-based literacy. Cope and Kalantzis write that their approach "relates to the increasing multiplicity and integration of significant modes of meaning-making, where the textual is also related to the visual, the audio, the spatial, the behavioural, and so on. . . . Meaning is made in ways that are increasingly multimodal—in which written-linguistic modes of meaning are part and parcel of visual, audio, and spatial patterns of meaning" (5). By embracing the idea of multimodal literacy in relation to comics, then, educators can help students engage critically with ways of making meaning that exist all around them, since multimodal texts include much of the content on the internet, interactive multimedia, many contemporary, newspapers, television, film, instructional textbooks, and many other texts in our contemporary society.

According to Cope and Kalantzis, the key concept the New London Group developed in thinking about issues of multimodality, literacy, and pedagogy is that of Design, "in which we are both inheritors of patterns and conventions of meaning while at the same time active designers of meaning" (7). In this theory of multiliteracies, the semiotic modes which function as design elements in the meaning-making process are "Linguistic Meaning, Visual Meaning, Audio Meaning, Gestural Meaning, Spatial Meaning, and the Multimodal patterns of meaning that relate the first five modes of meaning to each other" (7). The concept of Design not only engages with these multiple modalities, but attempts to mediate between socially constructed patterns of meaning and individual agency in the production of meaning. Or, as Kress writes, "the remaking [of meaning] on the one hand reflects individual interest and, on the other, owing to the social history and the present social location of the individual, also reflects broad socio-cultural trends" (156). Design is thus an attempt to explain how we actually engage with and make meaning through various communicative media from our locations as situated individuals, affected and constructed by the cultures in which we live, but not determined by them.

For the New London Group, the concept of Design consists of three elements through which we make meaning: Available Design, Designing, and the Redesigned. Available Design includes all resources for Design, including both "the grammars of language, and the grammars of other semiotic systems," and "order[s] of discourse," each of which can be seen as "the structured set of conventions associated with semiotic activity (including use of language) in a given social space" and "a socially produced array of discourses, intermeshing and dynamically interacting" (New London Group 20). In speaking of Available Design, then, we are talking about all the available resources for making meaning in both the production and consumption of multimodal texts; as producers and consumers of texts, these resources are what we have to draw upon within our multimodal rhetorical environments. Given these resources, designing is "the process of shaping emergent meaning [involving] re-presentation and recontextualization" (22). Designing allows us to take available resources and use them to shape meaning (as both producers and consumers) from multimodal texts. What results is a new layer of meaning and a transformation of the initial Available Design: the Redesigned. In the Redesigned, we see "neither a simple reproduction (as the myth of standards and transmission pedagogy would have us believe)," nor a "simply creative [meaning] (as the myths of individual originality and personal voice would have us believe)" (23). The Redesigned, in its creation of new meanings, provides more available resources for design (Available Design), thus completing the ongoing loop of creating meaning from the multimodal texts that we create and consume every day. As Kress writes, "Design takes the results of past production as the resource for new shaping, and for remaking" (160). The process of Design provides us a way to understand how we create meaning and a means to productively engage with multimodal literacies, including the multimodal literacies involved in reading comics.

Thinking about comics as multimodal texts in practice: *Polly and the Pirates*

In order to further flesh out the concepts of multimodality and Design in relation to comics, let me turn to an example taken from Ted Naifeh's all-ages comic *Polly and the Pirates* to show how these concepts operate when we read a comics text. As you can see in the first two pages from the first issue of *Polly and the Pirates* (Figures 1.1 and 1.2), all of these Design elements are present, including a textual and visual representation of the audio element.[6] Despite the existence of these multiple modes of meaning making, however, the focus in thinking about the relationship between comics and education is almost always on the linguistic element, represented here by the words in the word balloons (or, in the conventions of comics, the dialogue from each of the characters) and the narrative textboxes in the first three panels (which we later find out are also spoken dialogue by a narrator present in the story).

As discussed earlier, comics are often seen as a simplified version of word-based texts, with the words supplemented and made easier to understand by the pictures. If we take a multimodal approach to texts such as comics, however, the picture of meaning making becomes much more complex. In exclusively word-based texts, our interaction with words forms an environment for meaning making that is extremely complex. In comics and other multimodal texts, there are five other elements added to the mix. Thought about in this way, comics are not just simpler versions of word-based texts, but can be viewed as the complex textual environments that they are.

FIGURE 1.1 *Polly and the Pirates #1, page 1. Polly and the Pirates ™ and © 2012 Ted Naifeh. Published by Oni Press Inc. Used with permission.*

FIGURE 1.2 *Polly and the Pirates #1, page 2.* Polly and the Pirates ™ *and* © 2012 Ted Naifeh. Published by Oni Press Inc. Used with permission.

It is, in fact, impossible to make full sense of the words on the page in isolation from the audio, visual, gestural, and spatial modes. For example, the first page of *Polly and the Pirates* #1 opens with three panels of words from what the reader takes to be the narrative voice of the story. Why do most readers interpret the words in this way? Partially it is because of *what* the words say—how they introduce a character and begin to set up the story—but also it is because of the text boxes within which the words are enclosed. Most people understand from their experiences of reading comics at some point in their history that words in text boxes almost always contain the narrative voice of the story and denote a different kind of voice than do words in dialogue balloons. The shape and design of these text boxes deviate from the even rectangles usually seen in comics and instead are depicted more like scrolls, a visual element that calls to mind both the time period and genre associated with pirates. Not only does this visual element help to place the reader in terms of both time and genre, but it, along with lettering and punctuation, also aids in indicating tone, voice inflection, cadence, and emotional tenor by giving visual representation to the audio element of the text. We are better able to "hear" the voice of the narrator because we can see what words are emphasized by the bold lettering and we associate particular kinds of voices with the narrative voice of a pirate's tale, especially emphasized here by the shape of the text boxes. Both the visual and the audio thus influence the way we read the actual words in a comic, as can be seen in these three opening panels.

It seems to me, however, that the key to reading the comic lies in going beyond the way we make meaning from the words alone and considering visual, gestural, and spatial elements. Important visual elements to consider are the use of line and white space, shading, perspective, distance, depth of field, and composition. The gestural refers to facial expression and body posture, while the spatial refers to the meanings of environmental and architectural space, which, in the case of comics can be conceived as the layout of panels on the page and the relation between these panels through the use of gutter space. The opening panel depicts a ship, mainly in silhouette, sailing on the ocean; we are not given details, but instead see the looming presence of a ship that we are led to believe is a pirate ship by the words in the text boxes. The ship is in the center of an unbordered panel and is the only element in focus, though its details are obscured. The unbordered panel indicates openness, both literally and metaphorically, and this opening shot thus acts in much the same way as an establishing shot in a film, orienting us both in terms of place and in terms of genre. The second panel pulls in closer to reveal a silhouetted figure standing on the deck of the ship. She is framed between the sails, and the composition of the panel draws our eyes toward her as the central figure in the frame. She is clearly at home, one arm thrust forward while the other points back with sword in hand, her legs anchoring herself securely as she gazes across the ocean. The third panel pulls in even farther to a close-up of her face, the top half in shadow and the bottom half showing a slight smile. She is framed by her sword on the left and the riggings of the ship on the right, perfectly in her element, yet obscured from our view. Here and in the previous panel, gestural and visual design indicate who is the center of the story and the way in which she confidently belongs in this setting. At the same time, the spatial layout of the page and the progression of the panels from establishing shot to close-up and from unbordered panels to bordered and internally framed panels help us to establish the relationship of the woman to the ship and to the story; as we move from one panel to the next, we must make connections between the panels that are implied by the gutter. Linguistic, visual, audio, gestural, and spatial elements combine in these first three panels to set up expectations in the reader for the type of story and its narrative approach. Taken together, these elements form a multimodal system of meaning making.

What happens in the fourth panel serves to undercut these expectations as we find out that the narrative voice actually belongs to one of the characters in the story, as evidenced by the shift from text box to dialogue balloon even though the voice is clearly the same as in the first three panels of the page. Spatially, we are presented with a larger panel that is visually dominated by the presence of a book called *A History of the Pirate Queen*. This book presumably details the story to which we had been introduced in the first three panels. The character holding the book is presenting it to someone but because of the composition of the panel, is also effectively presenting it to us, the readers. Thus, the gesture becomes one of offering this story up to us, a story that simultaneously becomes a romance as well as a pirate story as seen in the words the character says and the way she says them (with the bold emphasis on "dream" and "marry"). At this point, we do not know who this character is or to whom she is speaking and the answers to these questions will be deferred until we turn to the second page.

On the first panel of page two, we see three girls, each taking up about a third of the panel, with both them and the background in full focused detail. Both the words and facial expression of the first girl indicate her stance toward the story, while the words and facial expression of the second girl indicate her indignation at the attitude of the first girl (who we learn is named Sarah). The third girl, who the dialogue names as Polly, is looking to the right, away from the other two, and has a blank expression on her face. The next panel depicts the second and third girls, pulling in to a tighter close-up that balances one girl on either side of the panel and obscures the background so that we will focus on their faces and dialogue. The unbordered panel again indicates openness and momentary detachment from their surroundings. Polly is at a loss for words and is not paying attention to the other girl, as indicated by the ellipses and truncated dialogue balloons, as well as the fact that her eyes are once more pointing to the right, away from the other girl. Spatially, the transition to the third panel once more encloses them in the world that we now see is the classroom of a school in an overhead shot that places all of the students in relation to the teacher. The teacher's words serve to restore order to the class and, on a narrative level, give a name to the last of the three girls and the narrative voice of the opening page. The story of the pirates that began on page one is now contained within the world of school and we are left to wonder how the tensions between these two stories/worlds will play out in the remaining pages. As you can see, it is much more than words alone that are used to make meaning in these first two pages of *Polly and the Pirates*.

What I have just described is my own process of making meaning from these pages of *Polly and the Pirates* and, as such, is one of many possible meanings within the matrix of possibilities inherent in the text. As a reader, I am actively engaging with the "grammars," including discourse and genre conventions, within this multimodal text as I seek to create/negotiate meaning; such a theory of meaning making with multimodal texts acknowledges the social and semiotic structures that surround us and within which we exist, while at the same time recognizes individual agency and experience in the creation of meaning. Knowledge of linguistic, audio, visual, gestural, and spatial conventions within comics affects the ways in which we read and the meanings we assign to texts, just as knowledge of conventions within word-based literacy affects the ways in which those texts are read. For example, all of the conventions discussed above in terms of the grammar of comics would have been available to Naifeh as he created *Polly and the Pirates*, just as they are also available to me and to all other readers of his text.

These conventions form the underlying structure of the process of making meaning, while familiarity with these conventions, practice in reading comics, interest, prior experience, and attention given to that reading all come into play in the exercise of agency on the part of the reader (and writer). Structure and agency interact so that we are influenced by design conventions and grammars as we read, but are not determined by them; though we are subject to the same set of grammars, my reading of the text is not necessarily the same as that of someone else.

Reading and writing multimodal texts, then, is an active process, for creators, but also for readers who by necessity engage in the active production of meaning and who use all resources available to them based on their own familiarity with the comics medium and its inherent grammars, their histories, life experiences, and interests. Every act of creating meaning from a multimodal text, happening as it does at the intersection of structure and agency, thus contributes to the ongoing process of becoming a multimodally literate person. By helping students to become conscious and critical of the ways in which they make meaning from multimodal texts such as comics, teachers can then help students to become more literate with a wide range of multimodal texts with which they come in contact everyday. Complicating the view of comics so that they are not seen as simply an intermediary step to more complex word-based texts, teachers can more effectively help students to become active creators, rather than passive consumers, of meaning in their interactions with a wide variety of multimodal texts. The real power of comics can then be harnessed in the classroom as students are prepared for better negotiating their worlds of meaning. When it comes to comics (and other multimodal media), though, teachers are not the only or even the primary sponsors of multimodal literacy.

Comics and literacy sponsorship

In viewing comics as complex multimodal texts and the reading of comics as a complex form of multimodal literacy involving an ongoing process of Design, we open up possibilities for thinking about comics in the lives of readers. Add to this multimodal view of comics the idea that comics can be used in highly complex relationships of literacy sponsorship and we see the potential that exists when we engage with comics in meaningful ways. The concept of sponsors of literacy is one I borrow from Deborah Brandt's 1998 article of the same name. In that article, Brandt describes "a conceptual approach that begins to connect literacy as an individual development to literacy as an economic development," an approach to written literacy that I propose to extend to multimodal literacies as defined by the New London Group (166). Brandt defines literacy sponsors in this way:

> Sponsors, as I have come to think of them, are any agents, local or distant, concrete or abstract, who enable, support, teach, model, as well as recruit, regulate, suppress, or withhold literacy—and gain advantage by it in some way. Just as the ages of radio and television accustom us to having programs *brought* to us by various commercial sponsors, it is useful to think about who or what underwrites occasions of literacy learning and use. Although the interests of the sponsor and the sponsored do not have to converge (and, in fact, may conflict) sponsors nevertheless set the terms for access to literacy and wield powerful incentives for compliance and loyalty. Sponsors are a tangible reminder that literacy learning throughout history has always required permission, sanction, assistance, coercion, or, at minimum, contact with existing trade routes. Sponsors are delivery systems for the economies of literacy, the means by which these forces present themselves to—and through—individual learners. (166–7)

As will be seen later in this chapter (as well as in Chapters two, three, and four), mainstream comic book publishers such as Marvel, DC, and EC act as sponsors of multimodal literacy. When libraries use comics as a way to draw in so-called reluctant readers (see Chapter seven) or when teachers introduce comics into their curricula, comics are being used as a way to sponsor particular kinds of multimodal literacy. When churches use comics to get teens to think about the Bible (see Chapter five) or parents' groups sponsor comics about American heroes (see Chapter three), comics are being used as a way to sponsor yet another kind of multimodal literacy. When non-profit groups form partnerships with comic book publishers, as was the case with the Children's Television Workshop and Marvel Comics in the 1970s, they are acting as sponsors of multimodal literacy (see Chapter six). Again, the relationships here are reciprocal in that both the sponsored and the sponsor get something from the relationship; the sponsored is entertained *and* develops multimodal literacy (in an often complex relationship with the particular goal of the sponsor) and the sponsor receives, depending on the relationship, money, patrons, salaries, tax support, parishioners, pride, fulfillment, or some combination of these or other possible advantages. Advantages accrue to both in the relationship so that, in general, literacy sponsorship is beneficial to both the sponsor and the sponsored.

These examples emphasize the positives of literacy sponsorship from various institutional perspectives, just as I am, for the most part, emphasizing the positives of literacy sponsorship from the readers' point of view. But are there negative ways in which to view this literacy sponsorship? Certainly Fredric Wertham thought so, as evidenced by his influential 1953 book *Seduction of the Innocent*. A psychiatrist, Wertham wrote *Seduction of the Innocent* as a warning about what he saw as the many possible detrimental effects of comics on children, including juvenile delinquency, abnormal sexual development, and illiteracy. The problem, as he saw it, lay in the "extreme avidity" that children demonstrated toward comics and the graphic nature of most comics that glorified violence and sexual depravity while simultaneously impeding the development of print literacy (50). Wertham baldly asserted that "Comic books are death on reading" (*Seduction* 121). He went on to write,

> Reading troubles in children are on the increase. An important cause of this increase is the comic book. A very large proportion of children who cannot read well habitually read comic books. They are not really readers, but gaze mostly at the pictures, picking up a word here and there. Among the worst readers is a very high percentage of comic-book addicts who spend very much time "reading" comics books. They are bookworms without books. (*Seduction* 122)

Simply put, children who read comic books were not really reading, they were simply looking at the pictures as a way to avoid engaging in the complex processes of learning to read words. The problem, according to Wertham, was that in reading comics children focused far too much on the image to make meaning and avoided engaging with the written word, a semiotic system that Wertham clearly saw as both more complex and more important. According to Wertham, these "comic-book addicts" were not gaining specialized literacy through their relationship with comic books, nor were they even beginning on a path toward more developed word-based literacy. Rather, their addiction—much like what is often supposed of an addiction to drugs—led them away from the world of literacy (and respectability) and toward the worlds of juvenile delinquency and sexual depravity.[7]

The comparison of comics to drugs is an apt metaphor for thinking in complex ways about the literacy sponsorship I am describing here. Wertham's comparison of literate practices to drugs is not a new idea. Rather, the connections go back to antiquity when thinkers such as Gorgias and Plato compared the effect of words to the effect of drugs. For example, in his *Encomium of Helen*, Gorgias argues that

> The effect of speech upon the condition of the soul is comparable to the power of drugs over the nature of bodies. For just as different drugs dispel different secretions from the body, and some bring an end to disease and others to life, so also in the case of speeches, some distress, others delight, some cause fear, others make the hearers bold, and some drug and bewitch the soul with a kind of evil persuasion. (53)

According to Gorgias, words *do* have an effect on the soul, just as drugs have an effect on the body, and this effect can be positive (such as delight) or negative (such as distress). Similar claims can be made of the effects of other literate practices, such as reading comics or other multimodal texts; they cannot be seen as wholly positive or wholly negative because the use of literacy embodies the full spectrum of possible consequences. Even Wertham acknowledged as much, writing that although "[a]ll comic books with their words and expletives in balloons are bad for reading . . . not every comic book is bad for children's minds and emotions" (*Seduction* 10). Moreover, even a particular literate act may be viewed as simultaneously positive and negative, depending on the perspective from which one views that situation.

To these ends, Plato used the term *pharmakon*—a notoriously slipperly and ambiguous term that can mean everything from drugs to poison to remedy to charm to medicine (to name only a few possible meanings)—as a metaphor for thinking through a variety of literate practices and the shifting attitudes toward those practices. Just as the attitude of the medical establishment and general public toward smoking is very different now than it was in 1953, so too are most people's attitudes toward comics different now from those expressed by Wertham and others in 1953.[8] As well, just as the use of a drug such as coffee may be viewed as both positive by the user (*Coffee helps me get through my day of tedious meetings*) and negative by the user's doctor (*Your excessive use of coffee is causing ulcers*), so may the reading of comics be seen as positive by the user (*Comics help me to escape and deal with the confusing world around me*) and negative by the user's parent (*You need to quit reading comics and go play outside*). Even the same person can see drugs in different lights depending upon the particular situation (the pleasure felt during a night of drinking versus the feeling the hangover induces the morning after), just as that person can see literate practices differently depending upon the situation (the pleasure felt during a night of reading comics versus the feeling the next morning of not having finished the assigned homework). In invoking the classical comparison of drugs to literate practices, I wish to complicate the idea of the relationship of literacy sponsorship and to establish that this relationship is often ambiguous, neither wholly positive or negative, much like any individual's experience with any particular version of literacy.

If we return to the definition of literacy sponsorship, we can see that Brandt argues that *every* sponsorship of literacy involves gaining an advantage of some sort (including teachers through salaries and job satisfaction and parents through pride in their children). That is not to say that those sponsored get nothing from the relationship. For example, the literate practices learned in reading comics not only provide pleasure for the reader, but they also provide transfer value to other forms of literacy, both multimodal (such as the internet, film, or television) and alphabetic. This transfer value was, unbeknownst to me at the time, a side benefit of reading comics that helped prepare me for other kinds of multimodal texts I would encounter in my later life. The comic book companies in the 1970s, however, had no investment in my other forms of literacy and would gain little or no advantage in the promotion of other kinds of literacy. While comic book companies did not denigrate or critique other forms of literacy when I was growing up, neither did they overtly push children to engage in other literacies; their interests as the sponsors of literacy concerned the promotion of the reading of comics in general and their comic books in particular. By examining my own experience as a child growing up reading Marvel comic books, I want to flesh out the basic ideas of multimodal literacy sponsorship before moving on to specific moments in the history of comics.

The making of true believers: Marvel Comics as a sponsor of multimodal literacy

The comics industry's sponsorship of my literacy ensured that I, along thousands of other kids, would plunk down my allowance each week to purchase their products, happily consuming the cliffhanger stories that would necessitate the purchase of next month's issue. The serial nature of comics, especially of Marvel and DC, pushed readers to spend their limited capital on not just comics, but particular series of comics in which the reader became interested. But more than that, Marvel (and, I think, to a lesser extent DC) sought to create a coherent universe in which events in one title affected the events in another title. Spider-Man might team up with Thor in an issue of *Amazing Spider-Man*, only to see the conclusion of the story happen in *The Mighty Thor*. As a result of this overarching cross-title narrative, there was a sense with Marvel comics from the early 1960s on (certainly through the 1970s and, even more so, today) that in order to understand the fabric of the Marvel Universe and its continuity, you really needed to read every title. Marvel was not only concerned with sponsoring the multimodal literacy of comics, but they specifically wanted to sponsor such literacy as it related to their own comics. The desire to create a need for your product and then sell more of it than your competition lies at the heart of every business endeavor, but Marvel was legendary in its attempts to create the loyalest of loyal readers (who Stan Lee variously called True Believers, Marvelites, Real Frantic Ones, and other names designed to create a collective identity) who would identify completely, if not exclusively, with Marvel Comics/comics. As a sponsor of literacy, Marvel implied that comics were not only important, but that they should form one of the central literate behaviors for children through young adults (a view that ignores the notion that comics should be seen as a stepping stone to higher forms of print literacy).

But what makes a reader decide to engage with the multimodal story within a comic book? For the answer to that question, let's turn to the cover of *Nova* #1 (see Figure 1.3). As I looked at the

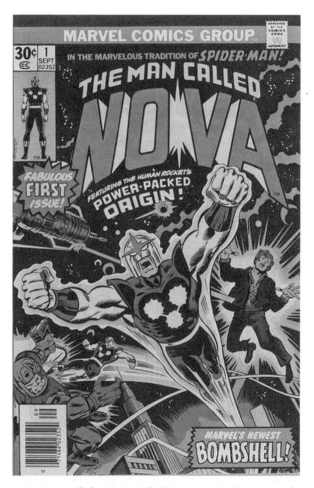

FIGURE 1.3 *Cover of The Man Called Nova #1. © 2012 Marvel Entertainment, Inc. and its subsidiaries.*

cover on a summer afternoon in 1976, I knew that it was not, strictly speaking, part of the story, but was nonetheless extremely important in determining whether or not I would even give the story a chance. Given a short amount of time and a limited amount of resources (a 1-dollar allowance), the comic book buyer (much like book buyers everywhere) decided quickly whether or not to take the book from the shelf and leaf through it (and then perhaps purchase it). Seen in these terms, the cover was an important initial space of Design because it determined whether or not any more Design would even take place. It is useful, then, to think about the cover as what Gerard Genette calls a paratext or confluence of paratextual elements, those elements that surround the narrative text itself. As Genette writes, "the paratext is what enables a text to become a book and to be offered as such to its readers and, more generally, to the public. More than a boundary or a sealed border, the paratext is, rather, a *threshold*, or—a word Borges used apropos of a preface—a 'vestibule' that offers the world at large the possibility of either stepping inside or turning back" (1–2). Designed with the purpose of creating interest in the comic that will then lead to its purchase, the cover of *Nova* #1 draws on available design resources to create a cover, itself a paratext, that literally acts as a threshold for its potential readers as they decide whether to step inside or turn back.

As a 10-year old, the cover of *The Man Called Nova* #1 caught my eye partially because of the art (visual design), the written text (linguistic design), the visual portrayals of bodies and facial expressions (gestural design), and the combination of all of these elements (multimodal design). The cover featured a collage of images, two of which were Nova in his yellow and blue costume, while one was Nova's alter ego Rich Rider being transformed into Nova by cosmic beams. In addition to these visual elements (that include elements of the gestural), there was a great deal of visual information, including the comic's new logo, the Marvel Comics logo, the price, the date, the Comics Code seal (itself a reference to the history of censorship in comics), and a number of written taglines designed to draw the potential reader into the book.[9] These written taglines promised that the book was "In the Marvelous tradition of Spider-Man!," that this "Fabulous First Issue!" featured "The Human Rocket's Power-Packed Origin!," and that Nova was "Marvel's Newest Bombshell!" A variety of colors were used for each of these blocks of text and jagged text-boxes were used to offset some of this written information. Exclamation points, a staple of comics, were also used to add to the urgency and excitement promised by the cover and the lettering of the written text further conveyed this physical and kinetic power. Combined with the distinctive red and yellow title banner of *A Man Called Nova*, written elements used the semiotics and grammar of a written system, while also pulling on the design elements of the visual to combine in multimodal ways that could be conceived as both hybrid and intertextual. That is, as we read (and write), we engage in acts of hybridity ("articulating in new ways, established practices and conventions within and between different modes of meaning") and intertextuality ("the potentially complex ways in which meanings . . . are constituted through relationships to other texts, either real or imaginary, to other text types (discourse or genres), to other narratives, and other modes of meaning") (New London Group 30). The cover and the multimodal narrative to which the cover hopes to pull you in operate as hybridized and intertextual sites of meaning making.

As a young but seasoned reader of comics, I immediately understood the intertextual reference to Spider-Man, the importance of and pleasure in an origin story (crucial to the superhero genre of comics), and the status of first issues for both readers and collectors of comics (often, of course, overlapping categories).[10] Further, the cover's other visual elements also operated as hybridized intertextual markers. For example, the movement lines that implied the speed with which Nova flew on the cover, and the force lines that surrounded both Nova's blow to Zorr, his alien enemy, and the cosmic rays that struck the young man soon to be revealed as Rich Rider, Nova's alter ego, drew on the semiotic traditions of comics for their meaning. As a comics reader, I could have quickly interpreted what these lines were designed to represent while also making connections both to other comics (how does this implied movement compare to Spider-Man?) and to other textual forms (how does this implied narrative that moves from origin to fighting what must be an alien menace compare to science fiction novels, fiction, or television?).

The three images of Nova/Rich Rider worked both as a collage (a form with which readers would be familiar from not only comics, but certainly from magazines, television, and film) and as the kind of implied narrative I just mentioned, with each operating as a panel in the narrative sequence. The creation of panels here operated especially well for readers familiar with the semiotic conventions of comics because comics readers are so used to sequential art implying a narrative continuity that they easily see the images in this collage as panels with implied gutters representing the passage of narrative time. In this way, the whole of the issue, from origin to warding off an alien menace was encapsulated in the cover's opening collage. Finally, the central image of Nova that dominated the cover showed him in his distinctive blue and yellow costume flying at a very high speed (notice the movement lines), muscled arms outstretched toward the reader in a gesture of power, mouth open and jaw locked in an expression of intensity. The gestural intersected with the written and the visual in a hybridized form that referenced many other possible texts; each reader would take the available resources of Design (slightly different for each reader) and in the process of Designing create the Redesigned; the results of this process would then determine whether or not the reader opened the book.

The real question, then, was whether or not the cover would seduce a young reader (i.e. me) into buying the comic. And if it did, what would that seduction entail? If we listen to Wertham, comics are clearly in the business of seducing innocent children toward a set of literate practices (though he would never have seen these practices as literate in any way) that were imbricated in a way of thinking and being in the world that led to illiteracy, juvenile delinquency, and sexual depravity. For Wertham, the idea of seduction in comics was more than purely metaphoric:

> Comic books stimulate children sexually. That is an elementary fact of my research. In comic books over and over again, in pictures and text, and in the advertisements as well, attention is drawn to sexual characteristics and to sexual actions.. . . That is not the free development of children, that is a sexual arousal which amounts to seduction. (*Seduction* 175)

He went on to detail what he saw in early 1950s comics: the ways in which the illustrations of women emphasized their sexuality, the sexual situations that were detailed, and cases like the "subtle atmosphere of homoeroticism which pervades the adventures of the mature 'Batman' and his young friend 'Robin'" (*Seduction* 190).

These pervasive depictions of deviant sexual behavior, he contended, interfered with the natural sexual development of children through an unhealthy process of seduction; he was especially concerned that the "Batman type of story may stimulate children to homosexual fantasies, of the nature of which they may be unconscious" (*Seduction* 191). Did *The Man Called Nova* excite such fantasies? After all, Nova is described on the cover of issue #1 as "Marvel's Newest Bombshell!" Was he meant—consciously or unconsciously—to be seductive in that way? This question can never be answered, but it does lead to some other, more important ones. For example, did the reading of Marvel comics stimulate its young readers sexually? What place did these comics play in the sexual development of their readers? Perhaps this link between comics and burgeoning sexuality accounts for some of the shame of which Jonathon Lethem writes when he describes his experience sharing comics as a child in the 1970s as both "miraculous and pornographic" (13). As one of the central forms of literacy for many children in the 1970s, including myself, comics certainly played a part (along with other forms of literate practice) in the formation of identity as we thought through how we fit into the world, including how we fit as developing sexual beings. In the comics I read, I saw physically beautiful people (both male and female) interacting in situations that might be sexually charged (such as a kiss), unconsciously coded (such as the relationship between mentor and teen sidekick), or *seemingly* non-sexual (such as flying, which involves an adolescent fantasy of power). In retrospect, I can see that reading these comics (along with watching television, reading print books, attending school, and so on) gave me ways of thinking and being in the world and ways to deal with burgeoning sexuality. In this way, sexuality was certainly tied to literacy, even though I (or, I suspect, most other children) would have been unable to see it at the time.

Therefore, it is important to consider the role sexuality and seduction can play in the relationship that develops through literacy sponsorship. If comics like *A Man Called Nova* operate at an unconscious level of sexual seduction (even at the often discussed level of adolescent power fantasies), let me ask again, what is entailed in that seduction? As discussed earlier, the cover of *A Man Called Nova* #1 operates as a kind of paratextual gateway, beckoning the reader toward what lies hidden under the covers. For developing adolescents, there is certainly an element of sexual fantasy that lies within those covers, but that fantasy is always already wrapped up with the particular kind of multimodal literacy I have been describing (just as it is wrapped up with other forms of literacy). That is, sexual seduction is wrapped up with seduction (and possible addiction) to a particular kind of literacy that entails a particular way of thinking and being in the world.[11] Wertham saw this seduction as the worst possible situation for children because he saw children as having virtually no agency in the relationship and powerless before the seductive/addictive sway of comics. However, as I have tried to show, the relationship of seduction/sponsorship set up in this dynamic can also accrue tremendous benefits on the one being seduced/sponsored, especially if we think in terms of Design and grant a much larger degree of agency to comics readers than was granted by Wertham. The seduction/sponsorship embodied in comics such as *A Man Called Nova* is complicated and, like the earlier metaphor of drugs, is neither wholly positive nor negative but instead relational, with all of the complexities and disparate agendas that word entails.

The use of written, visual, and multimodal design on the cover of *Nova* #1 highlights how *Nova* #1 operates as a hybrid text that exists within the specific conventions associated with comics, while at the same time drawing on many other available resources for Design. The cover of *Nova* #1 articulates the possibility of these conventions in new ways through the juxtaposition of multimodal elements and the intertextual referencing that these elements imply. These conventions influence but do not determine how we read and react to texts since each person who engages with a text such as *Nova* #1 is situated differently with respect to not only comics as an order of discourse, but with respect to all other orders of discourse that might interact and influence us as we read the text. As I looked at the cover to that first issue of *Nova*, I was both consciously and unconsciously bringing to bear a vast array of design resources in ways that were heavily influenced by both comics as an order of discourse, but also the social situatedness of a 10-year-old white boy growing up in rural Alberta. My knowledge of comics was enough to convince me, for example, that the comparison of Nova to Spider-Man should translate into action and humor (because everyone knew Spidey's fights were great and that he had the best one-liners in comics) and that origin stories were important in understanding characters.

However, since I was not old enough to have read Lee and Ditko's earliest Spider-Man comics, I could not entirely grasp that the series' creator, Marv Wolfman, intended the series to be a nostalgic throwback to earlier days of superhero comics in which there was no concern for comics to be "relevant" to the world around them, as was happening to varying degrees in many 1970s comics in response to the social upheavals of the late 1960s. Wolfman was clearly working against such a trend, trying instead to create a comic that was, in his own words, "fun, goofy, and traumaless" (n.p.). In many ways, then, *Nova* can be seen as an intertextual backlash against this trend toward "relevance," and, indeed, it is likely that many readers in 1976 did read it this way. As a 10-year-old boy with little experience of either older comics or the civil unrest of the previous decade, I did not. Instead, I read the cover of *Nova* #1 in ways that allowed me to make meaning within my own situatedness and experience with a variety of multimodal texts and their discourse conventions.

A Design approach to comics allows us to think more complexly about how meaning is created as comics are read, an approach that views readers of comics not as passive consumers, but as active creators of meaning. When I was 10, I looked at that cover, deciding quickly whether it might be worthwhile to take a closer look at what lay inside; I interacted with these paratextual elements, creating meaning through the process of Designing, using literacies acquired through the reading of not only comics, but written texts, visual texts, and people's bodies and facial gestures. In exercising such a multimodal literacy, I was interacting with comics like so many of my peers did then and a large number of children and young adults do today. As I read the cover of *Nova*, Marvel's sponsorship of multimodal literacy was rewarded in my purchase of the title that day and my ongoing purchases of that title each month. In this way, Marvel benefitted from the relationship, just as I did in my continuing development of alphabetic and multimodal literacies.

The complex case of comics and the sponsorship of multimodal literacy

In every case of multimodal literacy sponsorship, each institution has a narrow agenda and particular reason for using comics in the sponsorship of literacy. Comic book publishers are in the business of literacy sponsorship to make money. Libraries use comics to get readers into the library, but in general have been not very concerned with the development of complex multimodal literacy because comics are most often seen as a stepping stone to print literacy (although this attitude is certainly changing). Churches use comics to spread their teachings and promote membership; they are not very concerned with the ongoing development of multimodal literacy beyond the initial hook since, presumably, the reading of the Bible is the eventual goal. The sponsorship of multimodal literacy is simply the means to an end. Similarly, schools, parents' groups, and not-for-profit educational groups also sponsor multimodal literacy for their own purposes. In each case, the use of multimodal literacy that is being promoted has a particular cast to it, a particular inflection that reflects the agenda of the sponsoring institution. However, the readers who are sponsored may comply with or resist such agendas in ways that are often unpredictable to sponsors. In looking at these overlapping and sometimes competing agendas and the way that readers respond to them, we can see the complexities of how multimodal literacy sponsorship works across the single medium of comics.

Without a doubt the comics and manga read by children and young adults today have become increasingly complex in their Design, including their use of hybridity and intertextuality, while the accompanying literacies have become increasingly sophisticated, especially in their linkages to other kinds of multimodal literacies. Further, the issue of comics as a means of sponsoring literacy is more complex now than it was in the 1930s, 1950s, or even the 1970s. However, as Bradford W. Wright notes in *Comic Book Nation*, "Emerging from the shifting interaction of politics, culture, audience tastes, and the economics of publishing, comic books have helped to frame a worldview and define a sense of self for the generations who have grown up with them" (xii). Comics have, in other words, been central to the literate lives of both children and adults since their inception in the early 1930s, and the complex relationships of sponsorship throughout that history offer crucial insight into comics, multimodality, and literacy.

My hope is that this book will help us to push the conversation about multimodal texts and literacy beyond the usual focus on the internet, film, and television so that we can also embrace the complex multimodal literacies involved in reading comics. Moreover, my intent is that this in-depth look at one medium will provide some additional tools for examining the complex realities of how multimodal literacies are sponsored for people in their daily lives. In looking at a spectrum of types of literacy sponsorship from a variety of institutions over the past 70 plus years of comics, I want to offer some possible tools to think about comics and their complexities as they are used in the sponsorship of multimodal literacy. As such, *Graphic Encounters* is not a book of practical strategies on how to use comics in the classroom, but rather an attempt to use myriad examples from the history of comics in order to illustrate and complicate the idea of multimodal literacy sponsorship in relation to a single medium. While I hope that teachers, librarians, and other literacy educators will find much here to think about as they engage with students and their literacies, I likewise hope that those interested in comics will find that the concepts of multimodality and literacy sponsorship will offer fresh perspectives on the medium. *Graphic Encounters* is my attempt to accomplish these dual goals.

Notes

1   Throughout the book, I use the term "comics" to denote the medium and "comic books" to denote a specific type of material artifact—serial publications (sometimes colloquially called floppies), usually published monthly or bi-monthly, that use the comics medium by combining word and image to tell a story through a sequenced succession of panels and a fairly established set of narrative conventions.
2   Paul Lopes reports that in 1944 over 95 percent of boys and 91 percent of girls aged 6–11 read comic books, while 87 percent of adolescent boys and 81 percent of adolescent girls (aged 12–17) also read comic books. With the decline in the number of genres available and with the rise of superhero comics in the 1960s, female readership fell considerably. For a useful description of the history of comic book readership trends, see Jean-Paul Gabilliet's *Of Comics and Men: A Cultural History of American Comic Books*.
3   Many schools and libraries now see value in comics and integrate them to some degree in their literacy curricula. For a fuller discussion of the evolution of the thinking in libraries about comics, see Chapter Seven.
4   The collective of scholars is called the New London Group because New London, New Hampshire was the site of their initial meeting in September, 1994. At that meeting, a small group of ten scholars from the United States, Great Britain, and Australia came together "to discuss what would need to be taught in a rapidly changing near future, and how this should be taught" (Cope and Kalantzis 3).

5   See, for example, the relatively recent collections, *Defining Visual Rhetorics*, edited by Charles A. Hill and Marguerite Helmers, and *Visual Rhetoric in a Digital World: A Critical Sourcebook*, edited by Carolyn Handa. While these books present a very useful theoretical take on visual rhetoric, along with very useful material on such visual media as film, photography, advertising, quilts, and graphs, the closest either book gets to addressing comics is a very short section on political cartoons in Janis L. Edwards' essay "Echoes of Camelot: How Images Construct Cultural Memory Through Rhetorical Framing" in Hill and Helmers and a short excerpt from Scott McCloud's *Understanding Comics* in Handa. *Shaping Information: The Rhetoric of Visual Conventions* by Charles Kostelnick and Michael Hassett and *Integrating Visual and Verbal Literacies*, edited by W. F. Garrett-Petts and Donald Lawrence, also do not mention comics in their discussions of visual rhetoric.

6   *Polly and the Pirates* was originally a six-issue mini-series, later collected as a graphic novel.

7   I will return to Wertham and other critics of comics in subsequent chapters.

8   Much of what Wertham argued then about comics is now often attributed to video games.

9   See Chapter 4 for my discussion of the Comics Code in relation to multimodal literacy sponsorship. For a full description of the institution of the Comics Code and its effect on the industry, see Amy Kiste Nyberg's *Seal of Approval: The History of the Comics Code* and Bradford K. Wright's *Comic Book Nation*.

10 While Marvel comics of this period tended to restrict intertextual references to other Marvel comics and the so-called Marvel Universe, and to discourse and genre conventions of a general level, more recent comics (including those by Marvel) tend to be much more broadly intertextual in nature. For example, Bryan K. Vaughn's *Runaways* (original series 2003–4), an all-ages comic clearly aimed at the teen and pre-teen market, contains a barrage of references, not only to the Marvel Universe, but also Batman and Superman (via Kryptonite), Joss Whedon, *Buffy the Vampire Slayer*, *Girl Interrupted*, *Star Trek II: The Wrath of Khan*, *The A-Team*, *Jurassic Park*, Harry Potter, Saddam Hussein, the Menendez brothers, on-line gaming, and countless other texts and events.

11 The idea of the link between seduction, teaching, and rhetoric is most often associated with Plato's *Phaedrus*, a text that is implicitly about the ways in which education can and should operate. Though there are certainly valuable connections (and also major differences) between ideas of seduction in the *Phaedrus* and the ideas of seduction/sponsorship I have discussed in this chapter, a full consideration of these ideas is outside the scope of this book. Further research into the connections between multimodal literacies and seduction would be a welcome addition to the literature in the field.

CHAPTER TWO

Secret origins of literacy sponsorship

Having begun with examples that illustrate the book's major concepts, I want to turn to the origins of commercial comic books themselves. In briefly outlining the genesis of the comic book as a distinct type of commercial publication in the early 1930s, this chapter will begin by exploring the ways that early comic book publishers remediated the new form on older media (particularly the pulp magazines), and the varying motivations these early publishers, creators, distributors, and retailers had for sponsoring literacy. As well, this chapter will outline the strategies used to sponsor multimodal literacy in both the short and long term, and the effects of these decisions and motivations. In these early comic books and the subsequent explosion of titles following the appearance of Superman in *Action Comics* #1 in 1938, we can see the beginnings of the commercial comics industry and its particular, if still varied, kinds of multimodal literacy sponsorship, as well as the range of concerns that surrounded the use of comic books in the sponsorship of this literacy. Since the importance of Superman in this history, and indeed in the history of comic books, cannot be overstated, much of the chapter will focus on that character and the ways in which his introduction in 1938 and subsequent relaunch in 2011 can be viewed through a lens of literacy sponsorship. But first, let's go back to where it all began.

Comic books: The early years

Although comic strips had existed in American newspapers since the late 19th century, comic books as a commercial publishing concern only came in to existence in 1933, with the first of these comic books simply comprised of reprints of newspaper comics.[1] *Funnies on Parade*, the first center-stapled half-tabloid sized pamphlet that we would now recognize as a comic book, was published in 1933 by Eastern Color Printing Company as a promotional premium for Procter & Gamble. It is interesting and telling to note that the men behind this idea were not artists or even publishers, but sales people: sales manager, Harry I. Wildenberg and salesman, M. C. Gaines. The sponsorship of literacy in this case was the clear result of parents spending money on Procter & Gamble products and then redeeming coupons to acquire these comic books for their children. Proctor & Gamble sponsored literacy here in a relationship where continued literacy did not affect the way the sponsor operated. That is, it could have been any kind of giveaway product that children wanted to have. However, the fact is that it *was* a comic book and through the work of Eastern Color, Proctor & Gamble was, perhaps inadvertently, sponsoring literacy. I would point to the publication of *Funnies on Parade* as the first instance of comic books being used in the sponsorship of multimodal literacy.

Famous Funnies, what we would now recognize as the first commercial comic book sold on its own and not as an enticement for another product (thus eliminating the mediator in the relationship of literacy sponsorship), followed in 1934.[2] With the publication of this issue, Eastern Color became a comic book publisher, producing material for the consumer market at the newsstand. In making this transition from suppliers of incentives for other companies to publishers selling through established distribution channels, Eastern Color became the first direct sponsor of multimodal literacy through their commoditization of the comic book. Forging that connection with readers through the extant distribution channel of the newsstand was, as much as any of the factors noted above, what distinguished Eastern's efforts and presaged the imbrication of comics in the sponsorship of literacy for the next 70 plus years.

New Fun, the first comic book to include original material rather than reprints, followed soon after. This shift is important for a number of reasons, not least of which because it formed the basis for an ongoing relationship with customers (whose literacy the publishers were sponsoring) in which the kinds of narratives (and thus the kinds of literacy) offered could be tested through the mechanism of the market. Whether to avoid paying licensing or with the idea that the new material would be even more popular than reprints, publisher Malcom Wheeler-Nicholson and his National Allied Publications issued *New Fun* in 1935, in spite of the fact that distributors were wary of such a new and untested type of publication and reluctant to cede newsstand space to it. Despite strong early sales from *Famous Funnies*, such resistance is quite understandable since both the distributors and the retailers had to be aware of what would sell and therefore which titles should occupy the valuable real estate of their racks. As sponsors of literacy, they were highly cognizant of giving readers/consumers what they wanted since the concern was simply selling product. In other words, within early comic book production there was no other agenda (especially at the level of retailer and distributor) than to sell books; sponsoring multimodal literacy equated to monetary exchange for a product like any other product. Unlike the publishers, as we saw with Marvel in the last chapter and will see with DC later in this chapter, distributors and retailers did not care which publications sold, nor did they care whether the publications were pulps, comics, or other magazines as long as the product moved off the shelves. As sponsors of literacy, then, these distributors and newsstand retailers had almost no stake in the type of literacy that was being sponsored.[3]

Comic book publishers, on the other hand, did have a stake in the type of literacy being sponsored insofar as they wanted readers to pick up comic books rather than the other magazines that occupied the shelf space at the newsstand. Comic books were, of course, primarily a product and a way to make money for publishers and the type of literacy they were sponsoring and the effects of that literacy on those being sponsored did not, for the most part, matter to them—a reality that certainly contributed to the ongoing concerns about comics in both the 1940s and 1950s. Stan Lee, in *Origins of Marvel Comics*, corroborates this view in describing his first two decades at Timely (which later became Marvel Comics). Lee writes, "If cowboy films were the rage we produced a lot of Westerns. If cops and robbers were in vogue we'd grind out a profusion of crime titles" (13). The profit from comic books, however, depended on a specific kind of literacy sponsorship that would entice readers to develop skills in reading comics and an affinity for those comics. In fact, as Lee and Marvel discovered in the 1960s, specific strategies such as a shared narrative universe, ongoing continuity, and the cultivation of insider status could be cultivated to sponsor loyal readers and increase profits; strategies for multimodal literacy sponsorship, then, could be extended beyond simply giving the public what was already popular (though that strategy never goes out of fashion). The introduction of original material to comic books, despite the initial resistance to such unproven material at the level of distributors and retailers, ultimately proved to be the way to provide both the general strategies for sponsoring multimodal literacy through comics and, ultimately, the more long-term strategies involved in building a loyal readership, cultivated by both Marvel and DC.

Unfortunately for him, Wheeler-Nicholson did not prove to be a very adept businessman and he became ever more in debt to his distributor, Independent News, a company co-owned by Jack Liebowitz and Harry Donenfeld—the man who also owned the company that printed the covers of National Allied's books. By the time *Detective Comics* was published in 1937, Wheeler-Nicholson had formed a new company—Detective Comics Inc. (DC)—with Liebowitz and Donenfeld; by 1938, Wheeler-Nicholson had sold his interest to Donenfeld, the former publisher and distributor of inexpensive, and often lurid, pulp magazines.[4] I point out his other endeavors in publishing and distribution not to demonstrate that Donenfeld was a clever businessman (though clearly he was). Rather, it is important for two reasons: 1) distribution and production became more closely aligned and 2) the experience of the publication of the pulps served as a model for how to make the business end of comic books (and ultimately their sponsorship of readers' literacy) successful. I want to return to the question of distribution momentarily, but first let me take up the role of the pulps in the production of early comic books.

The relationship between the pulps and early comic books is one that has been commented on by several comics historians.[5] As Paul Lopes documents, many of the first wave of comics publishers had experience in publishing pulp magazines (easily the most popular type of American popular fiction in the 1920s and 1930s), including leading figures such as: Donenfeld from DC; Martin Goodman from Timely; Maurice Coyne, Louis Silberkleit, and John L. Goldwater who formed MLJ (which became Archie Comics in 1946); George T. Delacorte at Dell; and Lev Gleason, whose eponymous company would go on to publish *Crime Does Not Pay* (3–4). Moreover, most of the comic book genres—adventure, crime, western, romance, science fiction, jungle, and detective—as well as much of the art seemed to come straight out of the pulp tradition; even the superhero comics that were to make their debut with Superman's appearance in *Action Comics* in 1938 owe much to the pulp traditions.[6] The creation of familiar characters and serialized narratives also followed in the pulp tradition. In other words, comics remediated the pulp tradition, repurposing what had come before to create and develop a new medium, not in a linear manner so that comics simply replaced the pulps, but in a larger constellation of media in which influences work in multiple directions (as we shall see as we look at various moments throughout the history of the comic book).[7]

In this location of interaction, the publishers of the new medium of the comic book were using their experience with the publication of pulp magazines to develop the practices and content that would define the medium for the next 70 plus years. Not only were they adapting aspects and strategies of pulp publication, but they were clearly in competition with those same pulps (first in terms of shelf space and, ultimately, in terms of sales) as they sought to replace them on the newsstand shelves and in the hands of readers. Moreover, such remediation often necessitates some kind of change in the literacies needed to engage with the new medium and, thus, a change in the kind of literacies that are being sponsored. In the movement from the production of primarily alphabetic pulp magazines to the multimodal form of comic books, we can see the changed focus in literacies needed by readers and thus the literacies sponsored by the publishers; this change in literacy sponsorship is a crucial component in thinking about remediation, not only in this case, but also as we talk about digital media. As was demonstrated in the last chapter, comic book publishers have to be primarily concerned with the cultivation of a particular kind of multimodal literacy, with special emphasis on close connection with their own brands through the use of familiar characters and serial narratives (two key aspects that are remediated on the pulps). While early comic book publishers were able to import methods and ideas from the pulps, they had to adapt that knowledge to the production of multimodal texts and the sponsorship of this new literacy as they attempted to supplant the pulps as the predominant form of popular magazine. As Jay David Bolter and Richard Grusin point out in their discussion of remediation, "Each new medium has to find its economic place by replacing or supplementing what is already available, and popular acceptance, and therefore economic success, can come only by convincing consumers that the new medium improves on the experience of older ones" (68). What's at stake in this competition between media is not only short-term profit margins, but long-term control over the kinds of literacy that will be profitable to sponsor.

Though these new comic book publishers may not have known much about the production of comics narratives, they not only knew the key elements that worked in the pulps (such as action stories, recognizable characters, and serial narrative), but they understood and controlled a crucial aspect of the magazine publishing industry: distribution. According to Lopes, "The key to success [in the comic book industry] was the national newsstand and rack distribution network of newsprint media that was also key to the pulp industry" (10). Distribution was the key to sales since it was what ensured that the books were placed in front of the most potential buyers. Likewise, distribution was the key to literacy sponsorship for the new comic book publishers since the dissemination of the books into readers' hands had to happen in order for these new literacies to develop. As these new literacies developed, the affinity for comic books (this particular form of multimodal literacy) would continue to create demand for the product, reinforcing the relationship of literacy sponsorship between the publishers and the new comic book readers.

However, since these publishers were usually not able to provide the content for their books themselves (as they also had not for the pulps), they contracted out the production of the comics narratives to independent comic book production shops.[8] In the 1930s and 1940s, the shops were a crucial element in the way that comics were produced and, ultimately, in the way multimodal literacy was sponsored for comic book readers. Wright describes the shops this way: "Staffed with editors and freelance cartoonists, the shops sold completed comic book stories to publishers who lacked the resources or knowledge to produce their own material" (*Comic Book Nation* 6). Lopes adds, "The shop system and freelancing provided two basic advantages: it allowed new publishers to enter at low cost and allowed established publishers and comic shops to quickly respond to higher demand for their products" (10).[9] One of the major differences between early comic book production and later practices, however, is the amount of centralized editorial control that developed, especially within the major publishers of superhero comics, a strategy itself drawn from editors' previous experience with the pulps. In fact, as early as 1941, editors at DC, led by Mort Weisinger, increasingly began to oversee the narratives in order to maintain a greater degree of control over how their recurring characters were depicted so as to ensure that the kinds of stories being told were consistent with the editorial vision of the experience of reading a DC book. As Gerard Jones notes in *Men of Tomorrow: Geeks, Gangsters, and the Birth of the Comic Book*, "It was the character and appearance of creative continuity that mattered, not the writer or artist. This was the understanding that Mort brought from the pulps" (184). This kind of editorial vision and oversight would become even more important moving into the 1960s as Marvel, and later DC, began to promote the notion of a shared narrative universe that encourages readers to buy multiple titles (as can be seen in the discussion of Marvel in the previous chapter).

Despite such editorial oversight, it is important to note that there has always been a split between the production of comics narratives and their packaging/distribution in the material form of comic books. The writers/artists and the publishers/editors—and the shop owners who acted as intermediaries between the two—all had an interest in literacy sponsorship in that having readers take up the multimodal literacy of comic books benefited each of them in some way. While all parties were ultimately concerned with the number of readers (as seen in the number of issues sold), the sponsorship concerns were not identical from one group to another or even within groups. As writers such as Wright, Lopes, and Gabilliet all argue, the main concern of publishers in the early period was to package and distribute a product that people would buy. However, as will be seen in later chapters, publishers are not motivated solely by profit nor does profit alone dictate publishing practices. Similarly, writers and artists had to produce material that these publishers would buy since their continued contracts depended on sales as well. Many of these creators saw their production as an assembly-line process in which they would simply churn out product for money. Stan Lee, in remembering the conditions for writers in the early years, writes, "Comics have always been primarily a piecework business. You got paid by the page for what you wrote. The more pages you could grind out, the more money you made. The comic book writer had to be a comic-book freak, he had to be dedicated to comics; he certainly couldn't be in it for the money" (14). If not for the money, then, why write comics? Perhaps, as Lee suggests, it was, for some, the love of the medium. Others, however, clearly also saw the creation of comics stories as a way to communicate ideas to and instill values in readers, just as those who wrote in any medium might. The production of any comic book, then, involves multiple sponsors of literacy with multiple motivations for such sponsorship, just as the existence of that comic book sponsors the literacy of many different readers simultaneously. As will be seen in the next chapter, as comics became increasingly popular and the inevitable backlash against them came to pass, the multiple motivations of all of the parties involved in the production and distribution of comic books became increasingly complex.

On the threshold of greatness: The coming of Superman

From these first forays into comic book publishing, the industry quickly took off in popularity, especially between 1936 and 1939. Gabilliet attributes this rise in the popularity of comics to three factors: 1) the increase in themed magazines; 2) the increase in the number of publishers; and 3) the appearance of Superman in 1938 (14). The move to themed magazines can be seen, like many of the other features of early comic books, as a characteristic that was remediated on the successful use of the strategy in the pulp magazines. As seen earlier, the rapid increase in the number of publishers was facilitated by the use of the shop system, a feature remediated on the industrial logic of pulp publication. Finally, the introduction of Superman can certainly be seen to follow in the tradition of creating familiar, recurring characters that was a feature of the pulps.[10] No one could have known the impact this character would have on the publishing industry in general and the comic book publishing industry in particular. As Lopes so succinctly writes, with the publication of *Action Comics* #1, "National [DC] published the most important comic book in the history of American comics" (19).[11] The introduction of Superman sets the stage for not only the increased popularity of comic books in the 1940s and 1950s, but also presaged everything from the subsequent panics about comic books in those same decades to the resurgence of comics in the 1960s and the centrality of this character to DC's September, 2011 relaunch—a phenomena seen later in this chapter.

Themed comic books had existed since the first appearance of *Detective Picture Stories* in 1936, but it was *Action Comics* in 1938 that changed everything. Even more than *Nova* #1, the now iconic cover of *Action Comics* #1 (Figure 2.1) acts as a gateway, an important collection of paratextual elements that are designed to peak the interest of the readers and to push them to take the book off the rack to purchase and read. As the reader's eye moves down the page from the information about issue and date, it encounters the words "Action Comics" in a highly stylized—almost kinetic— font, the letters sloping down from right to left, effectively drawing the eye to the image below. With the linguistic, visual, and spatial aspects of the letters working together to convey action, the reader is then drawn down to the image of a man in a red and blue costume, the first glimpse of a character unlike any seen before.

Squarely in the center of the frame, the vividly colored costume becomes a beacon within the halo of yellow that infuses the scene as a whole; there is no doubt where our attention is to be focused. His expression is stern and his athletic posture connotes action. He lifts a green car over his head as it tilts down and to the right, again moving the eye in the direction of the action as the figure crashes the car against a boulder. Three figures are arrayed around the powerful man, two of them fleeing and one on his hands and knees; these characters not only provide a visual frame, but also provide a stark contrast to his actions and demeanor. More than that, though, their reactions provoke questions in the reader. Why are they running? Why do they appear terrified? What is their relationship to the man in the center of the frame? That man's intent here is ambiguous and it is the mystery of his motivations that provides part of the

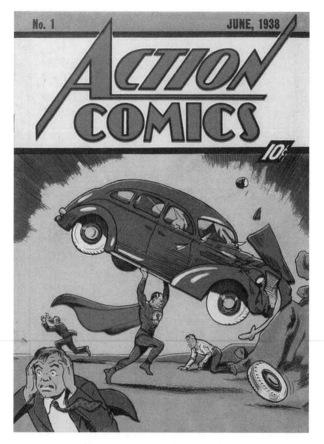

FIGURE 2.1 *Cover of Action Comics #1. © 2012 DC Comics.*

draw into the book. As you can see, the name "Superman" never appears as the name of the character anywhere on the cover. In his explication of this cover in *Supergods*, Grant Morrison writes that the "subliminal X" created by the angles of the lettering and the car mentioned above "suggests the intriguing unknown, and that's exactly what Superman was when *Action Comics* no. 1 was published: the caped enigma at the eye of a Pop Art storm" (7). There are no sound effects, nor are there words to help the reader understand what is happening. Instead, the choice to exclude sound provides a kind of tableau vivant as a threshold to this new book and character. Linguistic, visual, gestural, and spatial Design elements (with the visual depiction of sound withheld) thus come together to create this "vestibule" through which the world was about to enter in droves.

As a publisher, DC's short-term concern was simply to package and distribute the book efficiently and effectively so as to maximize the number of units sold and the resulting profit. Since DC had no way of knowing how popular the Superman character (and, indeed, comic books in general) would turn out to be, with the release of *Action Comics* #1 such short-term thinking predominated. That meant that long-term strategies for multimodal literacy sponsorship, through the cultivation of comic book readers generally and DC readers in particular, needed to be developed as the comic book industry evolved through trial and error remediation and experimentation. The immediate concern of attracting the attention of readers (as opposed to the long-term goal of holding that attention) can be seen before the book is even opened; the cover of *Action Comics* #1 was designed and drawn by Joe Shuster (likely with input from the editors at DC) to get readers to buy that particular issue and nothing more.[12]

From the cover of *Action Comics* #1, the intended message of the book was not at all clear so that at the moment prior to opening the book—as the buyer/reader stood at the threshold of entry— there was no way of knowing what kind of character this unnamed, costumed figure would be (or even if he was a hero or a villain). While the cover is designed to pull the reader in through its use of multimodal elements (including the creation of a mystery about who the character was), there is evidence that Harry Donenfeld, the publisher of DC, thought that the image of a man holding a car over his head would not work. As Wright reports in *Comic Book Nation*, a DC editor named Sheldon Mayer recalled that Donenfeld "got really worried. He felt nobody would believe it; it was ridiculous—crazy" (9). The initial print run was thus kept small—200,000 copies—and not increased until the fourth issue had sold out so that "by the seventh issue, *Action Comics* was selling over half-a-million copies each month" (Wright 9). Ian Gordon reports that "by 1941 *Action* Comics sold 900,000 a month, a figure close to 10 percent of the monthly sales for all comics" (132).[13] Clearly, Donenfeld was mistaken in his belief that the image was too ridiculous for people to take seriously;

despite being a long-time publisher of pulp magazines, he failed to recognize the important groundwork that both the content and art of those magazines had done in sponsoring the literacy of its readers. By remediating on that established base, comic books were not creating something out of whole cloth, but rather extending literacies and literacy sponsorships that were already extant. It's not surprising, then, that Superman, the most popular character of this new medium, would be a product of what Lopes calls "recombinant culture" (20). Superman was, in other words, a hybrid of comic art and pulp fiction. By drawing on these influences in new ways, the cover of that first issue worked as a threshold space through which buyers entered the fictional world inside, setting up expectations in readers while simultaneously creating an air of mystery about what might be possible within the narrative of the comic (and the narrative universe that was soon to follow). The stories fleshed out that world and Superman's character in ways that clearly connected with readers, just as the cover had promised.

"Champion of the oppressed": Sponsoring worldview through multimodal literacy

With the introduction of Superman, the centrality of recurring characters to the business model of the comic book publishing industry became much more entrenched and the focus shifted to the promotion of ongoing series. As creators, Jerry Siegel and Joe Shuster needed to concern themselves with using multimodal narrative to create a character that would become popular in terms of sales, thus ensuring their continued work. In doing so, however, they could also inject their own ideas about how readers should view the world (as they had in fact done beginning with his first appearance). Their sponsorship of multimodal literacy, while certainly concerned with sales figures and number of readers, could also focus on the promulgation of a particular worldview. In other words, this was literacy sponsorship that was not only monetary, but ideological.[14]

As David Hajdu writes, "With his debut on the cover of the premiere issue of *Action Comics*, published in June 1938, Superman distinguished comic books not only from newspaper funnies but from all major forms of entertainment then popular—magazines, radio, and the movies" (30). Despite the fact that comic books had been around since 1933, it was the popularity of Superman, and similar characters created in his wake, that launched the popularity of the medium and situated comics as a major venue in the sponsorship of literacy from that point forward. As has been argued earlier in this chapter, as comic books developed, they were remediated on both comic strips (in terms of form) and the pulps (in terms of content and distribution). Although Superman's character is clearly drawn in part from the pulps, Peter Coogan argues that superhero comics differ in significant ways from that source material, writing,

> Superhero comics thus break ideologically with the pulps that preceded them by presenting a world firmly divided between straight and criminal society. This break began in Superman's stories, but intensified as imitators sprung up and the comics publishers, particularly DC Comics, wanted to appeal to children and their parents by presenting moral heroes operating in a moral universe instead of the sometimes murky world of the pulps. (188)

Such a change in values—or at least in the purported values—represented in DC's books is an important component of the ways in which multimodal literacy came to be sponsored in the years immediately after Superman was introduced.

In the first issues of *Action Comics*, however, the reader is presented with a character that does not yet stand for "Truth, Justice, and the American Way." Rather than a forcefully patriotic character who embodies American values, Superman was, at this point, portrayed as a progressive force who defended those who could not defend themselves against all manner of oppression.[15] In Superman's alter ego, Clark Kent, we see the celebration of the common man, so prevalent in the popular culture of the period. Though the conception and mythos of Superman have evolved over time, at the beginning, Superman drew on the figure of the Western frontier hero (of which the urban detective is a variation) and his adventures demonstrated what Wright terms a way to "resolve the tensions of individuals in an increasingly urban, consumer-driven, and anonymous mass society" (*Comic Book Nation* 10). In the beginning, Superman was a character very much of the period in which he was created and the worldview being sponsored by Siegel and Shuster was one that valued not only the individuality of the tough guy as representative of the common man, but also the idea of the collective good as the way to honor those common people. Again, literacy sponsorship not only encompasses the economic, but also the ideological through the promulgation of a specific worldview.

Despite his prominence on the cover of the book, the first Superman story in *Action Comics* #1 was one of eight included in a book that featured multiple genres, including western, crime, occult, historical adventure, and sports. Protagonists included characters like Tex Thomson, Scoop Scanlon, Pep Morgan, Marco Polo, Sticky-Mitt Stimson, Chuck Dawson, and Zatara, the Master Magician. In other words, the superhero story in which Superman was introduced was only one kind of action story among many in an anthology format in which variety was designed to be one of the draws as DC tried to differentiate this magazine from all the others on the newsstand rack. Again, at this point, there was not yet the necessity of fostering an ongoing relationship of literacy sponsorship with readers; here DC's goal in sponsoring literacy involved attracting the initial attention of readers and convincing them to read this one issue among the many publications on the stands. Yet, by introducing this cast of protagonists, DC was using the idea from the pulps of establishing recognizable characters that could be used in future issues and/ or ongoing storylines. Scoop Scanlon, for example, appeared in the first 13 issues of *Action Comics*, as well as in titles such as *Cat-Man Comics* and *Terrific Comics* through the 1940s, while Zatara continued to appear as a character in DC comics, even up to the present.[16] Like the much more popular Superman, Zatara is one of a vast stable of characters who comprise the shared universe and continuity that DC has developed over its long history as one of their strategies for continuing to engage readers in a relationship of literacy sponsorship.[17] This anthology introduction of multiple characters, then, served the short-term goal of pulling readers in and selling the book, but also laid the groundwork for the longer-term establishment of reader identification with characters, first in ongoing, serialized stories for each character and, much later, in the creation of a shared universe for these characters.

FIGURE 2.2 *The first appearance of Superman, from Action Comics #1.*
© *2012 DC Comics.*

As seen in Figure 2.1, the first Superman story opens with a streamlined, one-page version of what would become a familiar origin story. In the upper left corner of the first panel, we see the title "Superman" in three-dimensional script we now identify as his typographical logo, with Siegel and Shuster's names directly below. After taking in this still mysterious title that seems to burst from the page (drawing on both the linguistic and the visual), the eye is drawn first to the explosive puff of blue smoke at the center of the frame and then to the rocket departing the frame to the upper right. Finally, the eye circles back down to the caption box in the lower right hand corner of panel, which reads "As a distant planet was destroyed by old age, a scientist placed his infant son within a hastily devised space-ship, launching it toward earth!" This caption helps the reader to begin to contextualize the mystery created by the title and the image of the rocket blasting out of the frame, but also creates the curiosity that encourages further reading. Moreover, in reading these words about the infant in the first panel, the reader cannot help but see the image of a toddler holding a chair over his head in the third panel as both panels are on the same tier. Not only do the words in the caption relate to the panel in which they are placed, but they also become connected to the visual dimension of an upcoming panel. By the time the reader gets to the third panel (having seen in the second panel that the rocket did, indeed, land on earth), the words of the caption that accompany the toddler's feat of strength, and the looks of astonishment by onlookers (elements likely not seen in the peripheral vision of the earlier scan), are not surprising: "Attendants, unaware the child's physical structure was millions of years advanced of their own, were astounded at his feats of strength." Rather, these words simply confirm what the reader has been piecing together in processing the multimodal elements of the first three panels and the relationships between those panels.

The next three panels, grouped together almost as one, detail Superman's powers visually, gesturally, and lingusitically: he is able to "leap 1/8th of a mile; hurdle a twenty-story building," "raise tremendous weights," "run faster than an express train," and "nothing less than a bursting shell could penetrate his skin!" While he does have superpowers, he is not yet omnipotent, as he would come to be over the next 70 plus years. His mission is clearly detailed in the next, text-only panel: "Early, Clark decided he must turn his titanic strength into channels that would benefit mankind. And so was created . . ." Readers are thus reassured about how the potential in the superpowers seen in the preceding panels will be used, while naming him Clark Kent connects him further to the human world. Situated in the last panel in this second tier of information, the ellipsis at the end of the text creates a brief moment of anticipation as the reader's eyes move down and left to the next tier of panels in which Superman is depicted for the first time in the story. Unlike the toddler in the first tier of panels, this next panel is not closely in the line of vision, thus creating enough separation to create tension. Of course, the reader has likely seen the figure in scanning the page on initial read, but the relational work between panels happens in a different way here. In this panel, Superman, in his brightly colored red, blue, and yellow costume, is depicted against a black background so that the image seems to float above the page. His knees are bent, arms out from his side, in a gestural pose that signifies he is ready for action. Below him is "Superman" in red lettering, the first concrete association between the mysterious figure on the cover and the character Superman. The caption, as it continues from this naming of the character, reads: "Superman! Champion of the oppressed, the physical marvel who had sworn to devote his existence to helping those in need!" Not only is the reader here reassured about the way the powers they have seen on this page will be used, but about how they should process the image from the cover of the book. Moreover, the mission statement expressed in these two panels was a clear indication of the direction Siegel and Schuster wanted to take this character and the ways in which they wanted to use him to sponsor a particular view of the world through multimodal literacy. The way they would follow through on that mission statement quickly becomes apparent as the story moves directly into the action of page two.

After a brief two-panel "scientific explanation of Clark Kent's amazing strength"—a comparison to the relative strengths of ants and grasshoppers—that completes page one, the second page opens with a panel that depicts Superman in the air, carrying a bound and gagged woman under his arm. The caption reads, "Delay means forfeit of an innocent life." The reasonable assumption is that the life in question is hers and that Superman is saving her, but this assumption is quickly complicated in the second panel. The unnamed woman is shown in the foreground of the panel, bound and gagged outside what the caption identifies as the governor's mansion, her expression and body language neutral so as not to offer many clues to the reader. Through visuals and body language, we see Superman departing the right of the panel as he says, "Make yourself comfortable! I haven't time to attend to it." What, exactly, is going on here? Through the next two tension-filled pages, where Superman overcomes obstacles such as a steel door and a bodyguard with a gun in order to see the governor, the reader still does not know what the relationship is between the first two panels in this sequence and what comes after those panels. However, those first two panels are always in the back of the mind during reading because of what Thierry Groensteen, in *The System of Comics*, calls arthrology, the network of panels formed by every story in comics form.[18] Within any comic, panels—what Groensteen sees as the base unit of the form—connect to each other either in sequence (restricted arthrology) or in a larger network of a page layout or entire work (general arthrology). It is this networked linkage of panels separated by several pages that creates the resonance on which the story and its resolution depend.

It isn't until a panel in which the governor calls the penitentiary (his action and concern shown visually and gesturally, and the destination of the call shown through his words) that the reader begins to get enough information to piece things together. In the next panel, a man rushes into the scene from the left, proclaiming, "Stop! The governor has pardoned her!" while a woman (different from the one in the opening panels of the story) kneels before a priest on the right side of the panel, her word balloon reading, "Thank God! I told you I was innocent!" It is, of course, in the gutter that the reader makes sense of what has happened by seeing that the action of the first panel (the call) causes the action in the second panel (the stopping of the execution); this connection between panels in sequence embodies Groensteen's notion of restricted arthrology. This sequence confirms that Superman has saved an innocent woman from the electric chair, while the following panel draws on general arthrology to make it clear that the woman tied up on the lawn is the real killer.

In the first four pages of Superman's career, Siegel and Shuster utilized both general and restricted arthrology, as well as the multimodal elements of comics, not only to pull the reader in to the story (through the creation and release of tension), but also to establish and demonstrate Superman's mission and, thus, a specific view of the world (which is further reinforced in the rest of the issue as Superman stops an abusive husband and confronts both a corrupt politician and a munitions manufacturer). As Thomas Andrae argues in his study, *Creators of the Superheroes*, in creating Superman, Siegel and Shuster demonstrated the New Deal populism of the time so that "[r]ather than battling mad scientists and supervillains, as he did later, the early Superman fought real life social ills" (15–16). Jones further comments that it "wasn't a coherent political statement, it was a New Deal Hollywood portrayal of a world where innocent people are hurt by greed and callousness and we could all use a primary-colored conscience to zoom in and knock us to our senses" (174). In creating Superman, Siegel and Shuster not only aided in the kind of short-term literacy sponsorship with which DC was primarily concerned at this point, but they also sponsored that literacy in such a way that it presented and endorsed a particular view of the world. Finally, in creating Superman and establishing the basis for his character and mythos, Siegel and Shuster laid the groundwork for the ongoing relationship of literacy sponsorship that DC would develop with its readers over the next 70 plus years.

In with the new, in with the old: The relaunch of *Action Comics*

This early version of Superman is not immediately familiar to most contemporary readers, who have been steeped in 70 plus years of a Superman mythos that is embedded within an always changing societal context and relationship of literacy sponsorship. Rather, we have to see it as having a family resemblance to the ways in which Superman has been portrayed in the intervening years as other concerns (the war against Germany, the various comics panics, the Cold War, etc.) have come to predominate. Still, as Umberto Eco argues in his essay, "The Myth of Superman," there has to be some consistency to the mythology underlying characters such as Superman, even as newer iterations of the character and stories of his adventures are published. Eco writes,

> The mythological character of comic strips [and comic books] finds himself in this singular situation: he must be an archetype, the totality of certain collective aspirations, and therefore, he must necessarily become immobilized in an emblematic and fixed nature which renders him easily recognizable (this is what happens to Superman); but since he is marketed in the sphere of a "romantic" production for a public that consumes "romances," he must be subjected to a development which is typical, as we have seen, of novelistic characters. (15)

What Eco usefully reads as mythology can also be read in terms of literacy sponsorship. That is, in sponsoring the literacy of several generations of comic book readers, DC as a publisher, through editorial control of the artists and writers, has had to balance the presentation of a character who is recognizably Superman with the exigence of producing narratives that feel compelling enough to pull readers in. While both this need for narrative invention and the underlying social contexts have produced iterations of Superman that mark them of a certain period (such as the fiercely patriotic Superman of the World War II period or the innocuous version of the immediate post-Code period), all of these versions of Superman are not only responses to specific rhetorical exigencies, but they can clearly be seen as variations on the same character. As long-term sponsors of literacy, it has always been crucial that DC maintain such a balance between novelty, relevance, and recognition in order to maintain established readers' interest while also bringing in new readers. If all the stories start to feel the same, readers will become bored and will no longer buy the book; if the character is not recognizable, they will become alienated and stop reading. In other words, comic book readers, as consumers of a serial format with recurring characters, want the reading experience to feel both comfortable and novel, two seemingly contradictory expectations. As a literacy sponsor who wanted people to continue to buy and read their books, DC had a very different problem going forward, as Superman became popular, than they did as they launched *Action Comics*. Short-term concerns about moving a single magazine became long-term concerns about how to keep readers interested in comic books in general and in their comics and characters in particular, while at the same time attracting new readers to those comic books. The problem of literacy sponsorship thus became much more complex, as we began to see in the case of Marvel Comics in Chapter One.

In the September, 2011 DC relaunch of its books, necessitated by flagging sales, many of these issues were at play. While a discussion of the entirety of the issues involved in the relaunch is outside the scope of this book, it is instructive to look at how DC, and the creative team of Grant Morrison and Rags Morales, approached the restart of *Action Comics*. In terms of Design, the cover of issue #1 has much in common with the cover of the 1938 version, including the familiar font used for the word "Action," its bottom-left to top-right diagonal forming an X on the page with the top-left to bottom-right movement of the action on the page. Unlike the 1938 version, however, the word "Superman" appears above the title, with the words "The New 52!" stacked directly on top of it. The mystery created by the figure on the cover of the 1938 version was no longer viable in 2011, given that Superman had become such an important figure in North American popular culture. Instead, as part of a company-wide relaunch, Superman needed to figure prominently and, thus, DC had to ensure that all readers would know that Superman was the protagonist of *Action Comics*, just as they needed to identify the book as part of the relaunch ("The New 52!" and the prominent #1). Linguistically, DC was mainly addressing the new readers they were trying to reach (one of the avowed goals of the relaunch) through the promise of a reading experience that did not require prior knowledge of years of accumulated history, mythos, and continuity, and through explicit linkages to Superman, a character well-known to people who do not read comic books.

Not only is Superman's name included above the title, but, as in the 1938 version, he is the central figure on the page. In this case, however, Superman is much larger and more prominent, the stylized "S" insignia rushing toward the reader as Superman seems to fly out of the page. According to Rags Morales, *Action*'s artist, his drawing was intended as a direct reference to the earliest incarnation of the character since this pose "was the Superman trademark, and it made him look like he was running" (*Action Comics* #2 n.p.). In this pose, his teeth clenched, muscles flexed, bullets are shown ricocheting off his body; the overall effect of this combination of the visual and the gestural embodies the "Action" of the title—what Grant Morrison has called "nonstop, kinetic, muscular action" (*Action Comics* #2 n.p.). All of these elements were designed to draw in new readers (both those new to comic books and those who stopped reading them for whatever reason), and to sponsor them in the way that the first *Action Comics* sponsored new readers in 1938. Selling books in the short term was still an important goal, with DC to some extent banking on the cachet of a relaunch and renumbering to draw in curious readers for the first month, thus creating a short-term profit for the company. Though DC knew that sales would drop off after the initial fanfare, the main goal was keeping as many readers as possible going forward, thus creating a long-term revenue stream. Unlike in 1938, however, the transition to sponsoring ongoing multimodal literacy was not one that would have to be invented, remediated as it was on the experience of publishers with the pulp magazines. Rather, DC would not only draw on its own experience in fostering ongoing multimodal literacy directed specifically toward its own comics, but, since it was a relaunch intended to increase its readership, would also remediate its efforts on what had been successful in other media.[19]

One of the successful media on which DC in part remediated itself for this relaunch was the Hollywood action film, as can be seen in the structure and pacing of *Justice League* #1, the first title in the relaunch. Both sales numbers and anecdotal evidence from retailers suggest that this issue—with its nonstop action and pithy, yet engaging dialogue—has been very popular with new readers. In talking with long-time readers, however, it is clear that their reactions were less positive, as they often critiqued the issue for seeming to be an extended storyboard for a film rather than a comics narrative. Herein lay the crux of the problem for DC: how to sponsor the multimodal literacy of new readers while also maintaining the sponsorship and allegiance of long-time DC readers. In using techniques from action films, DC hoped to draw in new readers who understood these conventions and could build a new multimodal comics literacy based on the multimodal literacies needed in reading action films. In doing so, DC ran the risk of alienating long-time readers steeped in the conventions and pacing of comic books who wanted to read a medium that was not remediated on film in this way.

In the same vein, long-time fans expressed mixed reactions to Superman's change in costume in *Action Comics* and similar aspects of the relaunch that changed the depiction of what had been familiar, recurring characters. Gone were Superman's familiar tights and red boots, replaced by jeans and workman's boots in an attempt to show what Superman was like in his first years as a superhero (in line with the concept of the relaunch).[20] After seeing the first images of the new Superman in the months prior to the publication of *Action Comics* #1, Scott Johnson, a writer for one of the many fan sites, expressed an opinion typical of many long-time DC readers. In a June 6, 2011 blog post, he wrote,

> Join DC Comics in the historic relaunch of the longest running comic series, when they ask the question, "What if Superman

were a lumberjack?" Don't get us wrong, we're really excited about seeing Grant Morrison's spin on the Man of Steel, but the cover image of *Action Comics* #1 makes Superman look like a steroid-pumping lumberjack. If this is supposed to be how Superman looked when he first emerged to the world as a superhero, we're really wondering how he transforms from an over-muscled hillbilly to the armored, hi-tech looking Superman in *Superman* #1. (n.p.)

Here we can see how changes to this recurrent (and much loved) character unsettled long-time readers who read comic books in general and DC comics in particular in large part for the familiarity of the ongoing, recurrent characters. However, we also see the desire for novelty in the way Johnson (and many others) were "excited by Grant Morrison's spin on the Man of Steel." In the promotion for the book (and on the cover), Morrison's name was prominent, an enticement to draw in regular comic book readers (whether DC or not) because of his reputation as an innovative writer in the medium. In continuing to sponsor the multimodal literacy of long-time readers during the relaunch, DC needed to strike a balance so that the characters appeared familiar but, at the same time, fresh and their use and promotion of established writers and artists was one way to do so. Couple this tightrope with the necessity of bringing in new readers and it becomes apparent the depths of the challenge that DC faced as it planned and executed the relaunch. As a commercial enterprise, sales are, of course, what matters, but the ability to move their product ultimately hinges on the complex ways in which they must continually sponsor multimodal literacy for a diverse readership.

As sponsors of literacy in their own right, Morrison and Morales (like Siegel and Shuster) have to produce books that readers want to purchase and read in order for them to continue to procure employment in the industry. That is, at a base level, their sponsorship of literacy is still tied in with market forces and with the monetary exchange between the reader and the publisher. As successful creators, their names do ensure a certain level of sales based on their track records of involvement in comic books and graphic novels that readers had found appealing in the past. Clearly, including those names in the advertising campaign and on the threshold space of the cover, coupled with the presence of the Superman character, drew readers in to the first issue: it sold almost 183,000 copies, second only to the relaunched *Batman* #1, according to a report on the Comic Book Resources website under the heading "DC Comics Dominates September's Sales." According to The Comics Chronicles, a website that tracks comic book sales, in the month prior to the launch, *Action* sold just over 40,000 copies, while *Superman* sold just under 37,000 copies (as compared to 118,000 copies after the relaunch). The fact that it sold 55,000 copies more than *Superman* #1, which had a different creative team, demonstrates how the presence of specific artists and writers with whom readers have a prior relationship of literacy sponsorship can help sell a book and help establish a new sponsoring relationship. However, unless the characters, narrative, and use of the medium (through both writing and art) met the expectations of those readers (including the incorporation of both familiarity and novelty), they would drift to other comic book titles or to other media completely. For new readers, Morrison and Morales had no ethos to carry over from their previous work, but instead had to establish it in the narrative. The presence of these multiple kinds of readers, the long history of the characters, and the rise of other types of media made the rhetorical situation of creating a comics narrative for a relaunched *Action Comics* just as complex as that which faced Siegel and Schuster in 1938.

Like Siegel and Shuster, who faced the challenge of getting the attention of readers of the pulps and other magazines, Morrison and Morales had to attract the notice of new readers whose attention was fragmented by a plethora of other media. Unlike Siegel and Schuster, who had to establish a new character that they hoped would become recurrent in his own series of adventures, Morrison and Morales were tasked with reintroducing a character with over 70 years of history and mythos, maintaining the interest of comic book readers while also attracting new readers. In doing so, Morrison and Morales, like Siegel and Shuster before them, attempted to move beyond concerns centered only on readership and sales and into literacy sponsorship that presented and endorsed a particular worldview. Neither creative team was at odds with the aims of their publisher (and, in fact, depended on packaging, distribution channels, and financial compensation from DC), but did not envision their roles as sponsors of literacy only in monetary terms. Interestingly, it was not just the idea of using Superman to forward a particular worldview that Morrison adopted from Siegel and Shuster, but the actual worldview itself. In his book *Supergods*, published less than two months before the release of *Action Comics* #1, Morrison wrote, "The original Superman was a bold humanist response to Depression-era fears of runaway scientific advances and soulless industrialism" (6). In reading the first two issues of his run on *Action*, it is apparent that Morrison saw parallels between these fears and what was happening in the world around him and created an updated version of the 1938 Superman in response. He had, in other words, remediated Superman on Superman.

In keeping with Siegel and Shuster's version, Morrison and Morales present a Superman who, while clearly superhuman, is no longer the omnipotent creature of recent portrayals. For example, at the end of the first issue, Superman is shown trying to stop a train, as if Morrison and Morales were visually asking the question, "Is he really more powerful than a locomotive?" As Morrison writes of Superman in the backmatter to *Action Comics* #2, "When he's hit by a train, he's not the Superman we've seen for the last 25–30 years. This is someone who can be hurt. I wanted to show he has limits" (n.p.). Morales goes on to add, "I love that he's been brought back down to Earth. That's the way it should be" (*Action Comics* #2 n.p.). Through a highly kinetic five-page sequence, Morrison and Morales utilize Design elements such as visuals (to depict motion), spatial relationships (to demonstrate action and reaction), gestures (to show Superman's facial expressions and body language), and words (to emphasize Superman's reaction to being hit by the bullet he says only "Ow," in very, very small print). At the end of this sequence, there is a final, full-page wordless reveal in which Superman is shown flattened by the train against the outer wall of the *Daily Planet* building. He appears to be unconscious and, in fact, it is not clear whether he is alive or dead, though the serial nature of the comic book form, especially in a first issue, makes his death highly unlikely. Still, while he has saved many lives by stopping the train, Morrison and Morales have clearly shown through visual, spatial, gestural, and linguistic modes that his actions have exacted a cost. As Morrison writes, "I constantly put Superman up against very physical objects: a wrecking ball, a tank, a train, solid stone. It was designed for the motion of that muscular, 1938 Superman—to really tie him into physical things, to big, heavy objects" (*Action Comics* #2 n.p.). Morales adds, "Superman back in the '40s was more relevant than Superman of recent years, because things hurt him. There was a danger to that" (*Action Comics* #2 n.p.). Further, along with restoring Superman's vulnerability to injury, Morrison and Morales also chose to emphasize his humanity through his Clark Kent identity. Taking their cue from Marvel comics of the 1960s in which the vulnerabilities of the superheroes' alter egos form a central part of the narratives, Clark is depicted as anything

FIGURE 2.3 *Action Comics* #1 *(New 52), page 1. © 2012 DC Comics.*

but superhuman: we see him flustered, doing laundry, behind on the rent. Just as Siegel connected Superman to everyday people by giving him Clark Kent as an alter ego, so does Morrison use this tactic to emphasize Superman's humanity and his connection to common people.

From the first pages of *Action Comics*, Morrison and Morales signal that this version of Superman is not the one to which readers have become accustomed, but rather one that hearkens back to what Siegel and Shuster sought to do with the character. In a narrative arc of eight pages—likely in homage to the eight-page stories prevalent in early comic books—Morrison and Morales introduce a version of Superman who is once again concerned with stopping social ills such as oppression and corruption. As seen in Figure 2.3, the first page consists of five horizontal panels stacked on top of each other. Panel one acts as an establishing shot of a posh high-rise apartment and introduces two men in conversation, including Glenmorgan, who the reader will soon identify as the villain. The second panel has all the elements in exactly the same configuration, including the gestures and body positions of the figures in the apartment, with one significant change: on the left-hand side is a set of red motion lines. By reading panel three, in which we see a crouching figure depicted from behind, the stylized S insignia the clear focal point of the frame, the reader is able, through interpreting the gutter between panels, to make the connection between the motion lines of panel two and the figure in panel three. Panel four shows Superman facing forward, fist clenched and muscles taut, standing beside the two men from panels one and two. As well, all three figures are shown at a canted angle, a cinematic technique that disturbs the readers' desire for a straight and ordered composition. Superman's dialogue, in two word balloons just above the heads of these two figures, reads, "Rats. Rats with money." There can be no doubt to whom those words pertain. Finally, the last panel shows Superman's face in extreme close-up on the right-hand side of the panel, his eyes glowing red in a way that signals he is not human. To his left are two men pointing guns at him; his dialogue, in two word balloons above their heads, reads, "Rats with guns. I'm your worst nightmare." In this first page, through dialogue, body language, panel composition, visuals, and the arthrological connections of panel layout, Morrison and Morales have introduced a character who is angry and has a clear target for that anger, a target that will come more clearly into focus in the coming pages.

Rather than moving to a reveal on page two that clarifies some of these issues regarding Superman, Morrison and Morales instead focus two pages of narrative on the police and the carnage that Superman has left behind in the apartment. The reader is here put into the same position as the police as they see the damage and try to understand exactly what this character is all about. The last two panels of page three depict the initial encounter between Superman and the police as he stands on the precipice of the balcony and the police yell, "Put that man down, you maniac!" and Superman replies, "Sure, officer, I'll put him down . . ." The reader's gaze shifts to the final panel which shows Superman from the chest up, insignia front and center, eyes still glowing, and a terrified figure (who the reader recognizes from page one as Glenmorgan) held above his head. "Just as soon as he makes a full confession," Superman continues, "To someone who still believes the law works the same for rich and poor alike." Here is the reveal: the reader flips to see a two-page spread in which Superman, shown for the first time in a full body shot and framed at the center of the spread, stands on the narrow balcony ledge, a terrified Glenmorgan held aloft while four police officers level their guns at him. Continuing his dialogue from the previous two panels, Superman says, in a jaggedly drawn word balloon that emphasizes his growing anger, "Because that ain't Superman." Nor is it the Superman contemporary readers have come to expect. After two and a half more pages in which Superman proceeds to scare Glenmorgan, he finally confesses: "I'm guilty! What do you want me to say? . . . I used illegal cheap labor . . . No safety standards . . . I bribed city officials . . . I lied . . . I lied to everyone." These eight pages use multimodal elements to attempt to entice new comic book readers (through the mystery of the character and his motivations and the depiction of action) into picking up the book, but also to draw in long-time readers of Superman by offering what would in 2011 seem like a radically different version of the character.

The main problem for Morrison and Morales, as it was for Siegel and Shuster, was how to attract readers and then to keep those readers, a key to their sponsorship that is completely in keeping with the sponsorship concerns of DC. However, Morrison and

Morales, again like Siegel and Shuster, demonstrate a desire to also sponsor a particular worldview, a move that is not necessarily (or even likely) in line with that of DC Comics. These two motivations for sponsoring literacy—the monetary and the ideological—come together not only in some creators, but, as we shall see in the next chapter, in some comic book publishers.

Notes

1 The origin of comics as a medium is outside the purview of this book and is a question that has been hotly contested by researchers. For a variety of interpretations of the early history of comics, see Roger Sabin's *Comics, Comix, and Graphic Novels*, Scott McCloud's *Understanding Comics*, David Kunzle's two-volume *The Early Comic Strip*, Jerry Robinson's *The Comics: An Illustrated History of Comic Strip Art*, and Coulton Waugh's *The Comics*.

2 Confusingly, three comic books published by Eastern Color in 1933 and 1934 bore the name *Famous Funnies*. While all three are important, it is the third of these publications that is generally regarded as the one that is the most important because of its form and impact on the industry.

3 For a useful description of these early comic books, see Gerard Jones's *Men of Tomorrow: Geeks, Gangsters, and the Birth of the Comic Book*.

4 According to Michael Feldman, in his posts to the online *Comix Scholars Discussion List*, Paul Sampliner was Donenfeld's partner in virtually all of his publishing ventures. Because of the roles they played within DC in terms of literacy sponsorship in this period, however, I have chosen to focus on Donenfeld and Liebowitz.

5 Part of the long tradition of popular fiction in America, pulp magazines, as noted by Lopes, date back to *Munsey's Magazine* and *The Argosy* in the 1890s. Noting the hybrid nature of comic books, Wright argues that "The earliest comic books derived directly from comic strips, but in many respects they owed more to pulp magazines" (2). Lopes argues even more strongly that the pulps "had the greatest direct influence on the structure and rules of art in the new field of comic books" (3).

6 For a more detailed description of the link between the pulps and superhero comics, see Peter Coogan's *Superhero: The Secret Origin of a Genre*.

7   In using the term remediation, I am picking up on a notion developed most fully by Jay David Bolter and Richard Grusin in their book, *Remediation: Understanding New Media*. Like many of the other concepts I discuss in this book, however, remediation is a concept that can be usefully explored in the context of comic books even though much of its current application tends to be in the digital realm. Of remediation, Bolter and Grusin write, "Our culture conceives of each medium or constellation of media as it responds to, redeploys, competes with, and reforms other media. . . . Media are continually commenting on, reproducing, and replacing each other, and this process is integral to media" (55). Further, as Paul A. Prior and Julie A. Hengst note in their introduction to *Exploring Semiotic Remediation as Discourse Practice*, remediation not only focuses on the media themselves, but also on "the location of any interaction—and its convergence of particular tools, people, and environments." (7).

8   Some of the larger houses did have in-house art departments to provide some content, but most publishers did not. Even the larger houses had trouble keeping up with the number of books that were being published, however, and relied to some extent on the independent shops.

9   Though the shops have passed out of existence, the content of comic books is still often provided by freelance writers and artists (who may or may not be under exclusive contract with a specific publisher), thus maintaining some distinction between initial production of comics narratives and the packaging/distribution of them.

10   For a full account of how this first Superman story came into print, see Jones's *Men of Tomorrow*.

11   The company was not known as National Comics (a part of the larger National Periodical Publications) until Jack Liebowitz merged DC and All American Comics in 1944. For more on this history, see Jones's *Men of Tomorrow*.

12   As reported by Larry Tye in *Superman: The High-Flying History of America's Most Enduring Superhero*, Jack Liebowitz claimed to have picked the image for *Action Comics* #1.

13   For the September, 2011 relaunch, DC initial print run of *Justice League* #1 was also 200,000 copies, a cautiously optimistic number in an equally uncertain time in comic book publishing. The book is now in its third printing. Unlike *Action Comics* of 1938, however, there is now little chance that an ongoing title will be able to sell half-a-million copies per month on a consistent basis.

14   Unlike David Hajdu, I believe that prior to the war (with its influence on the uses of popular media) and the first comics panic of the early 1940s (and its myriad influences on the comic book industry), there

existed a space in which creators could extol progressive ideas to their readers. Hajdu, on the other hand, writes, "*Action* and its ilk were not so much outlets for the errant impulses of their artists, writers, and readers, or vehicles for them to challenge social convention or authority, as blunt credenda of virtue and testaments to the goodness of America. With Superman, the comics assimilated" (31). While I do not argue that such assimilation would, indeed, come to pass, I instead see this happening slightly later, as the influences of the war and the first comics panic began to be felt.

15 In the words of Hajdu, "Portrayed in Siegel's early stories as the 'Champion of the Oppressed,' avenging battered wives and vindicating the unduly punished, Superman spoke directly to survivors of the Depression; he was an immigrant (from another planet) himself, and he embodied the Roosevelt-era ideal of power employed for the public good" (30). Moreover, as Wright points out, "Audiences familiar with the rather stiff and morally upright character that Superman later became would be surprised to discover that Siegel and Shuster's original character was actually a tough and cynical wise guy, similar to the hard-boiled detectives like Sam Spade who also became popular in the Depression years" (9).

16 *The Grand Comics Database* lists 700 appearances for Zatara since his introduction in 1938.

17 For a fuller description of continuity, see Chapter One.

18 In *The System of Comics*, Thierry Groensteen writes, "comics is not only an art of fragments, of scattering, of distribution; it is also an art of conjunction, of repetition, of linking together" (22).

19 Concurrent with the relaunch was DC's first significant push of digital comics, an opening up of the medium to a different type of interface remediated not on past practices of physical publication, but on digital technologies.

20 In the *Superman* title, also relaunched in September, 2011, Superman wears a slightly altered, but very recognizable version, of the familiar costume; it is set five years after the events in the Morrison/Morales *Action Comics*.

CHAPTER THREE

To blend in or stand out: Publishers' responses to "A National Disgrace" and the comics panic of the early 1940s

The introduction of Superman in *Action Comics* #1, as detailed in the last chapter, significantly altered the landscape of comic book publishing through its initial and ongoing popularity. If Superman was a product of what Lopes calls recombinant culture, a comic book creation that was a hybrid of the pulps and the comic strips, the success of this venture quickly helped move the comic book industry from strategies of remediation and into replication (20). That is, after the success of *Action* Comics, not only did DC continue to introduce superheroes such as Batman and Wonder Woman, but many other comic book publishers also tried to duplicate the character of Superman through the creation of their own superheroes. For example, Timely introduced both the Human Torch and Prince Namor the Sub-Mariner in *Marvel Comics* (which later became its company name) in 1939 and Captain America in *Captain America Comics* in 1941; these characters remain popular today after Marvel resurrected and updated them in the 1960s. Meanwhile, in 1940 Fawcett released *Whiz Comics* featuring

Captain Marvel, a character who would prove to be even more popular than Superman in the 1940s.[1] Besides these still recognizable characters, the late 1930s and early 1940s saw the birth of much less lasting characters such as Bozo the Iron Man, The Green Mask, The Flame, and The Shield, to name but a few.

While the hybrid nature of Superman can clearly be seen as an aspect of remediation as this new publishing industry attempted to invent itself, the explosion of attempts to capitalize on that success also represents a brief moment of stability within a dynamic industry. With Superman, DC seemed to have invented a model that worked so that superheroes quickly came to be seen by publishers as a viable avenue for at least short-term literacy sponsorship; according to Mike Benton, by the early 1940s, superhero titles had been published by 36 different publishers (176). As Stan Lee, who began as a comic book writer for Timely in the late 1930s, writes, "We simply gave the public what it wanted" (14). If the public wanted superheroes, the publishers were more than happy to provide them and to reap the short-term benefits of such sponsorship. Of course, the more successful companies were those that were able to convince the reader to not only continue to read comic books (as opposed to the other publications on the newsstand), but to read their comic books in particular. As we have seen, for Marvel and DC, the key lay in how to move from being short-term to long-term sponsors of multimodal literacy through the development of an ongoing relationship with readers.

With the introduction of Superman, there came increased importance of the identifiable, ongoing character to the comic book industry, just as it had for the pulps before them. And just as pulp publishers had begun to see the possibilities of introducing their characters across a range of media such as radio and movie serials, so did DC see marketing opportunities for the Superman character in the wake of his popularity in the late 1930s and early 1940s. By 1941 Superman's adventures could not only be read in comic books, but they could be heard on the radio, seen in cartoons, and followed daily in newspaper comic strips. What's more, Superman's likeness could be found on all kinds of products for children, including watches, toys, puzzles, and cereal. As early as 1941, then, DC had tapped into what we would today call media convergence, defined by Henry Jenkins as "the flow of content across multiple media platforms, the cooperation between multiple media industries, and the migratory behavior of media audiences who will go almost anywhere in search of the kinds of entertainment they want" (2). Not only was DC benefitting monetarily from their sponsorship of multimodal literacy through their sales of *Action* and *Superman* (reported by Jones to be around one and a half million copies per month in 1941 (158)), but through their very lucrative partnerships with other companies (such as newspapers, toy manufacturers, and cereal makers), they were also sponsoring other forms of literacies, both multimodal and alphabetic. Moreover, Superman's appearances in other media fed readers back to the comic book in ways that further bolstered DC's place as a long-term sponsor of a particular kind of multimodal literacy. Other media also supplied material for the ever-growing Superman mythos, with details such as the introduction of Kryptonite and the character of Perry White in the radio serials integrated into the narrative world of the Superman comic books. In this case, media convergence helped to solidify the importance of Superman as a character for millions of readers and as a property at the center of successful (and immensely profitable) multimodal literacy sponsorship for DC.

As we have seen in the first two chapters, this kind of multimodal literacy sponsorship is extremely complex. Throughout the history of comics, two concerns have continually emerged: 1) who gets to sponsor literacies through the medium of comics and 2) are comics an appropriate venue for literacy sponsorship (especially for children). Those involved in the debates about the use and value of comic books—including the first panic about comics in the early 1940s and the second, more famous panic that resulted in the introduction of the Comics Code in the 1950s—would certainly not have framed their objections in these terms. However, seen through a framework of multimodal literacy sponsorship, these two questions are central concerns and thus underlie both this chapter, which deals with the comics panic of the early 1940s, and the next chapter, which deals with the 1950s comics panic. The rhetoric of all sides in these debates and the various actions and reactions of all the involved parties demonstrate both the complex nature of literacy sponsorship in relation to comic books and the perceived importance of the stakes involved. By examining these two panics closely, we not only get a more nuanced picture of how comics have been used as a medium of multimodal literacy sponsorship, but also see how these questions (who gets to sponsor literacy and what are the appropriate venues for literacy sponsorship) remain central to debates surrounding all types of multimodal literacy.

Before I turn to the first comics panic and the responses of the comic book publishers, let me first briefly trace the continuing proliferation of comic books in the period after the introduction of Superman. Certainly no comic book publisher was quite as successful as DC during the period from 1938 to 1941, but despite the variation in success of individual companies, the comic book industry as a whole showed tremendous growth in sales from 1938 to the end of World War II.[2] The early 1940s were a very good time for comic book publishers: Ian Gordon reports in *Comic Strips and Consumer Culture* that "between 1941 and 1944 sales of comic books doubled from 10 million to 20 million copies despite paper shortages" (139). Gordon attributes much of this increase to the reading habits of servicemen and the fact that comic books were routinely supplied to soldiers, first through Library Service subscriptions to those posted overseas.[3] Once the title became readily available for purchase by soldiers at post exchanges, such distribution ended. As a distributor, the US Army acted as a sponsor of multimodal literacy for soldiers by making comic books readily available to them, especially through their subscription program. By the time the program ended, it was clear that soldiers were receptive to engaging in this kind of literacy since they were now willing to use their own money to purchase comic book titles.[4] Such sponsorship by a government agency during this period is striking, especially given the vehement attacks on comic books that began to be launched in the early 1940s.

However, while the rise in sales to military personnel certainly contributed to the increased popularity of comic books, in no way can it be seen to tell the whole story. As Gabilliet argues, "Reading comic books was a cultural practice that was practically universal among American pre-adolescents of both sexes," as evidenced in the 1944 survey he quotes that claims 95 percent of boys and 91 percent of girls, ages 6–11, read comic books (198). Certainly there were adults who read comic books (such as the military personnel noted above), but comics were, during this period, primarily intended for and embraced by young people. Comic books were, in fact, integral to the youth culture of the period, an idea Hajdu nicely captures in a passage from *The Ten-Cent Plague* that is worth quoting at length. He writes,

> Erratic, inelegant, often clumsy, but boundlessly energetic and wide-eyed, early comic books appealed to youngsters as a kindred species. Kids recognized in comics something resolutely, gloriously unadult. The books were "less grown-up" than "everything, including the Sunday funnies," recalled Jules Feiffer, who, at eleven years old in 1940, was an avid comic-book fan and already writing and drawing stories of his own, for pleasure, though the work (pieces of which he would keep for the rest of his life) was as good as some published in comics at the time. "The rowdiness, the crude drawing, the cheap printing, the fact that they were looked down upon—these are the things that made them attractive," said Feiffer. "There was practically nothing else that we thought of as ours in those days."

> At ten cents a copy, comics, like sodas and candy bars, were among the few things children of the post-Depression years could afford to buy by saving the pennies they could pick up on the sidewalk or earn by running errands, and they instilled a pride of ownership rooted not in adult conceptions of value, but in their absence. Parents considered comics worthless; therein lay their worth to kids. "I really loved comics . . . [and] I'd have to say that I probably loved comics so much, like I did, because my parents didn't give a damn about them," said Martin Thall, a New York City kid, ten years old in 1940, who, like Feiffer, was inspired to become a cartoonist himself. "I went to the newsstand every day looking for new ones, and if they weren't there, I would stare at the old ones again, every day, like I would find something new [in them]. My buddies and me talked about them all day. If you didn't know about comics, you were a nobody." Comics were the capital in the social economy of childhood, void among adults.

> Nearly all young people—boys and girls, loners, athletes, scholars, and debutantes—read comic books, and most of their parents did not. To read comics was to belong to a vast yet exclusive club, one whose membership was restricted primarily by age. (36–7)

In looking at these anecdotal accounts, it is clear that the dynamics of literacy were wrapped up with notions of identity. Comics readers in this period were engaged in a common discourse about a set of material and commercial objects, the knowledge of which gave them cultural capital among the group that identified with this discourse. What's more, involvement with these material objects not only meant taking on a discourse that involved thinking and acting in ways that would mark oneself as a member of the group, but taking on a literacy that pushed far beyond the strictly alphabetic.[5] The only way a kid could enter this discourse was to become immersed in the multimodal literacy that gave him or her access to the narratives, characters, and ways of thinking and being that were being discussed by other insiders who were also versed in this literacy; through this ongoing discourse, children effectively sponsored each other as they experimented with this new multimodal literacy. In sponsoring each other, readers interacted outside of the control of not only parents and teachers, but the comic book publishers as well, making meaning from these texts and forming identities by and for themselves as part of an emerging youth culture. Moreover, not only was the reading of multimodal literacy sponsored here but, as can be seen in both of these anecdotes, the production (or at least the possibility of that production) of multimodal literacy was also sponsored by kids as they began to see what was possible in this new medium. Multimodal literacy became a prized form of specialized knowledge, creating the kind of insider/outsider dynamic that Marvel Comics would so enthusiastically exploit as a sponsor of literacy in the 1960s.[6]

Brandt's definition of literacy sponsors is worth noting once more: "any agents, local or distant, concrete or abstract, who enable, support, teach, model, as well as recruit, regulate, suppress, or withhold literacy—and gain advantage by it in some way" (166). As detailed in the first three chapters, the comic book publishers, creators, distributors, and retailers acted as sponsors of this multimodal literacy and did so in order to gain a variety of advantages because of multiple motivations. Comic book publishers, especially at this stage, sponsored multimodal literacy in order to sell books and thereby make a profit. Like retailers, distributors did act as sponsors of literacy because they enabled children to buy and read various kinds of texts, but at this point they had even less concern than the publishers about what kind of texts they were selling (with the advent of the direct comics market, this would change for both distributors and retailers as their focus became narrowed to comics and the literacy needed to read them). From their perspective, there was very little difference between a comic book, a pulp magazine, a children's magazine, and a magazine about Hollywood: they were all products.

As Hajdu points out, the difference with comic books was that they were cheap enough for kids to buy and, because of their particular multimodal content, appealed to them rather than to their parents. Gabilliet writes, "Unlike children's magazines, which were published so as to appeal to parents, comic books were the first kind of periodical publication deliberately and specifically designed to be purchased by youngsters, thereby becoming part of the long-term transformation of youth into active consumers of the 1930s" (xviii). By attaching a relatively low cover price, comic book publishers were inadvertently sponsoring a literacy that created a coherent identity and group allegiance of comic book readers that was aligned with the emergence of a youth culture in opposition to that of its parents. As both consumer goods and examples of a new kind of literacy, comic books came to be closely identified with youth culture; children could make their own decisions about whether or not to buy comic books, which comic books to buy, and, through their reading and through conversation with each other, the meanings of those books. Their forays into this new literacy were being sponsored not by their parents, schools, or churches, but by each other and by companies who were more than happy to give them the kinds of characters and narratives they wanted to read and discuss. By putting comics within monetary reach of children and responding to their buying habits, as sponsors of literacy concerned primarily with monetary gain, comic book publishers effectively allowed children to have a large say in determining the kinds of literacy appropriate and available to kids. As comic books became identified with youth culture, with kids talking to each other about comic books and comic book publishers responding to their narrative tastes, critics began to become increasingly uncomfortable with the way comics had become a major venue for literacy sponsorship for children and the lack of official control over who was allowed to sponsor that literacy.

"A National Disgrace":
The first comics panic

The groundswell against comics began in earnest with the publication of Sterling North's article "A National Disgrace (And a Challenge to American Parents)" in the May 8, 1940 edition of *The Chicago Daily News*. In it, North acknowledged the overwhelming popularity of comics among children since the introduction of Superman, a phenomenon he called "a poisonous mushroom growth of the last two years" (56). He went on to write,

> Ten million copies of these sex-horror serials are sold every month. One million dollars are taken from the pockets of America's children in exchange for graphic insanity.

> Frankly, we were not perturbed when we first heard about the rise of the action "comics." We imagined as do most parents that they were no worse than the "funnies" in the newspapers. But a careful examination of the 108 periodicals now on the stands shocked us into activity. At least 70 percent of the total were of a nature no respectable newspaper would think of accepting.

> Save for a scattering of more or less innocuous "gag" comics and some reprints of newspaper strips, we found that the bulk of these lurid publications depend for their appeal upon mayhem, murder, torture and abduction—often with a child as the victim. Superman heroics, voluptuous females in scanty attire, blazing machine guns, hooded "justice" and cheap political propaganda were to be found on almost every page.

> The old dime novels in which an occasional redskin bit the dust were classic literature compared to the sadistic drivel pouring from the presses today. Badly drawn, badly written and badly printed—a strain on young eyes and young nervous systems— the effect of these pulp-paper nightmares is that of a violent stimulant. Their crude blacks and reds spoil the child's natural sense of color; their hypodermic injection of sex and murder makes the child impatient with better, though quieter stories. Unless we want a coming generation even more ferocious than the present one, parents and teachers throughout America must band together to break the "comic" magazines. (56)

North's attack on comics echoed earlier attacks on Sunday newspaper comics, dime novels, and pulp magazines. As well, in this account are many of the charges of the later, more damaging comics panic of the late 1940s and early 1950s: comic books present violence and sex (later linked by Wertham to a rise in juvenile delinquency); comic books are bad for children's eyes and nerves; comic books contribute to a coarsening of America's youth. North believed that comic books and the multimodal literacy needed to engage with them had to be replaced by quality, traditional children's literature, and the alphabetic literacy needed to engage with it. In North's opinion, there was simply no place for comic books in the reading lives of children.

The vehemence of this attack can be best understood through the lens of literacy sponsorship. Especially important are the questions I raised earlier of who should sponsor children's literacies, how those literacies should be sponsored, and whether comics are an appropriate venue for the sponsorship of children's literacies. Though North would never have used such terminology, the sentiments underlying these questions permeated his reactions to comic books, as seen in this section of "A National Disgrace":

> But, of course, the children must be furnished a good substitute. . . . The classics are full of humor and adventure—plus good writing. And never before in the history of book publishing have there been so many fine new books for children, or better edited children's magazines.
>
> The shame lies largely with the parents who don't know and don't care what children are reading. It lies with the unimaginative teachers who force stupid, dull twaddle down eager young throats, and, of course, it lies with the completely immoral publishers of the "comics"—guilty of cultural slaughter of the innocents.
>
> But the antidote to the "comic" magazine poison can be found in any library or good bookstore. The parent who does not acquire that antidote for his child is guilty of criminal negligence. (56)

The problem, as North saw it, was that teachers and parents were negligent in the way that they sponsored children's literacies, either by not being active in their sponsorship or by providing them with inappropriate reading material in their roles as sponsors. North regarded both parents and teachers as appropriate and important sponsors of children's literacies, and fundamentally disagreed with the ways that they had sponsored those literacies in the wake of the tremendous increase in the popularity of comic books since the introduction of Superman. Not only did North see comic book publishers as inappropriate sponsors of literacy for children, he regarded their sponsorship as dangerous because of the violent and sexual content that they produced in exchange for children's spending money and without regard for the welfare of their young readers. Clearly North did not see comic books as an appropriate venue for the sponsorship of children's literacies, but rather a kind of literacy that should be *withheld* from them. Not only was North a self-appointed representative of the conservative high culture to which he thought children should be exposed, but he was also an author of the kind of children's literature that deferred to that culture.[7] As a sponsor of literacy himself, both as an author who benefitted monetarily from the sale of his books and a reviewer who advanced the cause of children's fiction which presented "better, quieter" (and less left-leaning) stories that depicted a worldview in accord with his own upper middle class views, North clearly felt threatened by the growing popularity of comic books.

The emphasis in North's writing was on those who would, for better or worse, act as sponsors of literacy. But what about those being sponsored? What about the children themselves? What types of literacy sponsorship were important to them? Comic books, as both texts and consumer objects, clearly formed an important part of children's and adolescents' lives in this period, but, as Hajdu astutely observes, "North's piece served as a denial of the possibility that comic-book readers were reading comics by choice" (42). By spending their own money on comic books and/or convincing their parents to buy comic books for them, the very children who North depicts as unwitting dupes of the publishers were instead making active choices about the kind of literacy they wanted to practice (multimodal), the medium in which they wanted to engage that literacy (comics), and the kinds of characters and narratives they wanted to see within that medium (superheroes and other adventure stories). Contrary to North's assertion that the dollars were "taken from the pockets of America's children in exchange for graphic insanity," children of this period actively chose to exchange their money for a particular kind of literacy sponsorship in a reciprocal relationship that benefitted both parties, children and publishers. It was not the fact that children had no agency in the face of ruthless publishers that bothered North, but rather the fact that the cheap paper and printing methods of those publishers made comic books inexpensive enough that children actually *could* exercise choice with regard to the relationships of literacy sponsorship they entered. Allowing children such choice was, more than anything, what frightened North about the growing popularity of comic books.

Within a year of its publication, "A National Disgrace" had been reprinted in newspapers across the country,[8] generating many similar columns (including North's 1941 follow-up piece, "The Antidote for Comics") and news stories, touching off a debate about comic books and their appropriateness for children among parents, teachers, and librarians.[9] Suddenly the leisure-time reading habits of children were being closely scrutinized to see whether or not they undermined the kinds of literacy taught in schools and provided by libraries, the kinds of official literacy sponsorship sanctioned by the adult world. In other words, the debate centered around how children's (alphabetic) literacy would be sponsored and who would sponsor that literacy. For librarians and teachers, the popularity of comic books among children carried with it great potential for affecting and/or undermining the ways in which literacy sponsorship happened in schools and libraries.[10] As Nyberg, Beatty, and Lopes point out, during this initial iteration of the debate, educators and librarians engaged in spirited debate in their professional journals about whether or not comic books were physically, mentally, and/or morally harmful to children without coming to the kind of consensus about the damaging effects of comic books that would be seen in the postwar period.[11] What's important to note at this juncture is that North's call to action was heeded by enough parents, teachers, and librarians that the comic book publishing industry was forced to take notice and justify not only their product, but their role in children's lives.

"Standards of wholesome entertainment": DC reacts

By the time the overwhelming popularity of Superman became apparent, Jack Liebowitz had taken over most of the responsibility for the day-to-day operations of Detective Comics; he was, by this time, also a partner (with Charles Gaines) in All American Comics, which would be merged with DC into National Comics (part of National Periodical Publications) in 1944.[12] Unlike Donenfeld, Liebowitz clearly understood the value and future of comic books as a discrete publishing endeavor, rather than as simply one more commodity to be distributed and sold along with every other magazine published by Donenfeld, including decidedly adult titles such as *Pep*, *LaParee*, and *Spicy Detective*. In comic books, Liebowitz saw "something that could be built and sustained here, a kind of entertainment that kids liked better than pulps and would continue to if given reason for coming back" (Jones 164). Liebowitz understood the necessity of narrowing their focus and becoming sponsors of an ongoing multimodal literacy directed at comics in general and DC comic books in particular. In order to do so, Liebowitz decided he needed to distance DC from the other, more adult publications Donenfeld's companies had produced by doing everything he could to ensure that their comic books were seen as wholly unthreatening by the censors. To that end, Liebowitz hired Whitney Ellsworth as DC's new editor in 1940 and together they drafted an internal code for the artists and writers of the DC line. One crucial element was that there would be no more of the explicit violence of the early Superman and Batman books; DC superheroes would not intentionally kill any criminals.[13] By toning down the action of their comic books through such an editorial code, Liebowitz sought to position DC as an acceptable sponsor of children's leisure time reading, a move that would quickly pay dividends when North's attack on comic books was published a few months later.

In response to the mounting national debate surrounding comics, DC made a series of moves designed to further the position established by Liebowitz with the introduction of the creative code. Beginning with the publication of the October issues of its line of comic books, in the summer of 1941,[14] DC (and its allied company, All American Comics) introduced an Editorial Advisory Board and began to advertize its existence within the pages of all of its books. Inside the cover of each of its comics books appeared a full-page "Message to Our Readers," subtitled "Introducing the EDITORIAL ADVISORY BOARD."[15] In a box on the left-hand side of the page were listed the members of the Advisory Board—Dr. Robert Thorndike, Ruth Eastwood Perl, Gene Tunney, Dr. C. Bowie

Millican, and Josette Frank—along with a brief notation on their affiliations. On the right-hand side of the page ran the text with DC's stated reasons for the introduction of the Advisory Board, along with a short paragraph outlining the qualifications of each Board member. The notice ran as follows:

Since the inception of this and other DC magazines, a rigid policy has guided the editors in their selection and presentation of editorial material. A deep respect for our obligation to the young people of America and their parents and our responsibility as parents ourselves combine to set our standards of wholesome entertainment.

Early this year we recognized the value of active assistance on the part of those professional men and women who have made a life work of child psychology, education and welfare. As a result we secured the collaboration of five Advisory Editors, each a leader in his or her respective field. In this issue we take pleasure in introducing them to you.

Dr. Robert Thorndike, of Columbia University's Teachers College, is well known for his distinguished work in the field of child education. His fund of experience and studies of children's reading interests have fitted him well to aid in guiding our editorial policies.

Ruth Eastwood Perl, Ph.D., has worked with children in the field of psychology for many years. Her activities in intensive research, as well as practical experience, have aided us in understanding more fully the findings and conclusions of specialists in child training.

Gene Tunney, former World's Heavyweight Champion, now a successful businessman. At present on active duty as Lieutenant Commander, in charge of Physical Fitness Program, U.S. Navy; a member of the Executive Board of the Boy Scout Foundation, and of the Board of Directors of the Catholic Youth Organization.

Dr. C. Bowie Millican, Department of English Literature, New York University, has noted the similarity of today's fictional heroes to the legendary heroes of another day—Hercules, Paul Bunyan, Samson, and mighty Thor.

Miss Josette Frank, of the Child Safety Association of America, and author of "What Books for Children" is an acknowledged authority in the field of juvenile reading. Her contribution to the DC magazines is actually three-fold: her monthly book reviews are a sound guide to the best in young people's books; her frequent movie reviews are helpful in selecting the best of current fare; in conjunction with the DC magazines themselves, she has contributed many helpful suggestions.

We believe parents and young people alike will welcome the addition of these outstanding experts to our Advisory Staff. As the number of comic magazines has increased so rapidly it has become more important than ever to discriminate between them. The "DC" at the top of our magazine covers is your guide to better magazines.

Sincerely,

The Publishers (n.p.)

DC's response to the public criticism of comic books was similar to publishers such as Dell and Fawcett: make one's corporate image and one's publications as palatable as possible to the parents, teachers, librarians, and lawmakers who shared North's concerns. That is, one strategy in response to the early comics panic was to stay the course in terms of the kinds of books that were published, but take steps to align the corporate image with the values of the community, setting one's company apart from the other comic book publishers in the eyes of the public and transforming it into an acceptable sponsor of children's leisure reading. Dell, for example, which focused on adapting Disney and other wholesome characters from the movies to the comics medium, could link their reputation explicitly to the way the public felt about the properties they had licensed to adapt. Since the adventures of Mickey Mouse and Donald Duck were not seen as threatening at the movies, neither was *Walt Disney's Comics and Stories* seen as threatening on the newsstand. Like Dell, Fawcett continued to publish its regular line, but emphasized their child-friendly humor as a way to deflect criticism from the company and its publications. As seen in the above announcement of the Editorial Advisory Board, DC (like Fawcett and Dell) continued with its same roster of titles, but rather than relying on its association with its licensed product or quietly emphasizing the child-friendly nature of its titles, DC aggressively asserted a new corporate ethos that was explicitly designed to position themselves as a publisher that understood and promoted the best interests of children in the development of their literacy. DC wanted to be seen as not just unthreatening, but as an exemplary sponsor of literacy and, in keeping with the possibilities Liebowitz saw in comic book publishing, one that was in it for the long term.

From the outset of DC's "Message to Our Readers," it is clear that DC was responding to the kind of attacks leveled by North and others against the comic book industry by positioning themselves as good corporate citizens (and literacy sponsors) who understood and took seriously their obligations to both parents and children. Further, the "Message" asserted that the people at DC were parents themselves, a nice rhetorical move designed to establish identification with parents who might be reading and an ethos of responsibility that would counter North's arguments. After all, if the people who worked at DC were parents and were worried about their own children's literacy, wouldn't it follow that the company as a publisher would only publish material that was in the best interests of children as readers? At least, that's the part of the argument that was implied here and the connection that the DC editorial staff wanted readers to make. But more important than the ethos that could be drawn from the common parental concerns shared by editors and parents of readers was the ethos that DC drew from the Editorial Board itself and the expertise of its members. The credentials and experience listed for each member of the Board were designed to bolster the corporate ethos through association, drawing on their expertise and authority as a way to make DC seem not just acceptable, but positive and beneficial as a sponsor of children's literacy. Of course, most of these names were not known to the general public and so their ethos stemmed from the titles and experience listed here by DC. Not so, however, with Gene Tunney, at first an odd name to find in this list of educators and child psychologists. As the former heavyweight boxing champion (1926–8), Tunney would have still been an immediately recognizable name to most people in 1941, a kind of celebrity endorsement for what DC was attempting to do with the introduction of the Editorial Advisory Board. Moreover, his past as a boxer and his stated association with physical education in the Navy created a connection between the act of reading comic books and the care and maintenance of the body; in essence, DC was making the argument that comic books, contrary to popular opinion, were not just for kids who wanted to hide in their bedrooms. Finally, the list of his involvements specifically linked him to both the Boy Scouts and the Catholic Youth Organization so that in the mind of the reader these associations would also extend to DC itself. Corporate ethos, and thus fitness for the role of literacy sponsor for children, was created in a variety of ways in this "Message to Our Readers" and in the ongoing presence of the Editorial Advisory Board it announced.

In addition to the establishment of the Advisory Board, DC also instituted a column written by Josette Frank entitled "Books Worth Reading" in which she reviewed current offerings in children's literature, an innovation touted by DC in the "Message to Our Readers." Examples of the kinds of books Frank suggested can be seen in her suggestions from the September/October 1941 issue of *Superman* in which she chose *Men Of Iron*, a book about knights published by Harper, and *Clear for Action*, a book about America's battle at sea during the War of 1812 published by Harcourt Brace. Similar in terms of adventurous themes to the content of the comic book, these suggestions were designed to appeal to young readers and to get them to see value in reading traditional books alongside comic books. An advocate of comics for children, Frank, "who received three hundred dollars per month from National to serve as a consultant" argued that "good comics far outweighed the bad nationally and that publishers such as National [DC] who had their own advisory boards were dedicated to cleaning up the industry and working with parents for the protection of the nation's children" (Beaty 110). In her capacity as consultant, Frank worked to show that comics could be as wholesome a medium as any other in presenting narratives to children. That work allowed DC to position itself as an ongoing sponsor of multimodal literacy in general and comics literacy in particular, while also trying to demonstrate that such literacy was not only compatible with traditional alphabetic literacy, but that such literacy, in very broad terms, supported the acquisition of alphabetic literacy, an idea much more thoroughly explored in the partnership between The Children's Television Workshop and Marvel in the 1970s.[16]

As part of this concerted effort at rebranding itself, DC also introduced a "Supermen of America" page in *Action Comics* and *Superman*. Though Gordon asserts that this page (and the fan club it represented, as can be seen in the button that children would receive when joining, shown in Figure 3.1) began in the October 1941 issue

FIGURE 3.1 *Supermen of America button.* © *2012 DC Comics.*

of *Action Comic*, it is clear that it had been established by 1939, part of the initial movement to add commercial value to Superman as a property. By 1941, however, it was also being used to offer "readers advice from Superman on the conduct of their lives" (Gordon 136). In the September/October 1941 issue of *Superman*, for example, Superman lectured readers on the topic of responsibility, the very notion that was being emphasized so strongly in the "Message to Our Readers." The columns' themes echo with those of that "Message":

> Greetings again, Members! There are many things that guide us in the practice of our daily lives and one of these is RESPONSIBILITY. By this, I mean our moral accountability not only to others but to ourselves.
>
> Each Member of the household, each Member of the community, the state and the nation has RESPONSIBILITIES, and they cannot be shirked. Father is obligated to earn the daily bread for the family, and Mother's duty lies in the care of the home and the raising of her family to be respectable, RESPONSIBLE citizens.

During your youthful years, you must learn to assume RESPONSIBILITY, for it is your dependability that will help shape the future of your community. It is not my intention to saddle you with unnecessary burdens, but I think it is only fair to you to point out that not one of you is morally and spiritually scott-free. You and I have duties to exercise, or to put it another way, RESPONSIBILITIES. We are responsible to our parents, our teachers and our friends as well as to ourselves. We have a RESPONSIBILITY to our community that only can be demonstrated by being upright and honest persons. This can be interpreted as social consciousness.

How can you prepare yourself for the moral obligations, the RESPONSIBILITIES which come with adult life? Now, if at all, is the time to lay the groundwork for a happy and secure future. Events abroad are robbing the youth of foreign nations of their opportunity to build moral structures for the future, but you, enjoying the blessings of peace and democracy, have nothing to prevent you from looking ahead and working towards a goal.

Take advantage of your schools; exercise your right to free worship. And do not overlook relaxation. Play properly in order to keep your body in trim and your mind clear and fresh.

Someone once remarked, "Youth must be served." That is quite true, but RESPONSIBILITY must be shared, and so, by the same token, youth must also serve.

Sincerely,

Clark Kent (n.p.)

Appearing in the same month as the "Message to Our Readers" that introduced the Editorial Advisory Board, this column reinforced the ideas of obligation and responsibility that DC was attempting to project onto themselves as publishers, while at the same time extending that concept to its young readers. Nominally written to Members of the Supermen of America Club, this column is as much directed at parents and acts in tandem with the introduction of the Advisory Board to position DC as not only harmless to children, but rather as beneficial to their moral education. DC would be responsible as a publisher and through their comic books they would be able to instill values like responsibility (and physical fitness, as per the linkage to Gene Tunney on the Advisory Board) to the youth of America. In other words, as sponsors of literacy, both multimodal (in the comics stories) and alphabetic (in columns like "Supermen of America"), DC was attempting to show that they were interested not only in profit, but in the inculcation of mainstream American values to America's children.

It is also important to note that DC used word-based argumentation, with both elevated diction and a serious tone, in these appeals to parents in order to defend the worth of the comics stories they published; though appealing to children through multimodal means and positioning themselves to become long-term sponsors of multimodal literacy, DC realized that parents needed to be convinced through alphabetic literacy. In dealing with the exigencies of the moment, DC, along with publishers like Fawcett and Dell, responded by keeping within the relationship of literacy sponsorship they had already established with children and making that relationship acceptable or seemingly beneficial to parents, teachers, and educators. Other publishers would, however, take a different tack, as seen in the 1941 introduction of titles such as *Classic Comics* by the Elliott Publishing Company and *True Comics* and *Real Heroes* by the Parents' Institute.

"Truth is Stranger and a Thousand Times More Interesting than Fiction!": The Parents' Institute, educational comics, and multimodal literacy sponsorship

While the efforts of DC to portray itself as a good corporate citizen and appropriate sponsor of literacy seem to have placated many critics, there were still a substantial number of people who saw comic books as dangerous to the intellectual and moral well-being of children and who did not see superhero comics as at all appropriate material in children's literacy development. For example, an editorial from the January 6, 1941 *New York Daily Mirror* argued, "There can be no defense except absolute prohibition of the comics by all parents for their children. It is not a case of selecting good comics among evil ones. They are 99 percent bad and nothing short of complete prohibition as far as possible will protect the child" (n.p.). A later article, in the November 20, 1942 edition of *The New World* (written well after DC had instituted its Editorial Advisory Board) entitled "Comics and Comic Books Are No Longer Comical," agreed on some points, but did not dismiss the medium of comics out of hand. While describing some possibilities for positive uses of the medium, the writer explicitly attacked the superhero genre:

> It is a poor defense to say that these stories portray the triumph of justice over villainy and crime. The damning argument against these gaudy publications is that they introduce the child to an unreal world peopled by scheming sirens and cold-blooded murderers and are the worst possible education for children whose minds are too impressionable not to retain some residue of the dangerous nonsense poured into them. (553)

The way in which comic books were aimed at children was particularly troubling to this writer because these fantasy stories—the "strong meat on which the youngsters have been fed"—may already have "destroy[ed] their taste for more wholesome fare" (549). Still, unlike North, and later Wertham, who viewed reading comic books as inherently damaging to children and inferior in every way to reading alphabetic texts, this writer did see some possibility for positive uses of comics by reframing the focus and content of the stories being told and using the interest of children in the medium to get them to engage with more uplifting fare.

It was this idea of substituting "good" comics for "bad" comics that led to the publication of the kinds of titles of which this writer approved: "Perhaps the issuance by *Parents' Magazine* of a new type of comic book and of a series of picture stories by the Catechetical Guild dealing with the lives of Christian heroes . . . is the beginning of a more widespread effort toward replacing the paganized, erotic comics by something that parents may, with easy consciences place in the hands of their children" (549). As the writer from *The New World* and several publishers had begun to see, comics as a medium and comic books as material objects could be used for purposes other than strictly making a profit. Sponsoring multimodal literacy through comic books could be a very effective way to instill values, both civic and religious. The religious comic book to which the writer referred is *Topix Comics*, distributed by the Catechetical Guild to students in Catholic schools beginning in 1942. This was a model of substitution in which the sponsor of multimodal literacy did not derive monetary profit from the relationship of sponsorship, but instead sought to influence the worldview of students through the use of comic books by encouraging them to engage with the religious subject matter. Such an approach acknowledged the popularity of the medium with children and rather than condemning it, attempted to use it as a tool for conveying information and influencing the way children thought. Religious publishers, both non-profit and for-profit, along with churches, pastors, youth leaders, and parents have continued to utilize comic books in this way ever since.

Comic books, the writer of "Comics and Comic Books Are No Longer Comical" argued, could also be used to instill civic values of which adults would approve and that would accord with what was being taught in schools: "In launching three new publications—*True Comics*, *Real Heroes*, and *Calling All Girls*—[the Parents' Institute] seek to instruct and uplift rather than horrify and degrade young minds" (555). The sheer popularity of comic books showed that children not only liked them, but were, in fact, delighted by them. Publishers such as the Catechetical Guild and the Parents' Institute seemed to be asking why not use comic books to do what children's literature had always purported to do, delight *and* instruct, by changing the subject matter of the narratives presented in them? Substitution of good comics for bad (rather than North's idea of literature for comics) thus became the second major response to the early 1940s critiques of comic books.

In the March 1941 issue of *Parents' Magazine*, Katherine F. Lenroot, Chief of the United States Children's Bureau, wrote an editorial entitled "Our Children's Heritage" in which she argued, "we must push forward toward the all-important goal of incorporating all our children into the heritage and destiny of our nation, and of developing in youth that sense of justice, that identification with the purposes and history of freedom, which alone can make democracy secure" (15). Consonant with those sentiments, in that same issue, Clara Savage Littledale's article "What to Do About the 'Comics'?" introduced *True Comics* and their new comic book publishing venture to the *Parents' Magazine* readership—the parents of the children who were reading comic books. In it, Littledale picked up on North's idea of substitution ("of course, the children must be furnished with a good substitute"), but instead of the wholesome (alphabetic) children's literature that North clearly intended, Littledale expanded this idea so that it included replacing problematic comic books with morally and intellectually uplifting ones. She wrote, "Because substitution is better than prohibition, the publishers of 'Parents' Magazine' are launching 'True Comics' and so enabling you to offer your children a magazine that is worthwhile" (26). As a publisher, they had "come to the conclusion that a suitable substitute for trashy comics magazines needs to be provided—a new magazine for children patterned closely after the comics, a magazine that shall be *very like* yet *very unlike* the comic magazines as we now know them" (emphasis in original; 27). Littledale announced a very different approach to North's criticism of comics than we saw from DC. Rather than trying to burnish their ethos as a publisher and sponsor of literacy, the Parents' Institute, publisher of *Parents' Magazine* and an already well-respected authority with regard to what was best for children, made the decision to enter into the publication of comic books as a way to expand the available choices for children. As Littledale wrote, "faith in children is the inspiration for this new magazine, since those who are responsible for it believe that boys and girls instinctively recognize and want what is worth while, and if, as in the case of the cheap comic magazines, they seem to have gone astray, it is only because we have given them nothing better" (93). The logic here was clear: if children were going to read comic books anyway, comic books should be provided that would be wholesome, educational, and beneficial.[17] In taking this tack, the Parents' Institute rejected North's argument that reading comics was inherently bad for children, while agreeing with his argument that the content of comic books currently being published was not beneficial to the children who read them. Substitution here was about content, rather than about the type of literacy in which children should be engaging.

By substituting what they deemed as trashy content with material seen as educational and uplifting, the Parents' Institute was intent on making comics *very unlike* what was being published at the time. However, they also realized that comic books also needed to be *very like* those being published in terms of excitement and action if children were going to buy (or ask their parents to buy) them so they could be read and discussed with other comic book readers. In "What to Do About the 'Comics'?" Littledale went on to write, "Every page in this new comic magazine is filled with action and excitement. But the heroes are not impossible creatures. They are real" (27). While it's hard to imagine that stories about Simón Bolívar or Winston Churchill would ever be able to compete with Superman or Batman in the imaginative universe of children, there was certainly an acknowledgement here that these new comic books needed to be more than didactic. They needed to not only instruct, but to delight. In a September 1941 advertisement in *Parents' Magazine* for *True Comics* and *Real Heroes*, both the need for action and the rationale behind the insertion of educational content are emphasized: "*Color and action-pictures are demanded by the youth of America today. Let them have worthwhile stories told in this technique.* . . . The publishers of *Parents' Magazine* offer these two popular-style publications as an antidote for the poison of cheap, lurid 'comic' fiction" (emphasis in original; 38). While agreeing with North that the comic books being published were a kind of poison to the literacy of children, the Parents' Institute sought to concoct a very different antidote than that proposed by North.

As publishers (and would-be sponsors of multimodal literacy), the Parents' Institute viewed *True Comics* as primarily apart from, though certainly supportive of, the more official literacies of the educational system. However, they did allow for the educational possibilities of their proposed comic books. In her introduction to these books, Littledale wrote, "While *True Comics* is primarily for children's leisure time amusement, it is believed that many schools will find this new magazine of the greatest help as supplementary reading for history and social science courses" (93). In suggesting possible educational uses of their comics, Littledale here went even further than the editors at DC in arguing for the benefits of these new comic books; the substitution of these new, beneficial comic books in children's leisure reading would be augmented by their possible value as supplemental teaching tools. Not only would *True Comics* be beneficial in inculcating values in children consonant with those of parents, teachers, and American society in general, this multimodal text could be used as another way to help students understand material in school. In effect, Littledale was arguing here that multimodal literacy and alphabetic literacy could be used in tandem to draw on the strengths of both ways of making meaning, much as the Children's Television Workshop and Marvel would draw on these possibilities in the early 1970s. Littledale asserted that by introducing titles such as *True Comics* and *Real Heroes*, the Parents' Institute would be giving children something much better, not only substituting the good for the bad in children's leisure reading, but ushering in the possibility of the uses of comics in partnership with the official literacy practices of schools. The Parents' Institute thus sought to position themselves as a very different kind of publisher and as a sponsor of multimodal literacy that would be much more than merely acceptable to parents and teachers. By laying out their philosophy of comic book publishing so explicitly, both here and in editorials in the comic books themselves, the Parents' Institute inserted themselves into the argument about the value of comics and announced to the adult world how they intended to sponsor children's literacy and how comics ought to be used in that sponsorship. The issue, according to the Parents' Institute, was not that the multimodal literacy of comics was inherently problematic, but that those sponsoring this type of literacy did not use their position of sponsorship for the benefit of children and society, but only for profit. As a publisher, the Parents' Institute would be a literacy sponsor unlike their competitors in the comic book publishing industry.

Under the direction of George Hecht, the Parents' Institute, through their publishing arm, the Parents' Magazine Press, thus began to publish comic books in response to this ever-burgeoning comics industry that, in Hecht's mind, emphasized entertainment over education and profit over the welfare of its readers. Rather than remediating his version of comic books on pulp magazines as many other publishers had done, Hecht instead looked to other alphabetic texts that emphasized true events as the model for his new multimodal texts, such as *Reader's Digest* and *Life*. Echoing Littledale's introduction to the new line of comic books, Hecht wrote in the editorial introduction ("A New and Different Comic Magazine") that appeared inside the cover of the first issue of *True Comics* (pictured in Figure 3.2), "nowadays most of the comics no longer even try to be funny. They consist largely of exciting picture

FIGURE 3.2 *Cover of True Comics #1.*

stories which everyone recognizes as not only untrue but utterly impossible." Instead, of such impossible entertainments, *True Comics* and *Real Heroes* would offer true stories that would appeal to both parents (because they would be educational and adhere to parents' values), but also to children (because they would still be in comics form, but, as their motto claimed, "Truth is Stranger and a Thousand Times More Interesting than Fiction!"). Through these comic books, the Parents' Institute sponsored a parent-sanctioned multimodal literacy that was not primarily directed toward entertainment, but instead toward education and the attendant instilment of values such as reverence for authority and patriotism. In attempting to explicitly counter the effects of other comics texts on children's reading, the Parents' Institute sought to sponsor word-based literacy by using comics as an intermediate step to alphabetic texts and to teach readers about history, literature, science, and other subjects along the way. Of course, the comic book that most people identify with getting children interested in reading and aiding in the transition to "real" books is *Classics Illustrated*, introduced in 1941 as *Classics Comics*.

Inspired by the success of *True Comics* (the first issue of which, according to Gabilliet, sold 300,000 copies in 10 days) and the sales success his own company was enjoying in simply repackaging old comics material, Albert Kanter urged his idea of adapting literary works to the comics medium to his employer, Elliott Publishing Company. The result was the publication in October 1941 of the first issue of *Classic Comics*, pictured in Figure 3.3. As William B. Jones, Jr. writes in *Classics Illustrated: A Cultural History*, "Kanter was concerned that his children seemed to be drawn to comic books rather than the literary masterpieces on the family bookshelves. With an autodidact's fervor, he dreamed of a means of introducing young readers to the classic literature that had sustained him over the years" (11). What better way to introduce children to these classic texts than through a vibrant cover, such as the one shown below, which acts as a paratextual space, a threshold that invites children into the comic book, its multimodal content itself designed as an entry point to the alphabetic text on which the comic is based. In effect, the cover of *Classic Comics* #1 acts as a gateway to a gateway, a bright and inviting first step toward the kind of alphabetic literacy and cultural knowledge of which Kanter approved. All of the multimodal Design elements except the audio (or visual representation of the audio) are present here and work together to draw the intended audience into the comic book. The linguistic elements introduce the title of the book and the new series (Classic Comics) of which this text will be a part. Meanwhile, the visual, typographic elements of the adapted novel's title draw the eye to the words and simultaneously indicate that the story is a work of historical fiction through its stylized and ornate typeface. The vertically printed words along the book's spine—"Complete-Entertaining-Educational"—are there primarily

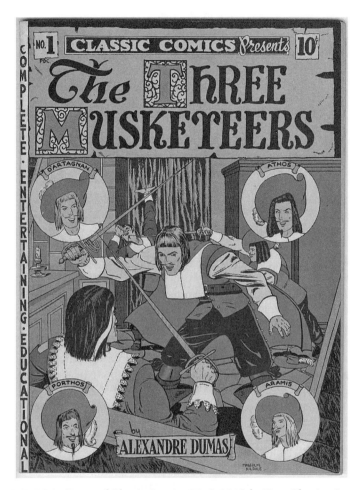

FIGURE 3.3 *Cover of Classic Comics #1. © 2012 by First Classics, Inc. All rights reserved. Used by permission of Jack Lake Productions, Inc.*

for parents and indicate that this comic will not be harmful, but will instead be educational for children; in effect, these words are an announcement of the publication's objectives and values. Through the visual and the gestural, an action scene is depicted in order to draw the interest of the potential reader. The colorful costumes and athletic poses involved in this fight scene mimic what children might see on the covers of the competing comic books, reassuring them that what was inside would be entertaining and not just educational. Finally, the scene is framed by headshots of the four main characters, an indication that what is shown here is part of their story and an invitation to potential readers to find out how they got into this predicament and how they will get out of it, thus creating an immediate attachment to the characters and their well-being.

The cover here takes on the dual function of drawing children in and reassuring their parents, both of whom are important targets in selling copies of the comic book, an outcome that is crucial for any publisher no matter what other motives they might have in publishing comic books. With *Classic Comics* (and later *Classics Illustrated*) that motive was the introduction of children to classic literature; the multimodal literacy involved in reading comics would be a step toward the alphabetic literacy that was prized by Kanter and (it was assumed) most parents. As a publisher, Kanter and Elliott Publishing were willing sponsors of multimodal literacy (in that they stood to make a monetary profit from sales of their comic books), but not ongoing sponsors in the way that DC and Marvel would try to be. That is, *Classic Comics* had no ongoing characters and no shared narrative universe and did not position their readers to stay with them for an extended period since the aim was for those readers to eventually graduate to the alphabetic literacy of the great literature that was depicted in each issue. Instead, Elliott was content to sponsor the multimodal literacy of children for a limited rather than extended period of time under the assumption that as one generation of children moved from comics to literature, the next would begin that same journey by picking up *Classic Comics*. In sponsoring literacy in this way, not only did Elliott Publishing work toward Kanter's aim of sponsoring alphabetic literacy, but they also attempted to ensure an ongoing stream of revenue by assuring parents that their comic books were a stepping stone and an aid to learning, rather than an end in themselves. As sponsors of literacy themselves, parents could condone these comic books as a useful intermediate step to alphabetic literacy. Despite these motivations, however, the fact remained that Elliott Publishing was also inadvertently sponsoring multimodal literacy through the publication of *Classic Comics*.

Like Elliott Publishing, the Parents' Institute viewed their comic books as an alternative to what had been available to that point and, to some extent, as a gateway to other kinds of texts and reading. More than abetting the transition to alphabetic literacy, in their not-so-hidden curriculum, *True Comics* and *Real Heroes* encouraged in children specific kinds of behavior and stances toward the world. Of course, any sponsorship of literacy involves those being sponsored adopting new ways of viewing the world, but in the case of the Parents' Institute, the expectations of the new worldview were overt and explicitly part of what they wanted to achieve in sponsoring multimodal literacy. This desire to instill specific values and to educate children can be seen in an ad for *True Comics*, *Real Heroes*, and *Calling All Girls* in the December 14, 1941 issue of *The New York Times Magazine*. While asserting that these comic books would be attractive to children because the "stories are told in the most interesting way possible—in full-color action pictures that look, to the child, like the other popular comics," the ad was clearly aimed at parents who would be interested in substituting "good" comics for those "popular" comics (32). The ad assured parents that "the vital difference is that [these comics] tell dramatic *true* stories about *real* people" and that "[e]ducators say *True Comics* adds to the child's knowledge by relating the exciting adventures of outstanding men and women of the past and present" (32). By portraying "outstanding men and women," the Parents' Institute was providing role models for children and portraying the particular values that they wanted to convey to their readers. For example, the first issue of *True Comics* (see Figure 3.2 above) included stories on Winston Churchill, the British Air Force, George Rogers Clark ("trapper, hunter, and guide of old Kentucky"), the discovery of the cure for yellow fever, the first naval submarine, the battle of Marathon, and Simón Bolívar. In these stories, certain values were clearly emphasized—courage, duty, freedom, innovation, patriotism, resilience, judgment, and sacrifice—as part of the transaction of literacy sponsorship. By ordering subscriptions to these new comic books, the ad claimed parents would be giving their children the comics they wanted, but they would also be giving themselves peace of mind about what their children were reading or, in other words, how their literacy was being sponsored. The ad was very explicit, delineating exactly what parents would get out of buying a subscription: "the assurance that what the child reads is not distorting his mind. Educators recommend these magazines because they tell the dramatic stories of real men and women whose words and deeds are part of world history" (32). Not only were these books educational, but the values in them opposed those that would distort children's minds found in other comic books.

As a commercial publisher, Hecht was very conscious of the need for all of the company's publications to make money, but unlike many other publishers of the period (including many comic book publishers), he did not see profit as the only motivation for these endeavors; profit was not the sole benefit to be derived from sponsoring literacy. Hecht was explicit on this point, as seen in *George Joseph Hecht: A Lifelong Commitment to Children*, a biography published by Parents' Magazine Press on the occasion of his 80th birthday and 50th year with the company: "I won't permit going into anything that doesn't render a useful educational service and which doesn't have a prospect of being profitable. Those are the two requirements. They don't have to make much money but they have to have good prospects. But I wouldn't go into any moneymaking project I cannot be proud of" (8). By entering into the publication of comic books, Hecht saw that the company could both profit and provide an educational alternative to the other comic book publishers such as DC, "what *Time* Magazine called 'the racketeers of childhood' who purveyed nearly 10 million comics a month to American youth in 'an over-seasoned diet of non-comic murder, torture, kidnapping, and sex-baiting" (*George Joseph Hecht* 33). Moreover, these comic books could be used as a medium through which to transmit the values that Hecht and the Parents' Institute deemed important. Given the content of the comic books produced by the Parents' Magazine Press, for example, it is not surprising that Hecht was quoted as saying, "I believe in the power of joint action, but I also believe that one person with sufficient determination and drive can accomplish the almost unbelievable" (*George Joseph Hecht* 26). As important as profit was the transmission of such values.

Like Kanter at Elliott Publishing, Hecht and the Parents' Institute clearly saw educational value in the way that the comics medium could introduce children to the world of alphabetic literacy through the process of scaffolding. Just as children could use *Classic Comics* as a stepping stone to the classic literature on which the comics were based, so could *True Comics* act as a scaffold for further investigation (through alphabetic texts) of the real people and the values they represented that were depicted in its pages. Hecht's thoughts on this aspect of comics can be seen in a broadcast of "America's Town Meeting" from March 1948 (a transcript of which was published in *Town Meeting* that same month), just at the beginning of the second comics panic. Here, Hecht and Al Capp argued the pro-comics side, while John Mason Brown and Marya Mannes argued the anti-comics side. With regard to the relationship between reading comic books and reading purely linguistic texts, Hecht said, "It's been definitely demonstrated that children who are readers, children who read comics, also are readers of books. Children who get the habit of reading, through the reading of comic strips, go on to read good books, too" ("What's Wrong with the Comics?" 15). However, it is important to note that later in the broadcast, Hecht goes on to say, "I think the educational and religious and industrial use of comics is just in its infancy. I think the schools and the churches will all in time be using comics as a means of mass education" ("What's Wrong with the Comics?" 18). In offering an alternative to the comic books on the market in 1941, the Parents' Institute viewed comics as a viable medium which could both serve as a scaffold for alphabetic literacy and as a multimodal medium through which multiple kinds of learning could happen.

How, then, did those involved in the publication of these new comic books attempt to achieve all of these goals? Each issue of *True Comics* took the form of a non-fiction anthology in comics form, with none of the recurring characters or serialization that readers would find in many of the fiction comic books. As we shall see in the next chapter, EC also eschewed recurring characters and serial narratives in an anthology format in the early 1950s to very different effect. Despite the enormous differences between the comic books published by the Parents' Magazine Press and those published by EC, what they did have in common was the problem of how to sponsor ongoing multimodal literacy (and thus ensure a continued readership) without familiar characters that would draw readers to the books. Speaking of EC, Les Daniels, in *Comix: A History of Comic Books in America*, argues that instead of "the concept of a continually featured character to guarantee a steady audience . . . stories of high quality would have to be presented in order to develop a market without the traditional come-on" (63).

While EC used the flexibility of this format to *critique and subvert* conventional values (as will be seen in the following chapter), the Parents' Magazine Press used it to *promote and sustain* those same values.

The first story in *True Comics* #1 (with a cover date of April, 1941), for example, told the story of Winston Churchill's life and through that telling emphasizes ideals of courage, duty, resilience,

FIGURE 3.4 *First page of "World Hero No. 1," True Comics #1.*

and judgment by holding Churchill up as an exemplar for young readers. Released months before Pearl Harbor and America's entry into World War II, the story nonetheless portrayed the figure of Churchill and the ideals ascribed to him as a bulwark against the dangers of Nazi Germany; like many comic book publishers, Parents' Magazine Press clearly sided with American intervention in the war and used stories such as this one to instill values in children that would be consonant with the war effort. The first page, pictured above in Figure 3.4, uses multimodal elements to introduce Churchill and to begin to build him up as a model of the kind of character children should emulate. In terms of visuals, the drawing of Churchill takes up the entire left side of the page, a layout used later in the issue to portray Simón Bolívar, "the liberator, patriot, warrior, and statesman" (56); the gestural mode here, through facial expression and posture, suggests gravitas and seriousness of purpose, as befits a world leader. His figure is superimposed over the Union Jack (linking him inextricably with country), his head level with the words "World Hero No. 1," which act as both the title of the story and an assessment of the character of the man. In other words, the spatial Design of the visual, gestural, and linguistic modes makes all the elements come together multimodally to create a meaning that is greater than the sum of the parts. By establishing this image of Churchill, creators George Harrison and August Froehlich attempted to create a resonance in the reader that would carry forward throughout the story, from the two panels on this page that introduced the concept of bravery to the final panel (shown below in Figure 3.5) that acted as a bookend to the opening images and further contextualized Churchill's role at the time of publication. In one of the few panels to include dialogue through the use of word balloons, this final panel offers an audio element from one of his most famous speeches as he is shown in a close up that is framed by the horrors of the war through which he is trying to lead his people. These framing devices, along with the story told in the pages between, are designed to hold the interest of children (the target readers), appease the parents of those children (an important sponsor of literacy for children and, by extension, another target market) by substituting good comics for bad, and to instill values of courage, duty, resilience, and judgment.

FIGURE 3.5 *Final page of "World Hero No. 1," True Comics #1.*

While DC, along with companies such as Dell and Fawcett, responded to the first comics panic by attempting to maintain an already established relationship of literacy sponsorship with children by making that relationship acceptable or seemingly beneficial to parents, teachers, and educators, publishers such as the Elliott Publishing Company and Parents' Magazine Press responded by substituting good comics for bad. With the advent of America's involvement in World War II, however, concern over comic books and their effects on children subsided, only to return again after the conclusion of the war. As we shall see in the next chapter, the second comics panic, while engendering some of the same responses, had much more far-reaching implications.

Notes

1 In fact, Captain Marvel proved to be such a popular character that DC brought suit against Fawcett for copyright infringement, claiming that the character was too much like Superman. Despite notable differences in the characters, DC won the suit.

2 As Gabilliet notes, sales figures have always been particularly important for the comic book industry since "their survival depended to a much greater degree on their sales than on their advertizing receipts" (134).

3 As Gordon reports, in 1943 and 1944 "the Army distributed at least 100,000 copies of [*Superman*] every other month, or about 10 percent of the comic's sales" (140).

4 Comics became such a part of the life of soldiers that in 1951 the United States Army hired Will Eisner to create a magazine entitled *PS: The Preventative Maintenance Monthly* in which he used comics to demonstrate to enlisted men how to repair and maintain the equipment they used as part of their duties. The best of these comics has recently been collected as *PS Magazine: The Best of Preventative Maintenance Monthly*.

5 As James Paul Gee writes in "What is Literacy?," a discourse can be thought of as "an 'identity kit' which comes complete with the appropriate costume and instructions on how to act and talk so as to take on a particular role that others will recognize" (1).

6 As Jones notes, the facilitation of fan identification can be traced back to Hugo Gernsback's editorship of the pulp magazine, *Amazing Stories*, in the late 1920s, yet another aspect of comic books and comic book culture that was remediated on the pulps. For more on early science fiction fandom, see Jones's *Men of Tomorrow*.

7 As Hajdu writes, "North appeared discontented with the prospect that young people might prefer a kind of book wholly unlike the ones he was writing" (42). Or, as Nyberg argues, "North's objection to comic books has its basis in the reaction of cultural elites to popular culture" (*Seal of Approval* 4).

8 In his follow-up piece, "The Antidote for Comics," published in the March 1941 edition of the National Parent-Teacher Association's magazine, North claims approximately 40 newspapers had reprinted "A National Disgrace."

9 Jones captures the moment succinctly when he writes, "Confronted in that apocalyptic moment with an alien entertainment form that had come from nowhere to infiltrate the taste of seemingly every child in America, adults reacted with a collective gasp" (170).

10 It is not surprising that librarians and public school teachers were so engaged in this early debate about comic books since "the former viewed themselves as charged with protecting the nation's literary heritage and the latter saw themselves as at least partially responsible for the safeguarding of American children" (Beaty 106).

11 I will return to the ways that libraries and librarians have positioned themselves in the debates surrounding comics and literacy later in Chapter Seven.

12 For a full account of the roles played by Liebowitz and Donenfeld in DC/National, see Jones's *Men of Tomorrow*. As Feldman has pointed out, however, Jones' account ignores the role of Paul Sampliner.

13 In *Superman: The High-Flying History of America's Most Enduring Superhero*, Tye goes even farther, arguing, "Not only did editors tell Jerry [Siegel] to cut out the guns and knives and cut back on social crusading, they started calling the shots on minute details of script and drawing" (49).

14 The cover date is always several months later than the actual publication date, as per standard publishing practices in the comic book industry.

15 The comic books included within the purview of the editorial board, as listed at the left of the initial notice, were *Action Comics*, *Detective Comics*, *Adventure Comics*, *More Fun Comics*, *Star Spangled Comics*, *All-American Comics*, *Flash Comics*, *Superman*, *Batman*, *All-Star Comics*, *All-Flash Quarterly*, and *World's Finest Comics*.

16 This partnership will be explored in Chapter Six.

17 This argument resonated at the time, as Beaty argues: "Many people found these efforts to fight comics with comics appealing because it seemed unlikely that the mass culture tide could be entirely diverted" (109).

CHAPTER FOUR

More at stake: EC, vampires, and the sponsorship of critical literacy

By the time 1941 came to an end, concerns over the effects of comics on the children of America had been replaced by the much more pressing concerns of World War II. So much had the tide turned away from the recent criticism of comics that by early 1942, comic book publishing was for the most part seen as part of the war effort, offering patriotic narratives of brave American and Allied forces defeating the Nazis and the Japanese at every turn, while of course proving financially profitable to publishers. Many in the comic book industry had, in fact, been advocating for America's entry into the war in the year leading up to the attack on Pearl Harbor and/or had been early supporters of the efforts of Allied forces during that period. As seen in the last chapter, for example, by early 1941 *True Comics* had already begun the work of instilling the kinds of values that would help prepare the American population for entry into the war. At Timely, Prince Namor, the Sub-Mariner, was fighting Nazi submarines in early 1940 and Captain America, in his first appearance in March, 1941 (released in December, 1940), famously punched Hitler in the face as startled Nazis looked on in horror. With so many Jewish creators and publishers involved in the industry, comic books "were particularly zealous in their creative assault on Fascism" (Hajdu 55). Hitler continued to appear on comic book covers throughout the war (as many as 50, according to Hajdu), his defeated or humiliated image a gateway and invitation to the narratives within that supported the war effort and delineated America's enemies.

Such pro-war narratives sponsored a multimodal literacy that instilled values consonant with mobilizing Americans for their entry into the war, values such as patriotism, sacrifice, bravery, and vigilance. In fact, superheroes often broke away from the narrative to urge the reader directly, encouraging children to do their part by collecting scrap metal and other materials that could be used for the war effort. At the same time, the absolutes of good and evil, especially in superhero comics, gave readers a clearly defined (and demonized) enemy, the antithesis of American values in the case of Hitler's Germany and a racialized and deeply racist version of the Other in the case of Japan. Such efforts considerably enlarged the number of "good" comics in the eyes of parents, teachers, and legislators, giving the comic book industry a respite from the criticisms of the early 1940s that would last until after the end of the war.

Even comic books which at first glance would not seem to be aligned with these values or concerned with America's involvement in the war took on the mantle of pushing for the war effort through the inclusion of such material as notices for war bond drives. *Crime Does Not Pay* was one such publication. Despite their support of the war, however, Lev Gleason Publications seemed unconcerned with making their publications palatable to teachers, parents, and concerned citizens. Destined for what Gabilliet calls "scandalous posterity," *Crime Does Not Pay* paved the way for a wave of imitators that would flood the market with violent crime comics by 1948 and precipitate the second comics panic of the late 1940s and early 1950s (27). In its connection to the documentary non-fiction approach of *True Comics*, its portrayals of authority figures and societal attitudes, and its sensationalistic depictions of violence, *Crime Does Not Pay* acts as a useful bridge to my discussion of the second comics panic, the Comics Code, and Entertaining Comics' sponsorship of literacy in the period leading up to imposition of the Code.

Crime Does Not Pay: "A Completely New Kind of Magazine"

From the time it debuted with July, 1942's issue #22 (taking over its numbering from the cancelled *Silver Streak Comics*), *Crime Does Not Pay* offered a documentary-style approach to the crime genre that focused on criminals rather than law enforcement. Rather than identifying with the hero trying to solve the crime, the reader was asked to be a more neutral observer of the purportedly accurate depiction of events in the comic. Remediated on true crime magazines such as *True Detective* and *Master Detective*, *Crime Does Not Pay* was not the first comic book of its kind, but was the first to offer such stark portrayals of a criminal underworld most comic book readers only knew through the filter of the superhero or detective genres. For example, in its first issue, *Crime Does Not Pay* offered stories such as "Crime Kings: The Real Story Behind Lepke, Mad Dog of the Underworld," "Officer Edward Maher and the Mad Dog Killers of Fifth Avenue" (the latter part of the title in much bolder and more distinctive type), and "The Case of the Twisted Cigarettes." Shockingly violent, these tales purported to present crime and criminals as they really were, with the final panel(s) showing the results of their crimes. For example, in typical fashion, the last panel of "The Mad Dog Killers of Fifth Avenue" shows a close up of a prison guard preparing an electric chair, with a caption that reads "These, as do all such lives, ended in the grim finality of the electric chair . . ." (n.p.). Even amidst such violence, ample support for the war effort was in evidence throughout this first issue of *Crime Does Not Pay*. Not only did each story begin with an image advocating the purchase of United States Defense Bonds and Stamps, but this issue included a superhero story, "The War Eagle," featuring a character specifically geared to fighting the war on the home front. In its beginnings, even the progenitor of the crime comic phenomenon of the late 1940s was on the side of truth, justice, and the American way.

In its documentary style and purported educational intent (to deter readers from a life of crime through examples of where such a life would lead), *Crime Does Not Pay* shared affinities with other books launched around the same time, such as *True Comics* and

Real Heroes. The column by Lev Gleason ("Crime Does Not Pay: A Completely New Kind of Magazine") inside the cover of the first issue makes clear the publisher's stated intent:

> But *CRIME DOES NOT PAY* is more than just a magazine. It is dedicated to the youth of America with the hope that it will help make better, cleaner young citizens. The object of the Editors is to bring home sharply, to make crystal clear, that CRIME DOES NOT PAY! Crime never pays, it is a sucker's game. Criminals are not heroes, they are not even brave or "nervy"—they are cowardly rats. Sooner or later they get their just reward. Their fate is prison and death.
>
> In these pages, then, you will see how one after another is brought to justice through the daring and cleverness of the officers of the law. Enjoy reading these exciting true stories. See for yourself the sad fate of crooks and criminals—and always remember that CRIME DOES NOT PAY. (n.p.)

Like *True Comics*, *Crime Does Not Pay* offered thrills and excitement in stories taken from real life, but unlike *True Comics*, it sought to work through a multimodal portrayal of negative behavior and the dire consequences of such actions (as seen in the panel with the electric chair mentioned above), rather than through the portrayal of positive values (as seen in the example from *True Comics* discussed in the last chapter). Of course, that documentary style was also highly sensational and the coda appended to each story often seemed to be artificially added only to satisfy the necessity of restoring the expected order, a criticism that was increasingly seen in the years after 1948 when the number of imitators began to rise rapidly. With the advent of such imitators, the level of sensational violence steadily rose, precipitating renewed attention to comic books and their effects on readers, particularly children.

There is no doubt that the stories were incredibly violent, a fact noted even by admirers of the series. In fact, in "Biro & Wood: Partners in Crime," the introduction to *Blackjacked and Pistol-Whipped: A Crime Does Not Pay Primer* (released in 2011), Denis Kitchen writes of the moral that was needed to accompany these "often-gruesome and sadistic stories," especially as parents and legislators turned their attention toward comic books and their content in the late 1940s and early 1950s (12). This moral, writes Kitchen, "was invariably supplied by the ending, when the criminal or gang was killed by the police or caught and punished. If a criminal who was effectively glorified throughout the previous pages was fried in the electric chair or hung by the neck in the last panel, the editors could sanctimoniously proclaim that crime does not pay, while simultaneously supplying an extra dash of violence" (12). However, there are those who argue for a more positive view of the series, as seen in both Daniels' *Comix: A History of Comic Books in America* and Jones' *Men of Tomorrow*. In the milder defense, Daniels writes that *Crime Does Not Pay* and other documentary-style comic books "came under attack for causing what they were actually only reporting" (86). Jones goes a step further, writing, "For all its perverse sensationalism, though, *Crime Does Not Pay* had a distinctive political twist. Many of its stories delved into the hard, poor environments that had produced their subjects" (194). For example, in issue #57, with a cover date of November, 1947, there appeared a story titled "The Short But Furious Crime Career of Irene Dague and Her Yes-Man Husband." In a series of three panels drawn by George Tuska, the two titular characters discuss their financial situation that precipitates their first foray into crime. Irene says to Glenn, "Sure it's chopped meat! What do ya expect, sirloin? We're livin' like tramps on your lousy pay—an' I'm tired of it, d'ya hear? We're gonna get money—if I have to rob it!" (n.p.). Glenn replies, "I'm not complainin'! It's just that I work an' work an' work an' I get no place!" (n.p.). Rather than portraying the couple as evil, the writer (uncredited in the book) instead provides a potentially understandable motive for their actions, while the artist depicts them as desperate rather than depraved.

From this angle, and despite its penchant for gruesome violence, the way *Crime Does Not Pay* was used to actually sponsor literacy, in both its target audience and its political outlook, was not limited to just purveying violent content for the sake of only profit. That is, if part of the intent was reportage and highlighting for the American public the class issues that were at the root of much violent crime, then the audience should not be seen only as the children who typically bought comic books during the period (though there were certainly children who read these books). Rather, if increased social awareness of the audience was part of the reason Lev Gleason might have wanted to sponsor such literacy (as can be seen in his left-leaning politics that eventually landed him in front of the House Un-American Activities Committee in 1946),[1] then it makes sense that adults would be an important target audience. In fact, as Gabilliet points out, advertisements for *Crime Does Not Pay* in other Gleason publications stated "Get 'Crime Does Not Pay'! Show it to Dad, he'll love it!" (37). By presenting a world in which the *status quo* wasn't perfect and a narrative that left room for questioning (even if order was finally restored in the last panel), Gleason, along with the creators/editors Charles Biro and Bob Wood, allowed for the possible development of critical questioning and critical awareness among their readers. Whether or not many of their readers would have grasped this possibility is an open question, but a case can certainly be made for a sponsorship of literacy that goes beyond the cynical equation of multimodal violence for money. Entertaining Comics (EC) later took this nascent possibility of societal critique and amplified it many fold.

"Horror in the Nursery": The second comics panic

As World War II came to a close, sales of superhero comics began to plummet and publishers began to experiment with a variety of genres—horror, crime, romance, western, humor—as they tried to find the next big thing. By 1948 the superhero was almost completely extinct and while other genres—including those made more palatable to parents and teachers in the early part of the decade by DC, Dell, the Parents' Institute, and Elliott Publishing— continued to do well, there was one genre to which every publisher was suddenly flocking: true crime.

Crime Does Not Pay had sold fairly well since its introduction in 1942, but beginning in 1947, sales increased dramatically. As Jones observes, audiences "suddenly wanted more ambivalent, more titillating stories of bad guys who lived it up at the expense of the good guys until they met a bloody end in the final panel" (237). Through their purchasing trends, comic book readers showed that they wanted to explore a more complex view of the world rather than the stark contrast between good and evil that seemed to be necessary during the war years. By 1948, seemingly every publisher was trying to get in on the act, introducing myriad imitations with titles like *Crime Must Pay the Penalty!*, *All-True Crime*, *Crime Can't Win*, *Crime Patrol*, and *War Against Crime*. All tolled, 40 publishers were producing crime comics by 1948 and, according to Kitchen, one in seven comic books sold in 1948 was in the crime genre (18). While perhaps not the biggest genre in terms of sales, crime comics were among the most high profile in 1948, drawing the renewed attention of critics. Chief among this new set of critics was Fredric Wertham who came to prominence with his March, 1948 interview with Judith Crist in *Collier's* entitled "Horror in the Nursery" and his article, "The Comics . . . Very Funny!" in the *Saturday Review of Literature*, published shortly thereafter. Almost singlehandedly, Wertham touched off the second comics panic that would ultimately lead to the establishment of the Comics Code in 1954.

Like Sterling North in his 1940 piece, "A National Disgrace," Wertham sounded the alarm about the morally deleterious effects of comic books: they were unsuitable and/or dangerous because they were aimed primarily at children. These attacks became more sustained with the rise of crime and horror comics in the 1940s. In "Horror in the Nursery," Wertham was quoted as saying that "The comic books, in intent and effect, are demoralizing the morals of youth. They are sexually aggressive in an abnormal way. They make violence alluring and cruelty heroic. They are not educating but stultifying" (22). Later in the interview, in response to the idea that comic books could be used to teach reading, Wertham went on so say, "Not only are comic books optically hard to read, with their garish colors and semiprinted balloons, but they are psychologically bad, turning the child's interest from reading to picture gazing" (95). In these ways, Wertham's critiques echo much of what North had written eight years before. However, there was a major difference in Wertham's attack and that difference lay in the connection he drew between the reading of comic books and juvenile delinquency and crime.

In "Horror in the Nursery," Wetham began to lay the groundwork for this connection between comic books and juvenile delinquency. He told Crist that "We do not maintain that comic books automatically cause delinquency in every child reader. . . . But we found that comic book reading was a distinct influencing factor in the case of every single delinquent or disturbed child we studied. And that factor must be curbed as it steadily increases" (22). He made an even stronger case for this point in his article "The Comics . . . Very Funny!" in which he provided a laundry list of specific instances of juvenile delinquency, all of which he saw as evidence of the link between reading comic books and the aberrant behavior he described. At the end of the article, he stated this link in unequivocal terms: "You cannot understand present-day juvenile delinquency if you do not take into account the pathogenic and pathoplastic influence of the comic books, that is, the way in which they cause trouble or determine the form that trouble takes" (8). It was this link to the perceived problem of juvenile delinquency that caught the attention of the nation and its legislators, eventually including Estes Kefauver, Chair of the Senate Subcommittee on Investigating Juvenile Delinquency.

Wertham further argued that there are really no "good" comics, including those based on the Bible and on classic literature, effectively dismissing the approach that George Hecht and Albert Kanter had used in attempting to substitute good comics for bad. For Wertham, the medium itself was the problem: "Even if the tiny percentage of so-called 'good' comic books could be used, that hardly justifies the existence of comic books *per se*. It's rather like saying that brothels justify themselves since they relieve the housing shortage by providing a few people with a place to sleep" ("Horror" 95). Meanwhile, Hecht was still making the case for the positive potential of comics, appearing along with Al Capp to defend the medium against John Mason Brown and Marya Mannes (author of the 1947 anti-comics article, "Junior Has a Craving") in a radio roundtable staged by America's Town Meeting of the Air in early March, 1948, as mentioned in the last chapter. Against Mannes's assertion that "comics can produce an uncivilized immature race" and Brown's hyperbolic claim that comics were "the marihuana of the nursery . . . the bane of the bassinet . . . the horror of the home, curse of the kids, and the threat to the future," Hecht remained steadfast in his defense of comics ("What's Wrong with the Comics?" 6, 22). In a seldom seen argument for this period and one that prefigures that of Scott McCloud, Hecht began by saying that "comics are really a new medium of communication, just as radio and television are new mediums of communication" ("What's

Wrong with the Comics?" 7). From there, he proceeded to reiterate an idea he had been stating since the introduction of *True Comics* in 1941: "there are good comic magazines and bad comics just as there are good books and bad books" ("What's Wrong with the Comics?" 7). For Hecht, reading good comics promoted reading in general, foreshadowing the scaffolding approach to comics described in Chapter 1. However, despite voices such as Hecht's coming to the defense of comics, the tide was turning against the comic book industry as more and more people began to take Wertham seriously.[2]

It was Wertham's influential 1953 book *Seduction of the Innocent* that was particularly instrumental in prompting the Senate Subcommittee on Juvenile Delinquency to investigate the comic book industry in 1954. In this book, Wertham continued to express his concerns about what he saw as the possible detrimental effects of comics on children, including juvenile delinquency, abnormal sexual development, and illiteracy. The problem, as he saw it, lay in the way comics glorified violence and sexual depravity while at the same time impeding children's development of print literacy; these problems were exacerbated by the "extreme avidity" which children showed toward comic books (*Seduction* 50). In fact, as it was for North, the real issue for Wertham and other critics of this period had as much to do with who would sponsor children's literacy and whether or not children should be able to have some choice in the types of literacies in which they engaged and the ways in which those literacies would be sponsored. For example, at the end of "Horror in the Nursery," Wertham is quoted: "We are not dealing with the rights and privileges of adults to read and write as they choose. We are dealing with the mental health of a generation—the care of which we have left too long in the hands of unscrupulous persons whose only interest is greed and financial gain" (97). Clearly, what's important here is who is allowed to sponsor literacy and in what way; in this attempt to regulate literacy, Wertham was in effect trying to position himself as a sponsor of literacy for an entire generation of children. Even more pressing, however, was the fear that children would exert control over their own literacy choices, including which sponsors they would choose. As Hajdu points out, "Encoded in much of the ranting about comic books and juvenile delinquency were fears not only of what comic readers might become, but of what they already were—that is, a generation of people developing their own interests and tastes, along with a determination to indulge them" (112). As important as these issues were for North in the early 1940s, they would become increasingly prominent as ever more overt cultural critique began to surface in the form of EC comics.

Wertham's major concern lay in the "moral disarmament" that crime comics caused in children (*Seduction* 91). As defined by Wertham, crime comics were not limited to true crime, but instead comprised nearly the entire output of the comic book publishing: "crime comic books are comic books that depict crime, whether the setting is urban, western, science-fiction, jungle, adventure, or the realm of supermen, 'horror,' or supernatural beings" (*Seduction* 30–1). Not only were children being exposed to sadistic violence and sexual depravity through these "crime" comics, but Wertham believed they were in danger of subconsciously imitating what they saw, especially through "identify[ing] themselves with the strong man, however evil he may be" (*Seduction* 116). According to Wertham and other critics like him, children would get the wrong kinds of ideas from comics and be prone to juvenile delinquency, exactly the concern shared by the Senate Subcommittee on Juvenile Delinquency.

Wertham, who would soon be called to act as a consultant to the Senate Subcommittee, argued that the scope of the problem was so vast that it needed to be dealt with on a societal level through the introduction of legislation at the state and/or federal level.[3] In fact, Wertham had been calling for such legislation since the publication of "Horror in the Nursery" in 1948. In the spring of 1954, Wertham seemed to get his wish as the Senate Subcommittee on Juvenile Delinquency convened in New York for three days of hearings. The most oft-cited testimony from those hearings came from two men representing opposing positions. The first was Wertham, who despite being an outspoken critic of comics was nonetheless also seen as a leading expert on comics and juvenile delinquency. The second was William M. Gaines, publisher of Entertaining Comics (EC) whose comics were cited as among the most lurid in terms of both violence and sexuality.[4] As seen above, Wertham clearly believed that comics caused children to imitate what they saw in them. Not surprisingly, being a publisher whose bottom line was deeply threatened by any legislation that would regulate the comics industry (and especially the genres he published), Gaines argued that comics were harmless entertainment that produced no lasting effects on children.[5] However, Gaines needn't have worried about government legislation as the members of the committee realized that legislation would be met with constitutional challenges (Nyberg, *Seal* 79). What he instead was faced with was the imposition of a self-regulatory code by the comics industry itself that was much more strict than anything that could have possibly been imposed by any legislative body.

Beware all monsters: The coming of the code

In August of 1954, the Comic Magazine Association of America was founded as a trade association with the express purpose of adopting an industry-wide comics code in an effort to change the tide of public opinion by demonstrating a unified commitment to what the publishers perceived as community standards.[6] The main targets of the Comics Code were crime and horror comics; of the three sections in the Code, the first was devoted exclusively to crime comics and the second to horror comics, while the third encompassed what are called "General Standards." While severe restrictions were imposed on how crime and punishment were to be portrayed in crime comics, the most severe restrictions were reserved for horror comics. Horror comics, which had become the most popular genre by the early 1950s, were on their way out, banished by the publishers in an exaggerated reaction to perceived public opinion.[7]

Of course, those comic book publishers that had not claimed a piece of the lucrative horror market had a vested interest in the demise of horror comics, just as those who profited from them, such as Gaines at EC, had a vested interest in doing everything they could to fight such a ban. In fact, *Archie* publisher John Goldwater was so involved with not only the establishment of the Code, but also its subsequent enforcement that he wrote *Americana in Four Colors*, a short book published in 1964 to commemorate the tenth anniversary of the Code (a revised edition was published in 1974 for the twentieth anniversary). In that volume, Goldwater wrote, "the self-regulation program has resulted in the elimination of the undesirable from the industry" (8). Later, in speaking of the elimination of horror comics under the auspices of the Code, Goldwater reflected, "There were never more than a comparative few of these published, but they caused a tremendous amount of furor, and were usually selected as 'typical' examples of the industry's product by those who chose to condemn the entire medium" (25). By eliminating such "undesirables" and establishing a commitment to perceived community standards, the Code was to have its desired effects.

The section of the 1954 Comics Code dealing with General Standards for horror comics reads as follows:

1 No comic magazine shall use the word horror or terror in its title.

2 All scenes of horror, excessive bloodshed, gory or gruesome crimes, depravity, lust, sadism, masochism shall not be permitted.

3 All lurid, unsavory, gruesome illustrations shall be eliminated.

4 Inclusion of stories dealing with evil shall be used or shall be published only where the intent is to illustrate a moral issue and in no case shall evil be presented alluringly, nor so as to injure the sensibilities of the reader.

5 Scenes dealing with, or instruments associated with walking dead, torture, vampires and vampirism, ghouls, cannibalism, and werewolfism are prohibited. (qtd. in Nyberg, *Seal* 167)

The extreme particularity of the last point is interesting in the way that it targets very specific parts of the industry, most specifically the titles published by companies like EC. For example, not only do the guidelines effectively remove vampire stories by specifying what is no longer permissible in horror comics, but as an added measure, vampires are explicitly prohibited. In effect, the vampire was not only staked, but its head was removed. Despite its brevity, the section of the Comics Code dealing with horror comics effectively ended the genre as it had been known.

In addition to these prohibitions on horror, the Code also dealt with the problem of sexual deviancy that had been outlined by

Wertham. Since vampires are not only effective in producing fear in their audiences, but also display thinly or not-so-thinly veiled sexuality, the prohibitions in the Code with regard to sexuality are also relevant here. In the subsection on Marriage and Sex, the Code stated that

1 Divorce shall not be treated humorously nor represented as desirable.

2 Illicit sex relations are neither to be hinted at nor portrayed. Violent love scenes as well as sexual abnormalities are unacceptable.

3 Respect for parents, the moral code, and for honorable behavior shall be fostered. A sympathetic understanding of the problems of love is not a license for morbid distortion.

4 The treatment of live-romance stories shall emphasize the value of the home and the sanctity of marriage.

5 Passion or romantic interest shall never be treated in such a way as to stimulate the lower and baser emotions.

6 Seduction and rape shall never be shown or suggested.

7 Sex perversion or any inference to same is strictly forbidden. (qtd. in Nyberg, *Seal* 168)

Vampire stories, especially those produced by EC, clearly flew in the face of all of these restrictions, portraying as they did illicit and violent sexual relations and seduction, eschewing the traditional values of the period, relying on the base emotion of physical need, and generally engaging in "abnormal" or "perverse" sexual acts. In this vein, as Carol Margaret Davison argues, "For all it 'disguises' sexuality, however, vampirism still delivers more of an erotic bang for the cultural consumer's buck. It elicits more titillation and generates more shock value per word/frame than any other graphically detailed sex scene possibly can" (27). In this quotation, taken from her introduction to *Bram Stoker's Dracula: Sucking Through the Century, 1897–1997*, Davison is writing about prose and film, but the idea applies equally well to the comics medium; through the use of vampires, comics creators could tread the margins of what was acceptable in the early 1950s in terms of displays of sexuality. However, as seen in the above guidelines, such depictions of sexuality were finally seen as too far outside what was acceptable, especially for material that was deemed to be for children, and thus expunged from what was possible in comics. As Goldwater wrote in 1964, the Code's seal on the cover of a comic book "provides an assurance to parents that the contents adhere in every particular to the tenets of the Code, and constitute acceptable reading material for young people" (30). Unlike the comics panic of the early 1940s which elicited a variety of responses from publishers, that of the early 1950s was met with a concerted response that would leave only the major, conservative publishing houses still in business.

In real terms, enforcement of the Code was in place because distribution companies would invariably refuse to carry comics that did not display the Comics Code Authority Seal (except in the cases of Dell, Gold Key, and *Classics Illustrated*, all of which were seen as conforming to community standards that were viewed as at least as stringent as those imposed by the Code). The importance of distribution cannot be overemphasized since the key to success was national newsstand distribution; the quality of a publisher's books would not matter if no readers or potential readers ever saw them. Thus, as a result of the Code and its restrictions, many companies went out of business, while others produced "a sanitized version of what had gone before" (Normanjon 12). This situation of self-censorship in the industry would not be effectively challenged for years to come.

From the reactions of critics to the Senate Subcommittee's investigation of comics to the imposition of the Comics Code, there was a vehemence to the attacks on horror comics that today seems out of proportion. What was it about horror comics that caused these kinds of reactions? Why were stories about vampires, for example, seen as so threatening? In order to take up these questions, I want to look more closely at the case of EC, whose titles, *Tales from the Crypt*, *Vault of Horror*, and *Haunt of Fear* were among the main targets of the Code; at the ways that EC sponsored literacy for a generation of horror comic readers; and at the reactions to their involvement in the lives of children from society in general and the comic book industry in particular. At the heart of this examination is the vampire, so vital a presence to the EC horror line; through this critical examination of the place of vampires in the early 1950s period of comics history, I will endeavor to shed additional light on what's at stake in struggles over literacy sponsorship.

The horror of comics as
sponsors of literacy

In many ways, the debate about the influence of comics on children is not that different from contemporary debates about the influence of other forms of popular entertainment, such as movies, television, music, or video games. However, the intensity of the scrutiny of comics and the subsequent self-censorship of the industry are unique. Why this elevated level of concern? Certainly there was much graphic content in terms of both language and sexuality in comics in the early 1950s, but this does not explain why the reaction was so strong. Of course, what all of these forms of entertainment have in common is that they represent a youth culture that adults usually do not understand and that always remains outside of their control. That lack of control over how children are spending their time and making meaning from the world is frightening to adults no matter what media or time period. It is, however, exacerbated in the case of comics because this activity involves reading, the province of not just adults, but of institutions such as schools and churches. Because literacy is so wrapped up with the ways in which we make sense of the world, it is easy to see why the shaping of literate behaviors is seen as so important, as seen in the discussion of the first comics panic. In other words, comic books were seen as so dangerous because the decision to read them usually rested with children rather than with their parents or teachers; children were choosing how their literacy would be sponsored and by whom. It is this battle over what children read and who is allowed to sponsor the literacy of children that makes the debate over comics so charged.

Since the acquisition of literacy involves taking on ways of making meaning in the world, horror and crime comics were seen as especially dangerous because they presented a vision of the world that was at odds with that of mainstream society. In an argument that could just as easily apply to horror comics, Wright asserts that

> The crime comic books put forth a remarkably perverse and horrifying image of the affluent society turned upside down.... the crime comics offered no way out. Their collective deconstruction

of the American dream promised no easy answers, only more of the same. They affronted the triumphalism of postwar America, and young readers bought it up by the millions. (*Comic Book Nation* 84)

Seen in this way, crime and horror comics offered young people a critique of the world of adults, a world for which they were being groomed for entrance. Such critiques threatened to disrupt the *status quo* and the assumptions on which early 1950s North American society rested. The Comics Code's prohibition of horror comics effectively stopped such critique and the opportunities for critical thought that were gained through reading them.

Why, though, was there a need to specifically prohibit scenes involving "walking dead, torture, vampires and vampirism, ghouls, cannibalism, and werewolfism," as was specified in the Code? Didn't the other, more general prohibitions against horror comics cover these specifics? In carefully delineating this list, the authors of the Comics Code precisely targeted the kinds of stories used to so effectively critique what was seen as normal in 1950s America, while at the same time crippling the publishers who relied on these stories to sell their titles. This was especially true of EC, whose horror comics—*Tales from the Crypt*, *Haunt of Fear*, and *Vault of Horror*—were a virtual catalogue of the types of stories specifically prohibited by the Code. Usually built on the reversal of audience expectations, EC horror stories served as ideal vehicles for cultural critique, with creatures such as vampires central to that critique.[8] While EC was in the business of publishing comics for profit, Gaines and his creative staff also had other goals in mind for their comics publications, as was made clear with the overhaul of their publishing program and the introduction of the "New Trend" line in 1950.[9] EC acted as a sponsor of literacy, developing a reciprocal relationship with young consumers, which was based on variations of tales associated with these aspects of horror; through that relationship, young readers developed a literacy that emphasized how to be critical of the world around them, while EC profited from their continued patronage of their comics line. It was, in fact, a mutually beneficial situation.

Terrorizing American culture: The pre-code vampire

To see the importance of vampires, zombies, werewolves, ghouls, torture, and cannibalism in EC comics, one needs to look no further than the last few issues of *Tales from the Crypt*, published in the months prior to the imposition of the Comics Code in 1954. Each issue of this immensely popular comic was comprised of four short stories, a format typical of EC's line of horror comics. The format, with its lack of recurring characters or ongoing plot, was a perfect match for the horror genre because the characters "usually end[ed] up condemned, mad, dead, or living-dead" (Wright *Comic Book Nation* 104). Though brevity held its own set of limitations, without the constraints imposed by serialized stories, there was virtually no limit on what could happen to the characters in service of the story the creators wanted to tell. Vampires, appearing in three of the final five issues of *Tales from the Crypt* (just as they often appeared in other EC horror titles), comprised one of the main vehicles that creators could use to critique the society in which they lived through a reversal of audience expectations. Given the frequency of their appearance in 1950s horror comics, it's no wonder that vampires were seen as so threatening to the authors of the Comics Code.

What exactly is it about vampires and vampirism that made these kinds of stories so appealing to creators and readers of horror comics? Vampiric tales are adaptable to the cultural contexts in which they are told, and draw their meanings from the lifeblood of those contexts;[10] they are, in effect, parasitic themselves. Moreover, the fear that they create is a fear that is generated not from the fear of death, but from fear of life *in that particular time and place*. By tapping into those fears, creators of horror comics could scare their readers by holding up a mirror of 1950s America, using vampires to show them why it was frightening and why they needed to think critically about it. As shape shifters who can pass for humans, vampires look like the person next door. They might be your boss, your best friend, or even your spouse.[11] This ability to pass for "normal" heightens what is possible in the vampire story and allows for myriad reversals of audience expectations, especially in the twist endings so prevalent in EC comics. Vampires thus speak to and draw their fear from whatever time and place conjures them.

The three vampire stories that appeared in the last five issues of *Tales from the Crypt* ("By Dawn's Early Light," "Clot's My Line," and "The Proposal") are all examples of invasions of the normal that serve to critique the social structure of the early 1950s. The first, "By Dawn's Early Light," appeared in *Tales from the Crypt* #42 along with three other stories, including a werewolf story, "Concerto for Violin and Werewolf." The cover of *Tales from the Crypt* #42 used an array of multimodal Design strategies to project a particular image and entice browsers to buy the book. The linguistic element is, of course, centrally important, from the title in its stylized font (designed to suggest horror through its use of jagged lettering) to the publisher information (which brands the comic for the prospective buyer by establishing an intertextual relationship with other EC comics) to the word "Terror" that occupies the upper left hand of the page (a not-so-subtle indication of genre that was expressly prohibited by the Code later that year). One of the most interesting visual elements is the series of portraits of The Crypt-Keeper, The Old Witch, and The Vault-Keeper, characters that recurred in all EC horror books as framing devices for the stories. Like the EC logo, these characters and their visual representation served a branding function that strengthened the relationship of literacy sponsorship that EC sought to create with its readers, much like the figure of Mr. Crime did in *Crime Does Not Pay*. These portraits are superimposed over a Jack Davis drawing that could be an interior panel within a comics story; the panel depicts a group of villagers about to drive a stake through the heart of a reposing vampire. Here the eye is drawn to the central image of the hammer poised above the stake as it literally bursts forth from the panel, at once implying its power to rectify the vampire problem and drawing the readers' eyes both up to the title of the comic and down toward the stake that will (we suppose) eradicate the vampire. In other words, Davis effectively designs the layout of the page to create spatial meaning. What's more, Davis has taken advantage of the gestural mode to create meaning, drawing all of the villagers agape, with facial expressions that clearly indicate fright, even as the two men in the foreground demonstrate both strength and fortitude in the moment before they stake the placid vampire. In this way, the visual, gestural, spatial, and linguistic interact as a multimodal paratext through which the reader will make meaning and draw conclusions about the comic as a whole.

Although each reader will negotiate slightly different meanings from this cover, potential comic book readers of the early 1950s were similar enough in their Available Designs that the above observations would hold for most potential readers. To the casual observer of this cover, the threat would seem to be contained, as the villagers have things in hand with the mallet poised above the heart of the sleeping vampire. To the average reader of horror comics in general and EC comics in particular, however, things were rarely, if ever, as they first appeared. Within the logic of the "panel" itself, the scene depicted is clearly meant to take place at night, a time when the vampire could awaken at any moment. As a single panel, bereft of its sequence, we as readers are not privy to the implied subsequent panels, but are only given a static moment in time, a concept that is antithetical to the comics medium. The next panel might indeed show the vampire's eyes opening, his hand wrenching the stake from the terrified villager, or any of a number of other possibilities. The key here is that since the cover is not a panel in sequence, we cannot know what will come next. Given their past experiences with the genre, however, readers of horror comics would have expected that things were not going to turn out well for the villagers. What's also interesting is that instead of engaging in the usual practice of depicting a scene from one of the stories contained in the issue (as happens in the other four final issues of *Tales from the Crypt*), Davis draws a scene from what we might call a classical vampire story even though the issue contains a contemporary vampire story of a very different order.

"By Dawn's Early Light," the vampire story included in this issue, was written by Al Feldstein and drawn by Jack Kamen and "presented" by The Vault-Keeper as The Vault of Horror feature, a clever cross-promotion that reminded readers of another title in the EC horror line. The story involves the quest of Frank Williams to understand what suddenly killed his fiancée, Joan Lorin. Recently returned from a trip to New York, Williams is unaware a vampire has been stalking the unnamed Illinois town where he lives. In a flashback sequence (denoted by the changing of the panel borders from straight to irregularly bubbled lines), his friend Harry tells him of the recent murders and of finding Joan with telltale puncture marks on her throat, a discovery that leads him and other concerned citizens to stake her to prevent her from also rising from the dead. After this conversation, Frank arms himself with a stake and walks home, along the way encountering the vampire fleeing from the scene of killing one of his victims. Frank gives chase and they end up back at the funeral home where Joan's body lies. In the kind of reversal that EC readers came to expect, Frank discovers that his best friend, Earl Boyd, appears to be the vampire. To make sure, Frank ties Earl up in the vampire's coffin, sure that if he is the vampire he will fall asleep at sunrise. In the last page (seen in Figure 4.1) the results of this test are revealed.

FIGURE 4.1 *Final page of "By Dawn's Early Light," Tales from the Crypt #42. © 2012 William M. Gaines Agent, Inc.*

The first tier of panels adopts the format of a standard nine-panel page grid and keeps the action contained within the boundaries of these three panels. All three panels show the relationship that has been established on the previous page between the two men, with Frank in the role of captor and Earl in the role of captive. This relationship is emphasized by the way in which the body language of the two men is portrayed (Frank is free in his movements, while Earl is hunched over and trussed) and the way in which the scene has been drawn (each panel is shown either from above or below to emphasize that Earl is in the subordinate position to Frank). As the regularity of the panels emphasizes, this state of affairs, the result of the previous page's shocking reveal that Earl is the vampire, is what Frank, and by extension the reader of the comic, believes to be true. That is, the visual, gestural, and spatial design elements emphasize what is the new normal: vampires walk among us, perhaps even in the guise of our best friends. However, the linguistic element works against this version of reality as Earl points to the printed time of sunrise on the calendar in order to exonerate himself from the charge of being a vampire. The next tier is comprised of two slightly larger panels as the narrative moves from exposition into action. In panel four, the dialogue between the characters and the text in the caption box (both linguistic), Frank throwing the stake away (a visual representation of the gestural), the hurled stake breaking out of the boundary of the panel (visual), and the way in which the stake points toward the action of Frank untying Earl in panel five (spatial), all point toward another reversal in what we (and Frank) think we know. Earl really isn't the vampire at all. Or is he?

By the end of the fifth panel, even as the audience focuses on Frank untying Earl, an act which is emphasized visually by the replacement of the detailed backgrounds of the first four panels with only darkness, the reader is cued linguistically that something is not right. Frank's speech, as seen in the word balloon, is represented as halting ("Y-Yeah") and tentative. Both the words (the linguistic element) and the way they are said or the way we are to imagine they are said (the audio element) work together to produce a sense of doubt in the reader about the outcome of the story. In the final panel of the narrative (but not the final panel on the page), it is finally revealed that Earl is, after all, a vampire as he attacks his purported friend, presumably signaling Frank's demise. Here all of the elements work toward the same conclusion; there is no longer any of the tension that has been produced in the first two tiers of information from the juxtaposition of elements. The facial expressions (including the tell-tale fangs of the vampire) and body language clearly convey the hunter and the hunted (visual and gestural); the background becomes red—a color associated, of course, with blood—with streaks of black that both represent motion lines as the vampire attacks and act as a visual link to the black background of the previous panel (visual and spatial); the text in the caption box and in the word balloons emphasizes the new reality of the situation and, through visual cues such as the bolding of text, both Frank's fear and Earl's triumph (linguistic and audio). Taken together as a multimodal whole, these design elements signify the final reversal of audience expectations.

There is, of course, every reason to believe that the reader has already taken in this panel when he or she first flipped to this page since it is notoriously difficult for comics creators to control this kind of eye movement in readers (Eisner, *Comics and Sequential Art* 41). Consciously or unconsciously, the reader is prepared for this final reversal by the layout of the page, just as she or he has been prepared for such reversals through previous experience with EC horror comics (which add to the Available Design the reader brings to this text). Like "The Proposal" and "Clot's My Line," vampire stories that appeared in the next two issues of *Tales from the Crypt*, "By Dawn's Early Light" use this reversal of expectations to pull back the curtain on American society in order to show what lies beneath. Just as "By Dawn's Early Light" questions the implied social structure of 1950s America by calling into question the concept of friendship and showing that beneath this concept is only self-interest, "The Proposal" similarly critiques the institution of marriage, while "Clot's My Line" sets its sights on popular entertainment and consumer culture. Moreover, through its triple reversal of audience expectations, "By Dawn's Early Light" implies that readers should not only question the appearance of the world around them, but they should be wary of those who try to convince them that everything is alright and that questioning is not necessary. This particular story has none of the gore or violence that precipitated the attacks on horror comics, but it is easy to see why the sponsorship of this kind of critical literacy would be threatening nonetheless.

Coda: The Vault-Keeper speaks

The last panel that helps to frame the story—a kind of coda delivered by The Vault-Keeper—explicitly states the relationship of literacy sponsorship EC sought to establish and maintain. Not only did Gaines and the staff of EC want young people to read *Tales from the Crypt*, but they wanted them to buy and read their entire horror line, all of which included similar stories that looked beneath the outward appearances of the American dream. Without a stable of ongoing characters, hosts such as The Vault-Keeper acted as guides to the critical worldview espoused by EC and links to the continuing sponsorship of a particular kind of multimodal comics literacy that emanated from and focused on EC. As seen in the virulent responses of critics and the harsh treatment of horror comic books by the Comics Code, such literacy sponsorship was indeed seen as dangerous. Of course, in many critics' eyes, all comics companies were vampiric in the way that they wanted to "turn" innocent young readers into comics readers and bleed them each month of not only their allowances, but of their very ability to read traditional print texts. Companies such as EC, however, were particularly troublesome because of the critical literacy they encouraged in teenaged and young adult readers.

No wonder so many people were made nervous by these comics since not only did they de-emphasize traditional print literacy, but their content was deemed objectionable in multiple ways, ranging from their lack of literary merit to their inclusion of violence and sexuality to their questioning of the *status quo*. In sponsoring children's and adolescents' literacy, comic book publishers such as EC were viewed as dangerous parasites on childhood reading, creating what Wertham called "bookworms without books," hollow shells being leached of not only their ability to read complex texts, but their very innocence (*Seduction* 122). The threat of the horror genre had to be contained and its particular brand of multimodal literacy sponsorship eliminated.

With the coming of the Comics Code, the vampire virtually disappeared from comics for almost 20 years and the use of vampires and other monsters for the purpose of societal critique for even longer. Changes to the Code in 1971 brought a rush to all things vampiric, but when vampires returned, they had no bite; their use as a medium of critique was exorcized as their very existence had been excised in 1954. The vampire returned in form, but the spirit of the EC vampire from the early 1950s was lost, along with the kind of literacy sponsorship it provided.

Despite the imposition of the Code and the restrictions it placed on the content allowed, there would soon be more uses of comic books, just as Hecht foretold in 1948: "I think the educational and religious and industrial use of comics is just in its infancy. I think the schools and the churches will all in time be using comics as a means of mass education" ("What's Wrong" 18). As will be seen in the following two chapters, such uses of comics would come into focus over the next 20 years.

Notes

1 For more on Gleason being brought before HUAC, see Jones's *Men of Tomorrow*.
2 A fuller description of the comics panic in the years from 1948–54 can be found in Nyberg's *Seal of Approval* and Hajdu's *The Ten-Cent Plague*.
3 See Nyberg's *Seal of Approval* for a full discussion of Wertham's arguments for legislating comics.
4 For a complete discussion of the Senate Subcommittee Hearings, see Nyberg's *Seal of Approval*. For a complete transcript of Gaines's testimony, see *Tales of Terror!* by Fred von Bernowitz and Grant Geissman.
5 Nyberg argues that "unintentional messages found in the comics— messages about violence, the victimization of women, or the making of criminals into heroic figures—lay at the heart of the dispute between Gaines and Wertham" (*Seal* 73).
6 Dell Comics, who at the time accounted for nearly one third of all comic sales, launched its own "Pledge to Parents" campaign and refused to join the Association, as did Gold Key, who steadfastly maintained that their standards were actually higher than those enshrined in the Comics Code. The other company that decided not to join was Gilbertson Publications, whose major publication, *Classics Illustrated*, was thought unlikely to be affected by the new rules.
7 Nyberg argues that the strictures on horror comics were put in place to show that the Comic Magazine Association of America was serious about the Code: "By sacrificing the horror comics, publishers hoped to demonstrate their sincerity of purpose in self-regulation" (*Seal* 113).

8 As Hajdu succinctly writes, "In EC's horror paradigm, the true graveyard was the living room of the American home" (179). Or, as Wright argues in "Tales from the American Crypt: EC and the Culture of the Cold War, 1950–1954," "EC's horror comic books were only the most extreme evidence of a calculated editorial strategy that set out to demolish the myths that informed Cold War America. . . . They were an exercise in cultural defiance, deliberately offensive to all those who championed selective 'traditional values' or claimed to speak for an 'American consensus'" (22).

9 The "New Trend" titles introduced in 1950 were *Tales from the Crypt, Vault of Horror, Haunt of Fear, Weird Fantasy, Weird Science, Crime SuspenStories,* and *Two-Fisted Tales.*

10 In *Our Vampires, Ourselves*, Nina Auerbach argues that "since vampires are immortal, they are free to change incessantly. Eternally alive, they embody not fear of death, but fear of life: their power and their curse is their undying vitality. . . . Because they are always changing, their appeal is dramatically generational" (5).

11 Auerbach writes that "vampires blend into the changing cultures they inhabit. They inhere in our most intimate relationships; they are also hideous invaders of the normal" (6).

CHAPTER FIVE

Oral Roberts discovers comics and Archie goes to church: Sponsoring multimodal literacy through religious comics

As can be seen in the preceding chapters, many of the subsequent possibilities for using comic books to sponsor multimodal literacy can be traced back to events in the formative years of the industry, especially between 1938 and 1942. Those years saw not only the advent of the recurring comics character with ongoing, serialized adventures, but also the introduction of Superman, the character most responsible for the development of comic book publishing, and many of the ways that multimodal literacy has been sponsored by major publishers ever since. As with any business, profit remained at the heart of this relationship, but as we have seen both in Chapters two and four, that relationship was often complicated by the ways in which creators attempted to sponsor particular worldviews through the comics (as seen with Siegel and Shuster, Morrison and Morales, and many of the creative staff at EC, with the blessing of their publisher). In addition, as seen in Chapter three, these years saw the first comics panic and the responses of the publishers to it, including the drafting of an in-house code for creators and use of an Editorial Advisory Board by DC, and the introduction of educational comics, such as *Classic Comics* and *True Comics*, by Elliott Publishing and the Parents' Institute. Finally, as discussed in Chapter four, these attacks and responses, along with the introduction of *Crime Does Not Pay* in 1942, prefigured the second comics panic in the late 1940s and early 1950s and the eventual imposition of the Comics Code. All of these issues and possibilities surrounding the use of comics and comic books to sponsor multimodal literacy can be traced back to this five-year period (1938–42) of innovation and remediation as seemingly everyone attempted to jump on the comics bandwagon in search of readership and profit.

In 1939, following on the success of Superman, eight new comic book publishers began to do business, including Fox Features Syndicate, Quality, Harvey, Better Comics, Lev Gleason Publications, and Timely Publications. That year also saw the start of MLJ, founded by Maurice Coyne, Louis Silberkleit, and John L. Goldwater (their first initials forming MLJ), and All-American Comics, founded by M. C. Gaines in association of Jack Liebowitz at DC. While the legacy of each company survives today—MLJ as Archie Comics and All-American as one of the forerunners of DC (responsible for such characters as Green Lantern, the Atom, and Red Tornado)—one of the most interesting aspects of both companies is the part that each played in the use of comic books to sponsor multimodal literacy within a religious context. Not only was John Goldwater of Archie Comics instrumental in the establishment of the Comics Magazine Association of America and the establishment of the Comics Code,[1] but, as we shall see later in this chapter, in the 1970s he would license Archie to Spire Comics for use in evangelical Christian comic books. Gaines, first at All-American and then later at his own Educational Comics, would publish the first religious comic book, *Picture Stories from the Bible.* While *True Comics* had ushered in the overtly educational use of the comic book, *Picture Stories* marked the introduction of the comic book for specifically religious education. Just as Hecht predicted in 1948, such uses of comic books were just beginning and would continue, moving from *Picture Stories from the Bible* and the Catechecial Guild's *Topix* in the 1940s to *Oral Roberts' True Stories* in the 1950s to Spire Christian Comic's use of Archie in the 1970s to manga versions of the Bible today. These examples provide a fascinating picture of the complex layers of literacy sponsorship in Christian uses of comic books.

In the beginning: *Picture stories from the Bible and Topix*

M. C. Gaines began his work in the comic book publishing business shortly after he took a sales job with Eastern Color Printing in 1933. In that capacity, Gaines was an integral part of three of the earliest comic books, *Funnies on Parade*, *Famous Funnies*, and *A Century of Comics*, all of which were published in 1933 and featured reprints of previously published comic strips. While the role he played in the conception and execution of these early comics has often been exaggerated, Gaines did arrange many of the corporate customers for these very successful promotional comics books,[2] including Proctor & Gamble, Kinney Shoes, and Canada Dry, among others. From there Gaines moved on to work as a book packager for George T. Delacorte at his new company, Dell Comics, and as a kind of talent and content scout for the McClure newspaper syndicate. Through their work at McClure, Gaines and Sheldon Mayer—an editor who often worked for him—became involved with Major Wheeler-Nicholson and, ultimately, Harry Donenfeld, Jack Liebowitz, and Detective Comics.

After the success of Superman, the material for which Mayer and Gaines had a hand in discovering,[3] Gaines worked to further entrench himself within DC through smart promotion of the popular new hero, both in his work on packaging the new *Superman* comic book and his involvement in *New York World's Fair Comics*, which featured Superman on the cover and was to be distributed at the New York World's Fair in 1939. While these projects were in the works, Gaines leveraged his good work to ask Donenfeld for the capital to start All-American Comics, a venture that he began in partnership with Liebowitz in 1939. It was, by all accounts, a very successful and lucrative partnership, but by 1944, it had come to an end, with Liebowitz buying Gaines's share and then immediately arranging the merger of All-American Comics and Detective Comics into National Comics.

Gaines walked away with a substantial profit and the rights to *Picture Stories from the Bible*, the first title for his new company, Educational Comics. Whatever his motives, it is clear that Gaines was committed to the idea of *Picture Stories from the Bible* and staked much of his future on its success. If Daniels is to be believed, *Picture Stories from the Bible* was Gaines's pet project, an effort on his part "to inject culture into the world of comic books" (62). This view accords with that of Jones, who writes that Gaines "sincerely wanted to do something wholesome and worthwhile" (223). Hajdu, on the other hand, paints Gaines in a much different, and much more self-aggrandizing, light: "A frustrated pedant in a field of Goliathan philistines, he promoted *Picture Stories from the Bible* by writing a historical treatise titled *Narrative Illustration, The Story of Comics*" (73). In his bio for that publication, Gaines greatly exaggerated his earlier contributions, claiming that he was the "[o]riginator of the comic book in its present form," also "credited with 'discovering' that super-streamlined hero of the young: Superman!" (15). Hajdu further erodes the picture of Gaines as a benevolent man of culture when he quotes Ivan Klapper, a former employee of Gaines in the late 1930s: "It was the strangest thing to me that Charlie Gaines was publishing all these Bible stories about love and kindness . . . and he was the nastiest son of a bitch on the face of the earth" (74). Whatever his private motivations, however, Gaines was nonetheless responsible for the first attempt to use the comics medium to present the Bible, much as Kanter had been with classic literature in *Classic Comics*.

The first issue of *Picture Stories from the Bible* went on sale in the fall of 1942 under the DC imprint with a cover (see Figure 5.1) that took its cues from the Design of adventure and superhero comics that predominated at the time, a strategy used earlier in the first issue of *Classic Comics*.[4] The main illustration depicts a physical confrontation, using both the visual and gestural modes to convey action that is designed to make an audience of comic book readers (who are used to kinetic action) notice the book and pick it up from the newsstand. In reading the comic, they would then encounter the same panel in "The Story of Moses and His Struggle for Israel," an arthrological or relational effect through which the reader would connect the promise of the cover (in terms of action) and the later fulfillment of that promise. As printed in the actual story, the panel is almost visually identical, with the only changes

FIGURE 5.1 *Cover of Picture Stories from the Bible #1.*

coming in the color of the sky (orange on the cover versus blue in the story), the shape of the panel/cover (square versus rectangular), and the addition of a motion line to help delineate the arc of the punch. As well, the panel within the story includes both a narrative caption box and a word balloon that help explain Moses' reaction to an Egyptian beating a Hebrew and the results of Moses' action. In the caption box we are told that "Enraged at such cruelty to his race, Moses killed the Egyptian," while in the word balloon, Moses is shown yelling, "This for tyranny!," words that echo the value in standing up against oppression espoused in both educational comic books such as *True Comics* and superhero comics such as *Captain America* (n.p.). The changes in the panel for the cover illustration streamline the image (by removing the motion line), provide a contrasting color for the striking use of the linguistic mode in the title font, and take advantage of the larger, rectangular cover size to imply the almost limitless space of the desert. Arrayed around the left, right, and lower margins of the cover are images of Noah, Joseph, Moses, Saul, Ruth, Jonah, and Esther, whose stories appear in the issue; each image is presented within its own circle in much the same way that the Three Musketeers had been presented on the cover of the first issue of *Classic Comics*. Here the appeal lay not in the development of a recurring character and ongoing narrative, but in making use of intertextuality by creating new, multimodally captivating versions of stories that were already known and loved.

In much the same vein as *Classic Comics*, the stories themselves were condensed adaptations, illustrated by Don Cameron and written/edited by Montgomery Mulford, a man with no track record in comics, but with experience in writing articles for church magazines. This brevity can be seen in stories such as "Noah and His Ark" (from Genesis Chapters 6–9) which is conveyed in just seven narratively economical pages, with the building of the ark and the loading of the pairs of animals each shown in just a single panel. Other stories were similarly episodic and condensed, adapted for young readers with relatively simple language and easy to follow illustrations and panel layouts. These Biblical adaptations were approved by a carefully assembled advisory board consisting of 11 members drawn from the leadership of Protestant, Catholic, and Jewish faiths. As with DC, the advisory board played an important role in public perception, though not in reassuring readers about the decency of content, but in ensuring an ecumenical approach to the Bible that would reach the widest possible audience. Further, as Mark Carlson argues, Gaines displayed "inspirational rather than explicitly religious intentions in publishing the series" (n.p.). Gaines, in the back cover matter of #2 of the series, wrote, "We see that the Bible lives today. Much of our civilization is based on its ideas. . . . A book which has endured so many centuries and has so powerfully affected the lives of so many people must commend itself to every American boy and girl" (qtd. in Carlson n.p.). In sponsoring multimodal literacy through the publication of *Picture Stories from the Bible*, Gaines aimed not only to make a profit, but at the same time to increase what E. D. Hirsch came to term cultural literacy, the general information that he deemed every American needed to know to understand a major newspaper; in fact, in *The New Dictionary of Cultural Literacy*, the Bible is the first entry (Hirsch, Kett, and Trefil 1–26). Like Kanter with *Classic Comics*, Gaines sought to provide access to the texts that he saw as foundational to the education of young people and, in this way, subtly inculcate them with the values that he believed undergirded contemporary society, unlike the later work of his son William and the creative staff at EC who sought to instill in their readers a critical literacy about contemporary society. Like Hecht and the Parents' Institute, Gaines saw that profit and educational goals did not have to be mutually exclusive; though the first two issues had lost money, Gaines clearly saw the potential for profit in the endeavor, as evidenced in his stipulation that he retain rights to *Picture Stories from the Bible* in his break from Liebowitz. Again, the important point to note at this juncture is that Gaines' intent, as seen in his use of an ecumenical advisory board and his statements that place the Bible within a framework of cultural literacy, seems to have been broadly educational in the sense of creating a common culture, rather than religiously sectarian.

Whatever Gaines' motivations were in publishing *Picture Stories from the Bible*, however, individual religious organizations could use the new comics as part of religious education.[5] Given the Catholic Church's history of using the visual in the religious education of the faithful in media such as stained glass and altar pieces, it is not surprising that they would be among the first religious organizations to see the potential in using comic books to sponsor a literacy that supported the teachings of the Church. Very quickly the Catholic Church "began to question the wisdom of leaving such a powerful medium exclusively in the hands of secular publishers" (Carlson n.p.). Such questioning led to the introduction of *Timeless Topix* (soon shortened to *Topix*) in the late fall of 1942 under the auspices of Father Louis Gale and the Catechetical Guild Educational Society, an organization devoted to publishing inspirational material for Catholic young people. These sixteen-page books focused on historical accounts of Christians who had shown courage and adherence to their faith in the face of adversity, including accounts of many saints and the events that led to their canonizations. Rather than simply presenting the Bible as a foundational cultural text, *Topix* instead used the multimodal form of comics to reinforce and strengthen a specifically Catholic faith.

Despite this move, the response of the Catholic Church as a whole to comic books was highly conflicted, as evidenced by Thomas F. Doyle's article, "What's Wrong with the 'Comics'?" in the February, 1943 issue of *The Catholic World*. Like North and other critics of comic books in the early 1940s, Doyle saw little of value in comic books, declaring, "The damaging argument against these gaudy publications is that they introduce the child to an unreal world peopled by scheming sirens and cold-blooded murderers and are the worst possible education for children whose minds are too impressionable not to retain some residue of the dangerous nonsense poured into them" (553). However, Doyle also saw possibilities "to instruct and uplift rather than horrify and degrade young minds" in the advent of educational comic books such as those put out by Hecht and the Parents' Institute, even as he doubted such substitution could stem the tide of the effects of all the other comic books on the market (555). While Doyle held out hope for the educational value of such secular comic books, he of course reserved the most praise for *Topix*, writing, "We believe that the new *Topix* stories render a real service to the children and parents of our nation. Now the desirable heroism of Christians whose courage and daring were directed into exemplary channels are portrayed" (556). Still, Doyle argued that none of these efforts would make any difference "until parents, in particular, are aroused to their inherent responsibilities" (556). That is, publishers such as the Parents' Institute and the Catechetical Guild could sponsor multimodal literacy that would contribute to specific kinds of religious and civic development in children, but unless parents also took an interest in sponsoring literacy in similar ways, the influence of the other comic books on the market would overwhelm those efforts. Again, the question of who sponsors literacy and for what purposes looms large.

Reach out and be healed:
Oral Roberts' True Stories

In 1947, so the self-authored story goes, Oral Roberts, a part-time Pentecostal pastor from Oklahoma, picked up his Bible as it fell open to a verse that would alter the course of his life: "I wish above all things that thou mayest prosper and be in health, even as thy soul prospereth" (3 Jn 1.2). As described in his obituary in the *Guardian* on December 15, 2009,

> Roberts decided immediately that it was all right to be rich. The next day he bought a Buick and God appeared, he said, telling him to heal people. Roberts then added this aspect to his tent revival meetings and a month later in Enid, Oklahoma, he cured, he said, a woman the use of whose hand had been impaired for 38 years. (n.p.)

Roberts would continue to emphasize physical healing as a key aspect of his ministry (the Oral Roberts Evangelistic Association) through not only his tent meeting crusades, but as one of the early pioneers of radio television evangelism.[6] Roberts's use of these media, in tandem with his emphasis on donations from his "partners" in these various audiences/congregations, worked to transform the way many Americans experienced religion in the latter part of the twentieth century. As Christopher Reed notes in the *Guardian* obituary, "his message of health and wealth held enormous appeal for poor Americans, often from ethnic minorities" (n.p.). As a result, by 1950, Roberts had an established radio network and a financial model to ensure the long-term success of his ministry. Despite (or perhaps because of) the successes of radio and television, then, the publication arm of the ministry remained Roberts' most important link to his followers or "partners"; by 1956, following the advent of the television series, a million people subscribed to Roberts' monthly magazine, *Healing Waters* (Harrell 130). Each partner pledged monetary support to aid with the ministry's various outreach efforts, including radio, print, and later television. Just as the Oral Roberts Evangelistic Association sponsored multiple kinds of literacy through multiple media, so did the partners effectively sponsor this sponsorship.

In 1955, the first Oral Roberts' comic book, *Happiness and Healing for You*, was released as an experiment in using comics for evangelizing and connecting with his partners. Produced by Malcolm Ater and Commerical Comics, *Happiness and Healing for You* was designed as a one-time giveaway/promotional comic book for Oral Roberts' crusades, featuring adaptations of two Biblical events, the story of Adam and Eve, and a version of the Gospel. The book seems to have been popular, as it was reprinted at least once (as evidenced by the two extant covers). Ater and Commercial Comics had produced comic books for such diverse clients as the American Gas Association, the Congress of Industrial Organizations, and the committee to elect George Wallace as governor of Alabama. The job, like all others Commercial Comics took on, was strictly work for hire, fulfilling the needs of the client through use of the comics medium, whatever the message might be. The benefit derived by Commercial in sponsoring the multimodal literacy of any of these diverse readers was thus strictly financial, while the motives of and benefits derived by their clients had as much or more to do with promoting specific political, religious, or world views as they did with any financial profit. Of course, in order for Commercial Comics to continue to get work and be successful financially, they had to ensure that the comics they produced met the goals of their clients.

The success of *Happiness and Healing for You* seems to have been quickly apparent to Roberts and those around him as they saw comic books as a tool to communicate with their partners, elicit testimonials from readers, reinforce the power of the live, radio, and television ministries, spread the Gospel, effect conversions, and solicit dollars to support every facet of the Oral Roberts Evangelistic Association. While this promotional comic book was aimed at both adults and children who would be in attendance at the tent meetings, the regularly produced comic that followed, *Oral Roberts' True Stories*, was more clearly designed with children as the target audience. Like the Catechetical Guild Educational Society in the early 1940s, Roberts saw the editorial and economic advantages of in-house production of comic books rather than outsourcing to a secular shop. *Happiness and Healing for You* was thus the only comic book publication not produced by the ministry itself.

According to the Christian Comics International website,[7] "Christian cartoonist Charles Lowe Ramsay was brought to Tulsa, OK in 1955 to help produce these new comics for Oral Roberts," working over the years as editor, art editor, and illustrator (n.p.). *Oral Roberts' True Stories*, which ran for 19 issues, was produced quarterly from 1956 to 1959. In 1959, the name was changed to *Junior Partners* and the frequency was increased to monthly publication; the series ran until 1961, with a total of 29 issues under the new title. Since the Comics Code had been in place for 2 years by the launch of *Oral Roberts' True Stories*, there would seem to have been little need for the substitution of good comics for bad. Such comics as those offered by the Parents' Institute with *True Comics*, Elliott Publishing with *Classic Comics*, or Gaines with his *Picture Stories from the Bible* would seem not to have been needed anymore, especially since the Code had forced companies such as EC out of the comic book business. Still, from a Christian perspective, there *was* a need to introduce comic books that showcased Christian values and Biblical teachings, just as there had been when the Catechetical Guild Educational Society introduced *Topix* ten years earlier. What's more, from Roberts' perspective, there was a need to promote not just Christian teachings, but a specifically *evangelical* version of Christianity. To this end, under Ramsay's direction, *Oral Roberts' True Stories* focused on the links between physical healing and belief in a tripartite God, and on an evangelical version of Christianity that emphasized the need for individuals to accept Jesus Christ as their personal savior.

From the outset, *Oral Roberts' True Stories* focused on faith healing through a combination of the adaptation of Biblical sources and the presentation of contemporary accounts. The first issue, entitled "The Miracle Touch," for example, featured the Biblical story in which Jesus heals a paralyzed man so that he can walk (taken from Lk. 5.18–25), while the contemporary story focused on a boy named Willie Phelps from Lynchburg, Virginia who was similarly healed through the "miracle touch" of faith, as channeled through the evangelist. Such stories reinforced the messages conveyed at the crusades and on radio and television in a way that was explicitly aimed at children, the "junior partners" who would (it was hoped) continue to see themselves as supporters of the Oral Roberts Evangelistic Association; *Oral Roberts' True Stories* was available only through subscription to partners or junior partners. Unlike the early issues of *True Comics* or the comic books issued by DC after the installation of its editorial board in 1941, there was here no attempt to explain the aims of the publishers to parents since these aims were presumably in agreement with those of the parents, many of whom would have been either "partners" in the ministry already or at least predisposed to its message. If a child whose parents were not already one of the faithful were to read the book, it would still be a chance to win the soul of that child for Christ, a clear aim of the comic book. In this way, the evangelical aims of the comic book were never hidden, but were directly conveyed to the child through multimodal means, rather than to the concerned parent through linguistic means.

This explicit message can be seen on the final page of the first issue, which features an invitation to join the "Christian Adventure Club." On the right-hand side of the page is an illustration of Oral Roberts, who has his Bible in hand and is smiling at the reader, an illustration that uses the visual and gestural modes to signify an open and welcoming presence as he invites children to join his flock. To the left of this illustration are the words through which the page attempts to witness to the reader, spatially arranged so that the welcoming nature of the illustration will carry over to the words themselves. The text of the evangelical message reads,

> Now I'm interested in knowing that you made a decision for Jesus.
>
> If you accepted Jesus as your personal savior after reading this book, just fill in the coupon below and send it to me. You will then be a regular member in our **Adventure Club** for boys and girls.
>
> If you were already saved before reading this book, but you want to join our club, just fill in the coupon and check the lower square.
>
> To those who send me this coupon, I will send **free** of charge a **membership card** and an Adventure Club **button** for you to wear.
>
> Write me today. If you have a spiritual problem, tell me about it. I want to help you.
>
> God bless you real good.
>
> Oral Roberts
>
> Tulsa, Oklahoma (n.p.)

In filling out the coupon at the bottom of the page, the child would indicate either that "I was saved **after** reading this book" or "I was saved **before** reading this book" (n.p.). Either way, response to the call represented readers who professed the particular kind of Christian faith espoused by Roberts and a pool of readers for whom this particular kind of literacy sponsorship had been effective. In this way, the Adventure Club can be viewed as at least partially remediated on clubs such as the Supermen of America from the early 1940s as membership in both clubs denoted a specific kind of brand loyalty created through the use of comic books and the multimodal literacy associated with them. For DC, that sponsorship translated generally into the creation of a comic book reader and specifically into a reader of Superman comic books.[8] For the Oral Roberts Evangelistic Association, that sponsorship was part of a larger ministry that included a variety of media. For them, the point in sponsoring multimodal literacy was not to create comic book readers, but rather to capitalize on the fact that children *were already* versed in the comics medium so that the sponsorship translated into converting souls to evangelical Christianity. In what was an appeal to help with the overt sponsorship of children's literacy, with the advent of *Junior Partners*, Roberts' partners were explicitly asked to give five subscriptions as gifts in support of the specific ministry to children and the ministry as a whole. Beyond that, the club began to foster the idea of partnership that formed the basis for Roberts' fundraising efforts. In this case, multimodal literacy sponsorship through the use of comic books promoted a particular view of religion and laid the groundwork for later monetary support of Oral Roberts' multi-pronged ministry.

The interweaving of the various parts of the larger ministry can be seen in full effect in the fourth issue of *Oral Roberts' True Stories*.[9] Like the first three issues of the series, both Biblical and contemporary stories focused on healing are told; this pattern would continue throughout the run, with the Bible story sometimes presented through preaching as a story-within-a-story. In order to emphasize the connection between them, both stories are titled "Released!"; this strategy of title repetition within an issue was used often by the creators of these comic books. On the first page of the book, we see a smiling medium shot of Oral Roberts petting his horse in the foreground of a bucolic, country scene. As in the earlier example of the Adventure Club, the illustration and his facial expression and body language are designed to welcome the reader into Roberts' peaceful world and to portray him as a trusted adult who only wants what is best for them. The text that occupies the top third of the page is his direct message to the reader, again connected spatially to the inviting and calming gestural and visual elements that comprise the rest of the page. The text reads,

Hello, kids! I'm Oral Roberts. I've been out here on the farm today riding my horse, Sonny.

I though I'd stop by and tell you a couple of stories, one from the Bible, and one that happened just recently. Both will thrill you.

I'll tell the Bible story in my own words and give names to people not named in the Bible so you can follow the story more easily. (n.p.)

In the way Roberts appears at both the beginning and end of each comic book, he serves the function of host, much like the Crypt Keeper, Vault-Keeper, and the Old Witch did in the EC comics of the early 1950s. That is, in a book without recurring characters, the character Oral Roberts serves to ensure continuity and a point of contact with the readers, as did the EC hosts. Moreover, just as the EC hosts were used to market the EC brand, so was Oral Roberts the focal point of the Oral Roberts Evangelistic Association, a brand that operated across media platforms and included not only comic books, but also radio, television, and public appearances. In other words, readers (and viewers and listeners) could identify with Roberts, and through him with the ministry as a whole, just as earlier readers could identify with the EC hosts, and through them with the EC line as a whole. However, while the EC hosts were used to sponsor a multimodal literacy in teens and young adults that questioned the *status quo*, Oral Roberts was here used to sponsor a multimodal literacy in children that supported an evangelical Christian narrative. Rather than inviting questioning, Oral Roberts instead invited children to join his flock of believers by accepting Jesus Christ. Bible stories told in the vernacular, along with contemporary stories of healing and faith, were designed to do just that as part of a larger cross-media ministry.

The first of the pair of stories titled "Released!" is a Bible story taken from Acts Chapter 3 and tells the story of Peter and John and the crippled beggar. The climax of the story takes place in a full-page panel (the left-side of a two-page spread) that depicts the moment of healing. John stands to the left of the panel, hands on his hips, looking on as Peter bends over the beggar and clasps his hand, saying (in a font that doubles in size by the time it gets to the final four words), "We have faith in God! In the name of **Jesus Christ of Nazareth, rise up and walk!**" (n.p.). The first panel on the right-hand page (which would have been at least peripherally visible from the time the page was turned), shows the beggar walking, his entire body framed within a bright yellow framed within a jagged border, as he says, "**I can walk!**" For most readers, the effect of the framing within the panel is to draw attention to the beggar's new-found mobility, but also to evoke the idea of a divine light, so that both the spatial and visual elements support the gestural (the beggar smiling and walking), the linguistic (his exclamation of joy), and the audio (the volume and tone implied by the large, bold font and exclamation point). What's more, this story emphasizes the notion that such healing can work through an intermediary who believes and acts in the name of Jesus Christ, who died and rose again (as shown in a two-panel sequence later in the story). The priests of the temple, however, do not believe or appreciate the efforts of Peter and John and their belief in Jesus Christ, depicted in the rest of the narrative and reiterated by the Oral Roberts character in the story's final panel, in which he sums up the theme and provides a transition to the second story, also called "Released!"

The story of Anna Williams was one of the most famous involving the Oral Roberts' ministry. Harrell describes the case and the publicity surrounding it in this way:

> On Monday, May 2, 1955, the newspapers in Wichita Falls, Texas carried a front-page story about a young air force sergeant's wife under the headline "Paralyzed, She Walks after Prayer." The story of Anna Williams was remarkable; it was picked up by the wire services, published across the country, and featured by ABC commentator Paul Harvey. The story was simple and powerful. Anna Williams had been crippled by a series of misfortunes: in 1951 she broke her leg in an automobile accident; and in 1953 she was "crippled by spinalitis." Since the onset of the last disease, she had been "paralyzed from the waist down" and had been confined to a wheelchair. While watching Oral's telecast on Sunday, May 1, Anna placed her hand over her heart during the healing prayer and, after its conclusion, asked her husband to help her stand. She began walking, tentatively at first, then with more confidence, finally borrowing high heels from a friend to dance about the room. Anna Williams became a celebrity in Wichita Falls, one of the most powerful testimonials ever received by the Roberts ministry, and the premier validation of the early television ministry. (128)

The validation received by the coverage of the secular media was a publicity boon that could not be ignored and the Roberts ministry chose to take advantage of it across its media platforms, including within the fourth issue of *Oral Roberts' True Stories*.

The four-page climax of the story opens with Anna and her husband Bill sitting down to watch Oral Roberts with another couple in a panel that sets the scene for what is to follow. The second page begins with a tier of two panels in which the television screen acts as a frame within the panel, both focusing the attention of the reader and emphasizing the fact that Anna is watching Oral Roberts on television; in the first, Roberts is shown kneeling beside a boy and saying, "In Jesus' name, **heal** this boy!," while in the second, the boy's legs are show on the television screen as he takes his first steps. Here the spatial (the frame within the frame), the visual (the depiction of the television screen and the action contained therein), the gestural (Roberts' touch and facial expression, as well as the boy walking), the linguistic (Roberts' words), and the audio (the emphasis on the word "heal" that indicates the intonation pattern for his speech) all come together to set the scene for Anna's own healing. The next three panels show Anna asking to be healed and her friend praying for this healing, while the final panel of the page once again focuses on the television screen as Roberts says, "If you will place your hand on your afflicted body and believe, God will heal you now!" Anna's request to be healed is thus framed by Roberts healing the boy and his invitation of healing to the viewers.

After the turn of the page, the narrative continues with a panel that again shows a close-up of Roberts on the television as he says, "And now Lord, heal afflicted bodies everywhere!" As in the Bible story that opened the issue, the moment of healing is contiguous with the result of that process because the reader cannot help but take in the several panels in which she walks, both on this page and the next one; the spatial mode thus helps create arthrological connections between the panels for the reader. At the moment of healing, in the page's second panel, Williams is visited by an almost ghostly visage of Jesus Christ, a transparent figure that is eerily reminiscent of Mr. Crime from the *Crime Does Not Pay* series. As this spectre bends over her, He says, "Anna, today I need your feet to walk for me. **Rise up** and **walk!**" Here the linguistic (Jesus' words), audio (the emphasis on "Rise Up" and "walk"), gestural (Jesus' body language), and spatial (the positioning of Jesus above

Anna within the frame) combine in the moment of healing which leads to Anna literally bursting from the last panel of the next page as she walks and shouts, "Oh Praise God! Praise God!" Through reading the gutter and making arthrological connections, the reader is pushed to make a causal connection. The piece ends with a page in which the readers are addressed by both Anna Williams and Oral Roberts. Again, through use of the gestural, visual, and spatial modes, these figures are designed to be inviting so that their words will have the greatest possible appeal, as Williams exhorts readers to confess their sins, believe in Jesus, and witness to others, and Roberts asks readers to write in to him with their own testimonials and/or spiritual problems.

Through the medium of comics, then, the Oral Roberts ministry could retell the story of Anna Williams and directly link it intertextually to an earlier Bible story as a way to reinforce the healing power of the television medium to their partners and their children. At the same time, they could use it to elicit testimonials from readers, spread the Gospel, effect conversions, encourage witnessing, and, by showing the effectiveness of both the comic book and the television show at performing all of these functions, lay the groundwork for contributions to the Oral Roberts Evangelistic Association. The Roberts ministry used comic books not to encourage comic book reading *per se*, but as part of a cross-media ministry in which comic books were an important component through which they derived a number of benefits in their sponsorship of multimodal literacy, ranging from converting new followers to communicating with their junior partners to inculcating loyalty to the ministry to increasing financial sponsorship from the parents of their readers. Through these comic books, the Oral Roberts Evangelical Association offered the sponsorship of a church-sanctioned multimodal literacy that was directed not (primarily) toward entertainment, but toward religious education. More specifically, they were concerned with the attendant instilment of values consonant with the doctrine of this specific denomination, and in support of the other media in the ministry. Of course, such an approach is not the only way that comic books can be used within a religious context to sponsor literacy. Another way can be seen in the work of Al Hartley, both while an employee of Archie Comics and during his tenure with Spire Comics.

Evangelizing in four colors:
Archie meets Spire

Al Hartley was born in New Jersey in 1921, the son of Congressman Frederick Allan Hartley, Jr. After returning from service as a bomber pilot in the Second World War, Hartley began his career in comics as a freelancer for companies such as Quality Comics, Ace Comics, Better Publishing, and the various incarnations of Martin Goodman's Timely Comics. As Nate Butler notes in his profile of Hartley, "By 1951, Hartley appears to have been freelancing exclusively in comics for Atlas/Timely/Marvel, either writing his own stories or drawing from Stan Lee scripts" in genres as diverse as crime, western, war, suspense, horror, jungle, and romance comics (n.p.). Hartley was still working for Marvel in the early 1960s, but was not one of the artists chosen to participate in the reinvention of the superhero line; Hartley did draw one early Thor story (1963) and write stories for both Iron Man and Giant-Man in 1965, but that seems to be the extent of his involvement with the Marvel superheroes. Still, even without being a part of the superhero renaissance, Hartley was nonetheless a success at Marvel through the 1960s as the artist of the popular Patsy Walker line of titles.[10]

The year 1967 saw the event that would define the rest of Hartley's life and career as a cartoonist: his conversion to evangelical Christianity, "brought about in part by seeing the effect faith had on his father despite failing health" (Spurgeon n.p.). As Hartley described in his autobiography, *Come Meet My Friend!*, by 1967 he was in a troubled marriage and was floundering both personally and creatively (9). He and his wife attended a prayer meeting on the advice of friends and, as a result, both of them became evangelical Christians. At the time, Hartley was drawing a suggestive feature called "Pussycat" that appeared in a number of Marvel's black and white men's magazines. After his conversion, Hartley "turned down the assignment and frankly told the publisher why" (*Come Meet My Friend!* 12). Other assignments stopped coming and he found himself out of work. Until this time, Hartley had viewed his part in producing comics (and thus sponsoring multimodal literacy) only in terms of the monetary benefit he derived as an artist and writer; he saw the money he earned from comics as the measure of his success (*Come Meet My Friend!* 10). However, after his conversion, the content of the material and the perceived effects that it would have on its readers began to play a part in his thinking; Hartley came to see the variety of possible benefits that could be gained through his sponsorship of multimodal literacy in his role as a comics creator. These possibilities started to become clear to Hartley beginning with a call from Archie Comics.

Hartley always maintained that the call from Archie Comics was part of God's plan that allowed him an avenue through which he could use comics to convey a Christian message. In *Come Meet My Friend!*, he described the way he came to work for Archie Comics:

> The editor of Archie comics phoned me, offering me the opportunity to draw the king of comics. I ought to point out that during my years as a cartoonist, no one had ever called me this way. Every relationship I had with a publisher, I had developed. No one had ever come to me. This time Hermine and I knew the Archie publishers had not just come to me. God had sent them. (12)

Within a short period of time, Hartley was not only drawing Archie and the gang, but writing their stories as well. Given Hartley's interpretation of his hiring by Archie Comics, it is not surprising that he would use this opportunity to embed Christian messages within these narratives, deriving benefit from his sponsorship as a creator that was not in concert with the publisher's motives for sponsorship.

While Hartley maintained that he always enjoyed the humor in writing the Archie characters, he quickly saw that he could do more with them: "Here was a chance for a Christian witness, on comic pages read by millions of kids. True, it had never been done before, but that fact simply reinforced my feeling that it was about time" (*Come Meet My Friend!* 15).[11] He went on to tell the story of one of his early forays into using Archie as a vehicle for Christian messages, a Christmas story in which Betty decorates her tree with ornaments with the names of all her friends. She then points to the star on the tree and says that it signifies her greatest friend of all. The story, however, was not at all well received by his editor, as Hartley later described:

> It certainly wasn't a forceful reference to Christ, but the editor at Archie Comics reacted as though I had included the Four Spiritual Laws in the story. Didn't I know that readers of all faiths read

Archie Comics? What was I trying to do? He really lowered the
boom on me. They changed the ending of the story and told me
never to try that again. (*Come Meet My Friend!* 15–16)

As can be seen from the editor's reaction, Hartley's Christian
message was in direct conflict with the aim of the publisher, at
least as perceived by this editor, to sponsor multimodal literacy
as widely as possible through the comics medium in an effort to
grow and sustain the readership of Archie comics. Despite this
conflict, however, Hartley was soon given license to create exactly
these kinds of stories that would serve his purpose of Christian
witness. In his obituary of Hartley in *The Comics Journal*, Tom
Spurgeon speculates on the reason for this reversal of course by the
editorial staff despite their initial concerns: "Hartley's stories were
well received, and when taken into account with his high rate of
production the cartoonist was considered an important company
asset. As such, he was given more of a free reign as a writer instead
of less" (n.p.). In other words, the mismatch in sponsorship goals
between Hartley and Archie Comics ceased to cause the same
amount of concern when viewed in terms of the overall situation
and the benefits that could be derived by the publisher in allowing
him more latitude. Hartley, of course, viewed the decision as part of
God's plan: "Then God opened the door wider! My editor told me
that I no longer had to submit plots and scripts for editing before
doing the illustrations for the comics. He gave me *carte blanche*
to write the stories, illustrate them, and just mail them in finished
without any editing whatsoever" (*Come Meet My Friend!* 16). It's
not surprising, given Hartley's ongoing interpretation of events, that
he would continue to inject Christian messages into mainstream
Archie comic books for the next several years.

Like the publishers and creators of *True Comics* and *Picture
Stories from the Bible* before him, Hartley was concerned with
substituting good comics for bad, first during his tenure with Archie
Comics and later with Spire Comics. Like the Catechetical Guild
Educational Society, though, he thought that the only real substitute
could be found in comic books with explicitly Christian messages.[12]
Further, like Oral Roberts, Hartley believed that the content needed
to not only be Christian in nature, but, more specifically, evangelical.
In *Come Meet My Friend!*, Hartley wrote, "In an age that throws
all kinds of negative, immoral content at its young people, to say

nothing of the insidious influence of outright pornography in many secular publications, what a persuasive spiritual impact Archie could have" (16). Later in the book, in discussing his 1972 adaptations of the Christian testimonial books *The Cross and the Switchblade* and *God's Smuggler* for Spire Comics, Hartley wrote explicitly about the issue of substitution: "Secular comics, like all literature, reflected a rapid decline in morals and philosophy. The art leaned more and more toward sadism and sex. The life-styles that were suggested were insidiously destructive. Thus, Spire Christian Comics offered an alternative. More than just offering clean content instead of filth, Spire offered God instead of the devil" (37). In words that echoed the accusations of the comics panics of both the 1940s and 1950s, Hartley made explicit his aims in producing evangelical comic books. Not only did Hartley understand what he perceived as the dangers of the medium, he clearly grasped the persuasive potential for a Christian comics creator like him.

By 1972, Hartley was regularly infusing his work at Archie Comics with Christian messages, often using the character of Betty to act as a witness and as the voice of/for the young Christian, just as he would in many of the books for Spire. Stories such as "Nostalgia Gets Ya!" from *Life with Archie* #129, published at the end of 1972 (with a cover date of January, 1973), in which the gang is somehow transported back to a time around the turn of the twentieth century, showcase both the clean content and the Christian message that Hartley sought to project. From the first panel of the book, Archie, Jughead, Reggie, Dilton, Veronica, and

FIGURE 5.2 *Final panel from "Nostalgia Gets Ya!," Life with Archie #129. TM & ©2012 Archie Comic Publications, Inc. Used with permission.*

Betty try to make sense of this world, discovering along the way that almost everything seems better to them—there is more respect for authority, women are treated more like equals, people take pride in their work and in their neighborhoods, and families seem to be much closer. On the last page of the book, in answer to the question of what the essential difference is, Veronica, alone in a panel as she looks out and speaks directly to the reader, suggests, "Y' know what I think it is? Everybody's going in the same direction! They have unity!" (20). In the next panel, Archie says, "Man! It would be great if **our** world could find that spirit!" and Veronica responds, "But **where** do you **look** for it?" (20). The final panel, which occupies the entire bottom tier of the page, depicts Reggie, Veronica, Archie, and Betty in a rowboat at the bottom right of the frame (see Figure 5.2). While the rest of the friends look to her, Betty's rapt gaze is directed up and to the left, toward the fireworks in the sky, as she says, "That's easy! You look **up**!" (20). Here the layout of the panel (Betty and the others at the bottom of the frame juxtaposed with the fireworks above), visuals (the majesty of the fireworks), facial and body language (Betty's rapt/peaceful gaze and the tilt of her body toward the heavens), and Betty's words all combine in an attempt to make the reader contemplate the possibility of God's presence in the world. Most readers would have understood that the reference is to God (for whom the fireworks act as a visual metaphor) as the "spirit" that Hartley, through his mouthpiece Betty, saw as the essential element that had been lost in the secular world he saw around him. Of course, not everyone would have the

FIGURE 5.3 *From "When You Witch Upon a Star," Sabrina the Teen-Age Witch #7. TM & ©2012 Archie Comic Publications, Inc. Used with permission.*

available resources for design to see the story as an allegory for the fallen state of the contemporary world and the necessity of turning back to God. However, even those readers who would not have seen this allusion would have understood the values that Hartley was espousing and the comparison between an idyllic (and clearly imagined) past and the much less satisfying present that Hartley constructed through what the characters said. While the story is overtly didactic in terms of the kinds of generic values it promotes, it is relatively subtle in terms of its Christianity, working on two levels in ways that some of Hartley's other mainstream Archie stories, and the later explicitly Christian stories for Spire, do not.

In his work at Archie Comics, Hartley saw the entire cast of Archie as potential vehicles for Christian evangelism, as he explicitly discussed in *Come Meet My Friend!*. He wrote, "Archie, the king of the comics, is actually an example of all the pitfalls that await every innocent pilgrim as he walks through life. What an incredible vehicle to present the need for Christ in our daily lives!" (16–17). To Hartley, the Archie characters "continued to be effective evangelists" through which he could show "the reality of Jesus Christ in the beautifully graphic medium of comic magazines" (33, 35). Even unlikely evangelists such as Sabrina, the Teen-age Witch, were enlisted by Hartley in his crusade to bear Christian witness. For example, in a two-panel sequence from "When You Witch Upon a Star!," Sabrina is shown sitting in a window seat, staring up at the night sky and thinking about her powers (see Figure 5.3). The first panel establishes the setting and mood of the short scene as it shows Sabrina in a full shot, her body canted forward in a way that conveys a kind of expectant posture toward the window, her face deeply thoughtful in its expression. Above her head, the thought balloon reads, "But I don't want my magic power to come from sorcery!" (4). The second panel shows Sabrina in close up, her expression identical to that of the previous panel, the same kind of rapt gaze seen on Betty's face at the conclusion of "Nostalgia Gets Ya!" Through a series of thought balloons, we are privy to the train of Sabrina's thinking: "The power I feel within me comes from a different source! And I want to use it in a different way—a **better** way!" (4). Later, in a direct reference to Psalm 23.5, Sabrina looks out from the page and tells the reader, "Aunt Hilda's pot is empty— and my cup runneth over!" (5). Despite her upbringing, Sabrina has become a good Christian who preaches love and kindness at every turn, causing her Aunt Hilda, in the last panel of the story, to lament, "Somewhere I made a mistake! But where? Where? Where did I go right?" (8). As in "Nostalgia Gets Ya!," here the message is relatively subtle, emphasizing the values of love and kindness much more than the message of Christian salvation.

Other stories (including some of those involving Sabrina) would, however, be much more overt in their Christian messages. For example, in "Solomon's Child" from *Archie Giant Series Magazine* #205 (cover dated January, 1973), a piece very reminiscent of the material soon to be published under the Spire imprint, Archie, Jughead, and Betty pick up a despondent young hitchhiker (drawn in a more realistic style than the three recurring characters, perhaps to emphasize the connection to the readers themselves). As they drive, stop for malts, and walk among the Christmas shoppers, Betty tells the young man the story of King Solomon and his efforts "to find the answers to life" (3). Virtually the entire conversation is conducted between the young, unnamed man—a stand-in perhaps for the reader—and Betty—Hartley's clear and unequivocal voice of Christian witness. Near the end of their talk, Betty comes to the point, telling him, "Solomon wrote his book for young people! He ended by saying, 'Recognize God in the days of your youth'" (4). When he responds, "I-I never really thought about God—He's never been part of my life!," Betty further pushes the issue, saying, "Solomon was very wise! There's a vacuum in your life without God!" (4). As a result of Betty's discussions with him, the hitchhiker decides to go home and pray with his parents. In the final panel (see Figure 5.4),

FIGURE 5.4 *Final panel from "Solomon's Child," Archie Giant Series Magazine #205. TM & ©2012 Archie Comic Publications, Inc. Used with permission.*

the young man is shown on the bus on the left of the frame, headed back to his parents. His change in outlook is indicated through gestural (his smile), linguistic (his words), and audio (the emphasis on "lift") elements. Positioned on the right of the frame, Archie and Betty see him off, with Betty's "God Bless You!" acting both as a farewell and as a benediction, her work as Christian witness done for the moment. Throughout the sequence, Betty and the young man are usually framed together within individual panels, the focus on their facial expressions and the words that pass between them so that the visual and spatial modes (the way they are drawn and how they are positioned in relation to each other) emphasize the gestural and linguistic (their facial expressions and words), which carry the text's main Christian message.

By this time most of the stories he was writing about Archie involved a heavy dose of spiritual content. As a result, he received a call from Archie Comics, who told him, "We're publishing comic magazines—not the Bible! You've got to slow up!" (35). Not even his high rate of production could save him this time. Hartley continued to work for Archie, but began to tone down the Christian focus. A month after being confronted by his editors, Hartley received a telephone call from the Fleming H. Revell Company about doing a comic-book version of David Wilkerson's *The Cross and the Switchblade* for their new Spire Christian Comics imprint. Hartley saw this call as the "greater Christian opportunity" for which he had been waiting (*Come Meet My Friend!* 36). In his initial meeting with Revell's editorial director, Hartley recalled that they prayed together, something he had never done in a business meeting:

> I'd prayed regularly about my work, of course, but it was a new experience to see that kind of faith and commitment touching the relationship of Christians involved in a business arrangement. More accurately, we were involved in the Lord's work and the business aspects were simply the means to the end. (36)

While profit for the company and financial remuneration for Hartley were still important aspects of the partnership, both clearly recognized that other benefits could be derived from publishing, in much the same way that George Hecht did throughout his career. In adapting and publishing a comic-book version of *The Cross and the Switchblade*, they would not only profit financially, but also derive the benefit of spreading an evangelical Christian message in ways that reinforced how this particular story was being told across other media platforms. As the partnership grew to include ever more Christian comic books in the Spire line, the evangelical reach of such multimodal sponsorship of literacy became much more explicit and sustained than anything Hartley had been able to do at Archie Comics.

Originally published in 1963, *The Cross and the Switchblade* had become a popular evangelical tool by the early 1970s; it was available as a paperback book and adapted not only into a comic book, but also into a feature film starring Pat Boone. The use of multiple media to present the story, both as an evangelical tool and as a commercial product, is detailed on the inside cover of the comic book, in an advertisement for both the paperback and the film, and an assurance to the reader that "This is a true story!" Here the book is described as "the story of [David] Wilkerson's

FIGURE 5.5 *Panel from The Cross and the Switchblade.*

dramatic call to minister to crime-hardened youth gangs in New York City's asphalt jungle!" The focus of the testimonial is on the conversion of Nicky Cruz, a gang leader who accepts Christ as a result of listening to Wilkerson in sermons, much like those depicted in *Oral Roberts' True Stories*, and in conversation, much like the one between Betty and the young hitchhiker in "Solomon's Child." As with these earlier evangelical efforts, the multimodal elements are designed to enhance the words that form the center of the Christian message, a good example of which can be seen in Figure 5.5. In this panel, which occupies the top two-thirds of the page, the reader is presented with a large picture of Cruz, his facial expression indicating that he is concentrating on the sermon's message that visually surrounds him; the spatial layout attempts to emphasize the way the message pervades his consciousness. The four depictions of Wilkerson use the gestural mode to animate his preaching style and help to give tonality to the words, the core of the evangelical message of God's love, forgiveness, and salvation. Not only is Wilkerson speaking to Cruz, but he is speaking directly to the reader at whom the questions and the message are ultimately aimed. Again, the multimodal elements work together to emphasize and focus the reader's attention on the explicitly Christian message of the text, just as they would for the rest of the Spire line that would soon follow.

Though they sponsored literacy for many of the same evangelical reasons as Oral Roberts did, the Fleming H. Revell Company and their Spire Comics imprint provide an interesting counterpoint for a variety of reasons. As a commercial enterprise, Spire Comics was concerned with financial remuneration, from both churches (who would purchase bulk order of comics for use in youth groups and for proselytizing, themselves then also becoming sponsors of multimodal literacy) and from individual consumers who would purchase the comics at Christian bookstores in much the same way that they would purchase mainstream comics at the corner drugstore. Unlike most other comic book publishers, however, Spire comic books were continuously reprinted throughout the 1970s and early 1980s because they were, like *Classics Illustrated*, seen to have a much longer shelf life than most other comic books. More importantly, they were kept in print because they were designed to be used as evangelical tools that, as far as Fleming H. Revell was concerned, contained a message that would remain relevant longer than a month or two. Of course, these comic books are no longer in print and are now often seen as dated and overly pedantic, just as *Picture Stories from the Bible* or *Oral Roberts' True Stories* would have seemed dated at the beginning of the 1970s. As seen in the examples throughout this book, the multimodal tools used to sponsor literacy through comic books are always used within and respond to the particular contexts in which they are produced and distributed.

Even before *The Cross and the Switchblade* was released, Spire had commissioned Hartley to do an adaptation of another evangelical Christian testimonial, *God's Smuggler*; the titles were concurrently published in September, 1972. Spire went on to publish many more personal testimonials by well-known figures such as Johnny Cash, Tom Landry, Andrae Crouch, Chuck Colson, and Corrie Ten Boom, as well as adaptations of stories from the Bible such as "My Brother's Keeper," "Adam and Eve," "Paul," and "Jesus." In total, Spire published nearly 60 comic books in the decade from 1972 to 1982, almost all of which were written and drawn by Hartley; Barbour & Company acquired the rights to many of the titles in the early 1980s and kept the books in print until 1988. But perhaps the most interesting project undertaken by Hartley and Spire was the partnership that they forged with Archie Comics.

Hartley quickly grasped the potential outreach that Spire Comics could have and, thinking back to his previous use of Archie comics to transmit Christian messages, hit upon the idea of creating original Archie comic books for Spire. It is worth quoting Hartley at length in order to understand his motivations and goals in such a venture:

> Archie would no longer be limited to an occasional witness as he now was in all my secular comics. In the Spire series he would be full blast for Christ on all thirty-two pages. No ads to break his stride, nothing at all to deflect the reader from a contemporary confrontation with Christ. Millions of kids all over the world are conditioned to reading Archie Comics. They love him. They identify with him. In the Christian Comic series, Archie would look the same and act the same, with one big difference: All the laughs and excitement and bloopers would just be hooks to get the reader's attention and lead him to Christ. The books looked

exactly like comics, but they were really supertracts. (*Come Meet My Friend!* 37–8)

Unlike other Spire titles that took the genres of Bible stories and testimonials and expanded them to the length of an entire 32 page comic book, the idea of using Archie was remediated on the idea of the recurring character as point of identification (rather than a host such as Oral Roberts) for readers. Moreover, while the didactic element remained firmly in place, Hartley seems to have been much more attuned to the necessity of delight and entertainment in creating material for children, while at the same time understanding not only the way in which comics appeal to children, but also the way that he could subvert their expectations in support of his goals. Writing in *Come Meet My Friend!*, Hartley argued, "No one expects to be confronted with the gospel in a comic. The reader begins reading in a familiar medium. If it's an Archie comic, the reader is with a familiar figure. The reading is fun and exciting. Then, in the middle of a familiar situation, there is a compelling ring of truth. Christ comes into focus and the reader sees how relevant He really is" (47).[13] Like any comic book creator, Hartley recognized that in order to sponsor multimodal literacy through the use of comic books, he had to catch the attention of the readers so that they would pick up the book and then hold their attention so that they would keep reading. The benefits of sponsorship, including both financial remuneration and the spreading of the evangelical Christian message, could only happen if he were able to grab and hold readers' attention. In Hartley's mind, using Archie gave him an invaluable tool to help him do so. The question would be how to acquire that tool.

Negotiating a licensing agreement with John Goldwater at Archie Comics to use Archie and the gang for such a venture would seem to have been an almost impossible task, especially given that Hartley had been told to severely curtail his Christian messages only a few months earlier. Not only was Hartley asking for permission to use a very valuable property for Christian evangelizing, but he was making that request to someone of the Jewish faith. When Goldwater agreed, Hartley claimed he was not surprised, noting, "Over the years, John and I had enjoyed several discussions about our faith. He was a man of deep moral and spiritual principles" (*Come Meet*

My Friend! 38). Certainly the idea of trying to convey a wholesome message was in line with what Goldwater had been practicing at Archie Comics for years and what he had been advocating more generally since the introduction of the Comics Code Authority. There is a sense in which their general sponsorship goals were in congruence, but the fact that Hartley sought to use Archie for explicitly evangelical Christian goals does seem to undermine both the long-term profitability of the character and Goldwater's own faith. However, perhaps because the Spire Archie comics were to be completely separate and directed toward a contained audience, these considerations were disregarded and a licensing agreement was struck, with no licensing fee charged (though it is likely that Goldwater and Archie Comics did see some share of the profits from the use of the Archie characters). Ultimately, though, we may never know how and why such a deal was reached as all records of it seem to have disappeared. As Johanna Draper Carlson reports, "When Archie Comics was asked recently to confirm some of the agreements, their response was a polite demurral because their records had been sealed and placed in storage long ago" (n.p.). What we *can* speculate is that Goldwater saw that the main reason for such a partnership lay not in the creation of loyal readers and increased sales of Archie Comics (though it is clear that monetary considerations did play a part). Instead, like the Parents' Institute, Goldwater seems to have been more concerned with the sponsorship of a multimodal literacy that centered on moral texts that promoted virtuous behavior, a fact that seems to have outweighed the doctrinal aspects of Hartley's work.[14]

Spire debuted their line of Archie comic books in 1973 with three titles, *Archie's One Way*, *Archie's Love Scene*, and *Archie's Clean Slate*, and between 1973 and 1982 went on to produce a total of 19 comics featuring the cast of Archie comics in a Christian context. At first glance, the comic books look much like those from the mainstream line, the major differences being the presence of the Spire Christian Comics logo in the top left corner of the cover and a higher cover price of 35 cents. In fact, of the three initial titles, it is only the cover of *Archie's One Way* that gives a clear indication that the content of the book will be explicitly Christian. In this illustration, placed below the large, stylized title and occupying the bottom two-thirds of the page, a police officer who is standing beside Archie's car (loaded with Archie, Veronica, Jughead, Ethel, Moose, and Betty) points towards a one-way sign in a manner that is ambiguous enough to suggest that he is actually pointing up. With an irritated expression on his face, the officer says, "Do you know this is one way?" Betty, her arms raised to the sky and her expression full of joy, exclaims, "This is cool! The officer is witnessing to Archie!" The words "one way" and "witnessing" are not only in a larger font than the rest of the dialogue, but are presented in bold red. Here the multimodal elements come together to announce the intentions of the comic book to the potential reader.

Archie's Love Scene is not nearly as direct, but instead implies that something slightly different is happening inside the book through its cover illustration in which the teachers comment on how happy the gang seems, how they do their homework every day and are never late to class, and how they seem to have no complaints. In front of these comments that form the backdrop of the panel, the gang marches forward, their expressions showing to the reader how happy they are. *Archie's Clean Slate*, on the other hand, could easily have been used as a cover for the mainstream Archie line. Here the cover illustration comprises a large illustration of Archie's face surrounded by a catalogue of the kinds of problems Archie had been getting into since his first appearance in 1941: Mr. Lodge yells at him as he sits with Veronica, he crashes his car, he doesn't have enough money to pay his bill at Pop's, he causes an explosion in the chemistry lab, Moose yells at him for talking to Midge, he causes Mrs. Grundy to be covered in foam, he runs into Mr. Weatherbee, and Ethel decides she loves him. Here Hartley draws on the available resources for design of readers familiar with Archie comics in order to bring them in to the book before revealing its Christian message, a strategy described by Hartley himself earlier in this chapter. In these three covers, then, we can see a variety of design strategies in using the cover as a paratextual gateway to the kind of literacy sponsorship Hartley and Spire wanted to establish, ranging from directly stating the evangelical purpose, to presenting the gang in a relatively familiar way but with an implied change, to creating a cover that looked as much as possible like a mainstream Archie book.

The format used for the Spire books followed closely that of the mainstream books, with a variety of short pieces that ranged in length from one to seven pages. While there are elements of the wholesome humor that Hartley saw as one of the main attractions of the Archie characters, the message here is explicitly Christian in ways that far surpass anything Hartley ever did at Archie Comics. Often the stories focus on either the problems of adolescence (i.e. popularity, the temptation to cheat on tests, the pressure to take drugs, etc.) or, as might be expected of a comic book produced in this period, on larger world problems such as pollution. For example, "Hot Spot," the first story in the book, centers on the problems both Archie and Ethel encounter in wanting to be popular. Partway through the piece, Betty puts her hand on Ethel's shoulder, smiles, and tells her, "Give God a chance in your life!" (5). After a full-page interlude depicting Psalms Chapter 8 (which connects this topic with that of environmental stewardship in one of the stories to follow), the story ends with a panel that focuses on a verse from Romans. Here the panel verse is placed within a caption box that is a physical presence within the narrative world, with Dilton peering around the side of it while Moose seems to hold it in place. Framing this caption box are the images of Archie reading the Bible on the right, his Bible pointing towards the verse, and Ethel on the left, her thumb also pointing to the verse. The words within both of their dialogue balloons are similarly designed to focus the attention of the reader on the Bible verse, the ultimate point of the story. This story then leads in to a one-page comparison of "Man's values" and "God's values," followed by a Christian guide to self-acceptance. These pieces work in tandem with each other to provide a Christian answer to the problems associated with the wish to be popular, while the next three stories pick up on the idea of environmentalism and place it within a Christian context. In both cases, the multimodal elements are used to focus readers' attention on the Christian answers to these two levels of problems.

The last story in this issue, entitled "Final Exam," has commonalities with "Solomon's Child" in that it introduces characters outside the normal cast of an Archie comic as catalysts and recipients for Christian witness. In the opening two pages, Jerry and Debbie taunt Archie and Betty as "Mr. Clean and the Fairy Princess" and tell them, "It must be awful—going to school with us sinners!" (27). Drawn in a more realistic style than the main cast, a style closer to the one Hartley used in his testimonial comics, Jerry and Debbie are shown drunk/high (as evidenced by the appropriate emanata, as well as by their expressions and body language) as they climb into a car and drive away. When Archie and Betty drive the same route, they discover an accident in which Debbie has been badly hurt. In a long series of panels that comprise the last three pages of the story, Betty comforts Debbie. In one panel, in which we see a close up of Debbie's battered face, she says, "Well, I want to live differently—I want a clean slate!" (30). The next panel, a long shot in which the entire scene including the wreck and Betty ministering to Debbie is visible, Betty replies, "God knows all about your life, Debbie—and he's willing to forgive you—for everything!" (31). Including the full scene in the panel is a design choice that attempts to link Betty's words about God to Jerry and Debbie's decision and its consequences in a way that will make the readers contemplate their own decisions and how they might be granted a similar "clean slate" by turning to God. Through Betty's ministering to Debbie at the site of the accident, Debbie is converted to evangelical Christianity and given what Archie calls, in the second last panel, "a new life" (32). The final panel shows Debbie being loaded into an ambulance on the left side of the frame, a new-found smile on her face, which one assumes is the result of her conversion. Archie and Betty are shown in the center of the frame, arms around each other as they gaze out to the audience, their faces radiating contented smiles, as Archie says, "And that's exactly the way God promises it!" (32). Behind them, the sun's rays shine through the clouds as if heaven has blessed the occasion of Debbie's conversion, the light out of a dark situation. Of course, not every reader will make such connections, but for many the available resources for design will push them towards these conclusions, as will the words that appear in bold red underneath the panel: "You can read God's exciting promise in II Corinthians 5:17" (32). As in the above examples, the thrust of the comic pushes the reader to its multimodally constructed internal Christian message and to the intertextual, linguistic message represented by the Bible verse.

Through their comic book publications, Spire and Hartley were able to build on the efforts of religious publishers such as the Catechetical Guild and the Oral Roberts Evangelical Association before them, using comic books to sponsor multimodal literacy both for monetary gain and for the promulgation of a specific kind of

Christian message. In their partnership with Archie Comics, however, Spire and Hartley went beyond what other religious publishers had done by yolking their message to a popular recurring character with a built-in readership, much like the Children's Television Workshop did in using Spider-Man to promote literacy through their partnership with Marvel. By engaging with these comic books, readers would have added to their available resources for design, thus increasing their multimodal literacy, much as they would have with any of the other kinds of comic books we have seen to this point. In doing so, readers would have, for the most part, understood the overt Christian messages, but the reactions to those messages would have run the gamut, just as they would have for readers of Siegel and Shuster's Superman, The Parents' Institute's *True Comics*, or EC's horror comics. The benefit lay in the possibilities created through the ability to convey such messages, an ability that could be enhanced through partnerships such as the one detailed here between Spire and Archie Comics or the one described in the next chapter between the Children's Television Workshop and Marvel Comics.

Notes

1 For a full description of Goldwater's involvement in the establishment of the Comics Code, see Chapter 4.
2 As Jones reports, "By the end of 1933, Eastern may have sold as many as 30 million pages of comics in just those three premiums" (100).
3 For more on the role that Mayer and Gaines played in the early publication history of Superman, see Jones' *Men of Tomorrow*.
4 Though the covers would soon become much less evocative and kinetic, the early covers are indicative of the ways that the series was initially marketed.
5 According to Hajdu, "[d]uring the war years, churches in some two thousand parishes across the country purchased volumes in a series of educational comics, *Picture Stories from the Bible*, for distribution through their Sunday schools" (72).
6 Roberts began his radio ministry in 1947, while his television evangelism began in 1954.
7 The Christian Comics International website is by far the most comprehensive source for material on the history of Christian comics.
8 Although Superman appeared in other media by the time the Supermen of America club was introduced, it was used specifically to promote the sale of his comic book adventures.

9 Beginning with the second issue, the numbering changed to 102 and carried on in this way until 119. The fourth issue was thus numbered 104.

10 According to Butler, "Adverts in his 'Patsy' titles were boasting of 'five to six million readers' at their peak, reportedly. In all, seven comic book titles were fully devoted to her—*A Date with Patsy*, *Miss America*, *Girls' Life*, *Patsy and Hedy*, *Patsy and Her Pals*, *Patsy Walker's Fashion Parade*, and *Patsy Walker*" (n.p.). Hartley's success with the Patsy Walker line would continue until 1967 when the last of the titles was cancelled as sales began to decline.

11 By "Christian witness," Hartley means telling non-believers about salvation through a belief in Jesus Christ and a tripartite God.

12 There was certainly a Christian message in *Picture Stories from the Bible*, but the Bible stories were presented more in the service of a cultural education that cut across the boundaries of faith.

13 In his Foreword to an anthology of Christian comics entitled *Proverbs and Parables*, Hartley also wrote, "We want the reader to pick up our books, be anxious to turn the page and to become totally involved in the story line" (VI).

14 Archie Comics asked that images from the Spire versions of Archie not be included in *Graphic Encounters* since they were produced under license and outside of the editorial control of Archie Comics.

CHAPTER SIX

Teaming up for literacy: Spider-Man, *The Electric Company,* and cross-media literacy sponsorship

EXT. BUS STOP

FULL SHOT of J. ARTHUR CRANK, who sits on a wooden bench, reading a comic book. Enter EASY READER.

> EASY
> Hey, what you doin'?

> CRANK
> What do you think I'm doing on *The Electric Company*? I'm reading. What else would I be doing on *The Electric Company*? Shooting fish?

> EASY
> Alright, alright. What you reading?

> CRANK
> What else? Spider-Man! He's my best.

EASY

I like him a lot myself. Say, listen. Speaking of Spider-Man, guess
who's going to be on *The Electric Company*.

CRANK

Mason Reese?

EASY

Nah.

CRANK

Why not, he's on everything else.

EASY

I *know* that. The man who's going to be on *The Electric Company*
is none other than Spider-Man.

CRANK

Get outta here. Easy, let me explain it to you. Spider-Man is in a
funny book—he's a cartoon guy, you know. I mean, he ain't no
real person. He's just a drawing. You know what I mean.

EASY

Suit yourself, my man. Suit yourself.

(*The Electric Company* Episode # 391, October 21, 1974)

For the 7–10-year-old viewers of *The Electric Company* in 1974,
the prospect of Spider-Man appearing alongside Easy Reader, J.
Arthur Crank, and the rest of their afternoon friends would have
been thrilling indeed, acting as yet another enticement for them to
watch the show. Since, as Crank points out, *The Electric Company*
was centered around the act of reading, further engagement with
the show by viewers was tantamount to further engagement with
reading. The introduction of Spider-Man in the above scene, a debut
that ushered in a three-year partnership between The Children's
Television Workshop (CTW) and Marvel Comics, marked the
advent of a complicated sponsoring of viewers' literacies by two
organizations with very different agendas. Beginning with this
appearance, a cross-media partnership ensued between Marvel
Comics and CTW based around short, self-contained narratives
that appeared on both the television show and in *Spidey Super*

Stories, a comic book introduced by Marvel, also in the fall of 1974. This chapter examines this partnership, the ways in which the two groups used their partnership to sponsor both alphabetic and multimodal literacies for their target audience, and the benefits each derived from such sponsorship of literacy. In looking at this partnership, I consider the ways in which cross-media story-telling begins at the earliest stages of children's literacy development and is complicated by not only the media used to deliver narratives and promote literacy, but also by the different motivations that animate the various sponsors.

Let's begin by looking at the way Spider-Man's introduction unfolds after Easy leaves Crank at the bus stop since it sets out the basic parameters of the rest of Spider-Man's appearances on the show. As Crank looks at the camera, he expresses his doubts directly to the audience (since Spider-Man is "just a drawing"):

CRANK

You tell me that Spider-Man's going to be on *The Electric Company*.

SPIDER-MAN

slinks silently into the picture, framed in an archway behind and to the left of Crank.

CRANK

I believe that, I gotta be some kind of dummy, you know what I mean. But, you know, I wasn't born yesterday. Old J. Arthur knows when somebody's pulling a joke on him and I ain't no dummy, know what I mean?

SPIDER-MAN

sneaks into the frame and picks up the comic book that Crank has left on the back of the bench.

CRANK

I mean, if I was gonna believe that, that Spider-Man is gonna be on *The Electric Company*, I'd have to be some kind of yo-yo, know what I mean?

As the scene progresses, Crank exits in pursuit of Easy (who he thinks has taken his comic book to read since Easy reads whatever he can find), while Spider-Man (still unseen by Crank, but clearly visible to the viewer) reads the comic book in the background. As Crank exits, the camera pulls in to a close-up of Spider-Man, and a word balloon appears above his head with the sentence "What a yo-yo!" The viewer recognizes that this sentence represents what Spider-Man is thinking because of the irregular edges of the balloon (in the shape of a cloud) and the series of circles that connects this balloon to Spider-Man's head. That is, the viewers use their knowledge of comic book conventions, gleaned from reading comics such as *The Amazing Spider-Man*, in conjunction with their developing alphabetic literacy to interpret what Spider-Man thinks about Crank. Here, as in all the live-action narrative sequences, Spider-Man never speaks. Rather, his thoughts and speeches appear in word balloons above his head, drawing on a familiar convention from comics in order to promote reading as a way for viewers to follow the simple narratives.

As we shall see, such strategies not only reinforced alphabetic literacy, but also multimodal literacies. As children encountered a scene such as this one, they engaged in the process of Design through a range of modalities (including Spider-Man's body language; the inflection, tone, and intonation of Crank's voice; the framing of Spider-Man in relation to Crank; the printed words above Spider-Man's head; the way the visuals suggest how these words should be read; and the way all of these elements come together) in order to interpret the meaning of this deceptively simple narrative. In doing so, children would have brought to bear their Available Designs in order to try to make sense of what was happening in the scene. After this viewing/reading experience was over, each child would incorporate this experience into their resources available for subsequent interactions with multimodal texts (the Redesigned). In other words, as viewers/readers engaged with narratives such as this one on *The Electric Company* and similar ones in *Spidey Super Stories*, they developed both alphabetic and multimodal literacies because of the combined interventions of CTW and Marvel Comics. Through both the Spider-Man segments on *The Electric Company* and the material in *Spidey Super Stories*, CTW and Marvel can be seen to be underwriting the literacies of their viewers/readers as these stories enabled, supported, taught, and modeled not only alphabetic literacy, but multimodal literacies as well. Clearly both organizations gained advantage through this partnership and through their involvement in literacy sponsorship, though their motivations, as we shall see, differed sharply.

In The Children's Television Workshop, we have a not-for-profit educational group whose existence is centered around the promotion of literacy (through television programs such as *Sesame Street* and *The Electric Company*); the advantage gained by CTW was that the sponsorship of literacy fulfilled their mission and satisfied their funding bodies. In Marvel Comics, we have a for-profit comic book publisher for whom the advantage in sponsoring literacy was less direct, but no less imperative to the success of their enterprise; by promoting literacies (especially multimodal literacies), Marvel hoped to create readers (and thus consumers) of their books, both at the time (for *Spidey Super Stories*) and in the future (for the rest of their comics). Both Marvel and CTW acted as individual sponsors of literacy, both here and in their other endeavors, but together their cross-media partnership presents a very interesting example of the ways in which such partnerships are complicated by the motives that inform each sponsoring partner. Before I examine this partnership in more detail, let me begin by providing some contextual background on the ways in which CTW and Marvel acted as literacy sponsors in their own rights.

We're gonna give you the power: *The Electric Company*

It was not long after the launch and initial success of *Sesame Street* that CTW began to plan its second series, *The Electric Company*, a show designed to explicitly teach reading through the use of television. This use of television in the educational content and intent of both shows was in line with the findings of the 1967 Report of the Carnegie Commission on Educational Television entitled *Public Television: A Program for Action*. The main conclusion of this report was that "a well-financed and well-directed educational television system, substantially larger and more pervasive and effective than that which now exists in the United States, must be brought into being if the full needs of the American people are to be served" (3). In the years immediately after the release of this report, the federal government put their financial support behind this initiative, funding programs such as *Sesame Street* and *The Electric Company*. As Joan Ganz Cooney, one of the cofounder's of CTW, recollects in the liner notes for the recent *The Best of The Electric Company* box set, "Lloyd Morrisett, Children's Television Workshop cofounder and chairman of the board, called and said the federal government was interested in emphasizing reading in schools and that money was probably available for a television series that would teach reading" (4). Through a partnership between the US Office of Education, Public Television Stations, the Corporation for Public Broadcasting, the Ford Foundation, the Carnegie Corporation, and the Mobil Corporation, money was indeed secured to support the development and production of *The Electric Company*. Funding in place, CTW began the process of initial research that would inform their decisions with regard to the target audience, approach, format, and curriculum of their second television series.[1]

In order to first establish who they were targeting with the show, producers began by consulting a panel of educational experts from around the United States. Cooney recalls that "The advisors suggested that the show be aimed at struggling readers in the second grade—children who were in danger of becoming academically disenfranchised because they were having trouble learning to read" (4). This general statement about whom they were trying to reach was then further narrowed and placed in context of their learning situations, as seen in *"The Electric Company* Final Report," published in 1978, the year after the show had finished its run. The report states,

> As part of the program's early development CTW's advisors designated "poor readers, 7–10 years old," children who had already tasted failure in school reading programs, and for whom television could provide a non-threatening and familiar alternative to the classroom experience. It was planned that the program be primarily for viewing in the home, a respite from the pressure—and perhaps even humiliation—of the classroom. (At the same time, it was hoped that teachers would also use the program and considerable promotional effort was to be aimed at them.) The target viewers and their peers were known to be steady and sophisticated television viewers. Televised reading instruction, if carefully designed, could take advantage of this visual sophistication. (6)

In thinking about how to best sponsor literacy for their target audience, CTW made two interesting moves when they decided to begin by scaffolding literacy learning on to viewers' experiences with watching and making sense from television. The first important point is that by beginning where the students were, the CTW tried explicitly to connect what children already knew with what they might be taught. Moreover, by designing the show to be primarily viewed in the home—seen here as a respite from the classroom—the show's producers attempted to build a bridge between the home space (where they exercised what James Gee calls their primary discourse) and the space of school (where they had problems with what Gee calls the secondary discourses they were expected to master). In this way, students could begin to see that there could be links between these different ways of using language. If this were the case, then, school might not seem so foreign or intimidating. Through viewing *The Electric Company*, students could begin not only to acquire basic reading skills, but they could also begin to move toward control of the important secondary discourses that comprised the school environment. Not only was literacy being sponsored in the sense that students learned simple decoding skills, the main focus of the program as laid out in the initial research, but it was also being sponsored in Gee's sense of literacy as the "control of secondary uses of language (i.e. uses of language in secondary discourses)" (23). Though CTW may not have termed it as such, the focus on scaffolding on what children already knew and making explicit linkages between home and school reinforced notions of literacy that go beyond the instrumentalist definitions of decoding that pervade much of CTW's research.

The second important aspect of CTW's thinking was the way they scaffolded the teaching of alphabetic literacy onto the skills that their viewers already had in viewing television, a medium that at first blush has little in common with alphabetic texts. In other words, the show's producers were using a multimodal medium (i.e. one in which viewers not only made meaning through the linguistic mode, but also through the audio, visual, gestural, and spatial modes) in order to promote alphabetic literacy which students would then presumably be able to transfer to the books they would encounter in school and other settings. Though multimodality may not have been what they called it, clearly those involved in *The*

Electric Company had some inkling of the ways in which meaning making encompassed more than just words on the page. While the focus of *The Electric Company* was always geared toward teaching children to decode linguistic/alphabetic texts, the producers of the show understood the ways in which meaning is created in multiple modalities and hoped to capitalize on this potential and the already existing expertise of their viewers in interpreting multimodal texts. Gerald Lesser, Chairman of the Board of Advisors of CTW, recognized this connection in his 1974 book, *Children and Television: Lessons from Sesame Street*, writing, "Although there are rare occasions when television will present either pictures or sounds, one without the other, its special capacity is the coordinated combination" (88). In *The Electric Company: An Introduction to the New Television Program Designed to Help Teach Reading to Children*, a paperback available to teachers and parents in the months preceding the launch of the show, Cooney also picked up on this idea, writing that "television, as a medium, has a particular set of advantages in the teaching of reading" (n.p.). She went on to discuss elements such as animation, music, and sound effects, all of which illustrate the kinds of meaning-making described by the New London Group in *Multiliteracies: Literacy Learning and the Design of Social Futures.* By drawing on these elements, not only would CTW be sponsoring linguistic/alphabetic literacies, but they would, whether they meant to or not, be sponsoring their viewers' multimodal literacies, no doubt a large part of what made *The Electric Company* such an attractive partner for Marvel Comics.

Make mine Marvel!: Marvel Comics

Since the literacies needed to engage with comics are multimodal rather than alphabetic, Marvel's interest in sponsoring literacy clearly lay in the sponsorship of multimodal literacy, rather than in the use of comics as an intermediate step toward increased alphabetic literacy. As I have been arguing throughout the book, when a reader encounters a comic, he or she is faced with a complex environment that requires interpreting material that is presented in a number of different modes simultaneously and in combination with each other. These modes of making meaning and the literacies needed to access them are present in both the television and comics media. While CTW sought to use these modalities (through children's previous experience with television and comics) to increase traditional print literacies, Marvel's interests instead lay in building on children's experience with these modalities (whether in television or comics) to foster an ever more sophisticated multimodal literacy that would then result in increased readership and sales of their comics. The fact that Marvel was seen also to be supporting alphabetic literacies brought with it the added bonus of positioning them as good corporate citizens, just as DC's Editorial Advisory Board had been designed to do in the 1940s.

Beyond a concern with sponsoring a multimodal literacy that would create and sustain a readership for comics in general, Marvel was necessarily interested in *which* comics children were choosing to read. To this end, Marvel sought to create a coherent universe in which events in one title affected the events in another title and in which characters might appear in each other's books. For example, Spider-Man might visit the Fantastic Four in a story that began in *The Fantastic Four*, only to have events further unfold in *Marvel Team-Up* and finish in *The Amazing Spider-Man*. In this way, literacy sponsorship for Marvel was tightly directed toward their own comics. As a commercial enterprise, such behavior is to be expected, but Marvel's efforts to create loyal readers were among the most pronounced in any medium. Marvel's strategy was to create a group of readers who would identify completely, if not exclusively, with Marvel Comics.[2] During Marvel's heyday in the 1960s, they had been incredibly successful in their sponsorship of not only multimodal literacy, but a multimodal literacy that pointed inward toward the shared universe of Marvel comics rather than outward toward any other kind of texts (including other kinds of comics). By the 1970s, however, Marvel had lost some of the cultural cachet it had enjoyed as a purveyor of cool in the 1960s and was rapidly introducing new titles and trying out a variety of strategies to entice new, younger readers to the Marvel fold. By partnering with CTW and *The Electric Company*, Marvel could not only sponsor the multimodal literacies necessary for readers to engage and enjoy comics, but they could also begin to instill a loyalty to the Marvel universe and its characters from the earliest stages of literacy development.

Teaming up for literacy

As *The Electric Company* entered its fourth season, researchers connected with CTW pushed for more inclusion of opportunities for sustained reading to supplement the attention given in the show to the decoding of single words. Within the magazine-style format of the show that utilized short, related segments in order to hold the attention of the viewer, the focus tended to be on strategies for sounding out and identifying single, isolated words. These researchers called for the "decoding of passages of print longer than a single sentence and embodying some narrative sequence" (*"The Electric Company* Final Report" 65). In order to emphasize the importance of reading in these sequences, it was imperative to produce "situations in which print would be critical (rather than irrelevant and 'tacked on') to the plot" (*"The Electric Company* Final Report" 64). As well, researchers realized that they needed to include more references within the show that would be familiar to their viewers and connect to the other interests in their lives; parodies such as "Julia Grownup," while funny to teachers and parents, were not connecting with the target audience, thus necessitating some re-thinking of the intertextual references that were being used in the show. Given these goals, the producers decided that one way to introduce narrative reading sequences was through the use of Spider-Man. In Spider-Man, CTW saw a character with whom viewers would be familiar, just as they would be with both J. Arthur Crank and Easy Reader. By incorporating "live-action sequences in which the familiar hero [Spider-Man] never spoke" and whose "speeches appeared in comic book style 'balloons' over his head,"[3] the producers of *The Electric Company* were simultaneously able to address concerns about both the lack of sustained reading and the necessity for more familiar references within the show.[4]

By all accounts, researchers at CTW and the producers of *The Electric Company* were pleased with the introduction and use of Spider-Man in these short narrative sequences. From their perspective, the partnership encouraged children to want to read and kept their attention focused on the show, rather than on other possible after-school activities; as seen in both *The Electric Company: An Introduction* and "*The Electric Company* Final Report," whether or not the show would appeal to and hold the attention of the target audience was always a central concern. Moreover, through the strategic placement of text within simple narratives (in the form of the main character's speech or thoughts), the emphasis was on reading as "a problem-solving endeavor, in which the purpose is to extract sense" (*Electric Company: An Introduction* n.p.). Without reading the text that was placed within the narrative sequence, it would be very difficult for the viewer to understand the story fully, which provided increased motivation to make sense from the linguistic text. Of course, in doing so, the viewers were also placing that text within the larger narrative, making sense of the entire story through audio, visual, gestural, spatial, *and* linguistic modes that all came together to create multimodal meaning. As sponsors of literacy, CTW understood the power of television (and its attendant elements) as an educational tool that could be harnessed to promote alphabetic literacy; CTW's mission was, after all, to promote reading. The partnership with Marvel and the use of Spider-Man in short narratives on *The Electric Company* afforded the opportunity to place the linguistic mode within a larger multimodal narrative and to make alphabetic literacy central to the multiple literacies necessary to understand the narrative fully. In this way, the partnership helped to promote the kinds of literacy that were important to CTW and to satisfy their funding bodies that they were successfully pursuing the work with which they had been charged.

According to "*The Electric Company* Final Report," the use of Spider-Man in *The Electric Company*

> provided considerable motivation to read and became extremely popular with viewers. Capitalizing on the popularity of these segments, a special *Electric Company* "Spidey" comic was designed for newsstand distribution as a way of providing additional reading matter of a controlled kind. This comic looked much like any other, but had carefully placed print, short messages, controlled vocabulary and was designed to encourage the poor reader to read rather than to merely rely on pictures. (66)

In addition to the live-action narrative sequences that appeared in the television show, the *Spidey Super Stories* comic book began to appear monthly at about the same time that Spider-Man debuted on *The Electric Company*. Along with *The Electric Company*

Magazine (which featured shortened versions of the comics), *Spidey Super Stories* was designed to reach "the at-home audience" as a way "to provide reading practice to reinforce the program and also draw attention to the program" (*"The Electric Company* Final Report" 72). From CTW's perspective, their forays into commercially available materials were designed to supplement what was happening on the show by both reinforcing its literacy lessons and addressing the all-important issue of viewer appeal. In reading *"The Electric Company* Final Report," it is evident Spider-Man and *Spidey Super Stories* were both seen as tools to be used to promote CTW's particular literacy mission and its sponsorship of alphabetic literacy. From CTW's perspective, the benefits of the partnership in promoting literacy to their target audience were clear, both in the formative research that led them to the introduction of Spider-Man and in the summative research that was produced after the show went off the air. What, then, were the benefits of the partnership to Marvel Comics?

Normally in these kinds of cross-media partnerships much of the answer to that question would lie in the licensing fees that Marvel would charge to the organization that wanted to use the Spider-Man character. However, in this case, Marvel allowed CTW to use Spider-Man as a character on *The Electric Company* without charging any fee. Certainly Marvel would benefit financially in the short term from sales of *Spidey Super Stories* (though only from the cover price since it contained no ads), but alongside their other titles (including *The Amazing Spider-Man* and *Marvel Team-Up*, both of which already featured Spider-Man), the sales numbers were never going to compare because of the limited appeal of the new book with its 7–10-year-old target audience and simplified stories. Rather, what Marvel had to gain was wrapped up completely in the way that the partnership would allow them to sponsor multimodal literacy in general, and comics literacy in particular, especially as it was directed in the long term toward Marvel comics and characters. The appearance of Spider-Man on *The Electric Company* and in *Spidey Super Stories* would help to develop multimodal literacies and, in doing so, introduce, engage, and/or sustain children in the act of reading comics by reinforcing the pleasures of these multimodal narratives. By ushering children into the practice of reading comics and supporting the necessary multimodal literacies at an early stage, Marvel hoped to create life-long readers and consumers of their products. The simple multimodal narratives with which viewers engaged on the show and in the comic book would—they hoped—yield to increasingly complex narratives, such as those in *The Amazing Spider-Man*, the kind of reading to which Marvel wanted the target audience to graduate. In this way, their literacy sponsorship paralleled CTW in that both hoped to use the basic stories as scaffolding on which they could build ever more sophisticated literacy and reading choices. Where they diverged, however, was the types of textual engagement and the types of texts that would be the goal of this scaffolding: CTW saw television and comics (both multimodal texts) as stepping stones to alphabetic literacy, while Marvel saw these multimodal texts as stepping stones to more Marvel comics, complex multimodal texts of a particular type.

Since the 1960s, much of Marvel's success had been built on the way that they were able to create a distinctive discourse community around their line of comics by creating a knowledge set that clearly marked who were insiders and who were not. As I mentioned earlier in the chapter, the key to this discourse community was the idea of continuity across all Marvel titles, a shared narrative world (known as the Marvel Universe) in which characters interacted with each other across a range of titles. By creating such a shared narrative world, as opposed to prior practices in the industry in which each title stood alone, often telling several unrelated narratives within one issue, Marvel pushed its readers to follow multiple titles, thus creating a shared canon of texts among readers.[5] By allowing CTW to use Spider-Man on *The Electric Company*, interest could be generated and sustained among the target audience, leading them first to *Spidey Super Stories* and then to *The Amazing Spider-Man* or *Marvel Team-Up*. Since many other characters from the Marvel Universe appeared in *Spidey Super Stories*, however, the intention was that it would act not only as a stepping stone to the other Spider-Man titles, but as a gateway into the Marvel Universe and the discourse community of insiders that were sustained by those narratives. For Marvel, the cross-media partnership and the sponsorship of literacy that it entailed constituted an initial step in the long process of enculturation toward Marvel fandom. For Marvel, as for CTW, literacy mattered, but in a very different way.

Beware of The Spoiler: Spider-Man's adventures on *The Electric Company*

The first appearance of Spider-Man on *The Electric Company* occurred on October 21, 1974, while the first issue of *Spidey Super Stories* appeared with a cover date of October, 1974.[6] In both instances, there was an effort to introduce Spider-Man in order to familiarize new viewers/readers with the character and to orient those already familiar with the character to the new context in which he would be appearing. In the television introduction, as seen in the opening segment of this chapter, J. Arthur Crank and Easy Reader are shown to be familiar with the character, both being avid readers of *The Amazing Spider-Man*; for Crank, the question is not *who* is this new character, but *how* can this fictional, comic book character make an appearance on *The Electric Company*. However, the viewers understood that Crank was also a fictional character and that *The Electric Company* constituted a fictional world. In such a scenario, it would have been perfectly acceptable that there be overlap between these two worlds, a view that was especially true for those familiar with Spider-Man and the Marvel Universe, since within that context Spider-Man often appeared in other character's books and vice versa. For those not familiar with Spider-Man, his appearance simply marked the introduction of a new character, albeit one who had a separate history and fictional world that could be explored in the future. It was not, then, that a fictional character was entering the "real" world, but that a character from one world was inhabiting another narrative space or a different fictional world. For many viewers, the introduction of Spider-Man to the show would activate the associations they already had with this character, helping to hold the attention of the target viewers (one of the main aims of CTW in incorporating Spider-Man into the show). For those unfamiliar with Spider-Man or not as familiar as active fans, the introduction of the character would pique the interest of the viewers in exploring the fictional world from which Spider-Man had been transplanted (one of the main aims of Marvel in incorporating Spider-Man into the show). In either case, Spider-Man would become one of the "attractive characters [who were] critical not only to building an audience but also to providing models for children to identify with, since the capacity to bring about learning through identification is an important aspect of instructional television" (*"The Electric Company* Final Report" 29). Clearly the idea of identification is important for the kinds of literacy sponsorship that were important both to CTW and to Marvel.

The first episode in which Spider-Man appeared followed the well-established magazine format the show had been employing since its premiere in 1971, with many short segments (20 in this case) combining to emphasize a small number of learning goals.[7] It also followed the producers' dictum that "no program in the series should require of the viewer that he have seen any previous program" (*The Electric Company: An Introduction* n.p.). However, there was careful sequencing within each individual episode with the goal of working toward a limited number of curricular goals; a number of segments interlocked in ways that used repetition to emphasize learning goals and build on the skills that were being developed in each short segment. For example, after the sequence that introduced Spider-Man and the title sequence that featured the show's theme song along with shots of the main characters, the show moved to a series of segments that focused on teaching the "tr" sound to its viewers. One of the segments involved an ongoing technique that involved the silhouettes of two heads in profile, facing each other. In the liner notes to *The Electric Company* boxset, Walter J. Podrazik describes the routine: "One would start a word, with the first few letters flowing from the lips. The other would finish the word, sending out the remaining letters. As the letters settled on the screen, the two heads would also speak each part, blending together for the complete word. It was speak-along phonics" (13). For example, the head on the left said "tr," the head on the right said "ick," and then the two together pronounced the word "trick." In this oft-repeated technique, viewers are taught to sound out words through multimodal teaching methods in which the audio (the sound of the words), the gestural (the shape of the lips as the sound is made), the spatial (the way heads frame the words that are being said), and the visual (the shape of the profiles and the way the words, visual representations themselves, emanate from the mouths) come together with the words to create multimodal meaning. By making sense of this multimodal phonics, the viewer could then begin to also make sense of the alphabetic cues in sounding out the letters into words. For CTW, alphabetic literacy was the goal, but along the way viewers were immersed in multimodal literacy.

Following a number of other segments that further elaborated on the lesson of the "tr" sound, developed viewer familiarity with the "ai" sound, and taught about punctuation marks, the first full Spider-Man segment began. The narrative commenced as a new Spider-Man theme song, written specifically for *The Electric Company* to supersede the theme from the 1960s cartoon, played over the image of Spider-Man fighting an as-yet unnamed, but at this point intimidating, villain. As the camera pulled out, the viewer realized that the characters appeared to be almost bursting from a comic book cover for *The Amazing Spider-Man*, an explicit connection to the main title in which Spider-Man appeared within Marvel's fictional world (and set of commercial properties). As the lettering of the comic book title came into focus (familiar already to many in the target audience), so too did the words "Spidey Meets the Spoiler" come into view in the lower left portion of the cover. The narrator's voice intoned, "On today's episode, Spidey Meets the Spoiler" and the camera pulled in to once more focus on the action of the fight, while the page was turned to reveal the panels of a comic book. The edges of several panels were visible, but the focus was on a horizontal panel at the top of the page that depicted Spider-Man swinging through the city, his power emphasized by the way in which the figure was not contained by the panel, an effect often used in superhero comics. In these first few moments of the narrative, the conventions of television (camera movement, editing, narrator's voice) combined with those of comics (drawn figures, paneling, lettering) to create a multimodal text for the viewer to experience and interpret. As in the sequence of short segments that emphasized the "tr" sound, multiple modes of interpretation came into play as the viewer had to interpret the gestures and body language of the characters; the sound of the theme music and narrator's voice; the spatial layout of the cover and paneled page as well as the camera movements that alter these layouts; the visual elements that include the comic book cover with its images and lettering; the hand that turns the page; and the drawings within the panels on the next page. Add to this the written elements of the comic book and episode titles and you had the kind of multimodal environment on which CTW hoped to scaffold alphabetic literacy and through which Marvel hoped to create and sustain an army of young Marvel Comics readers.

The addition of explicit comic book elements such as paneling to the television and animation techniques already in place on *The Electric Company* augmented what CTW was doing in the teaching of alphabetic literacy by adding modalities familiar to many of their viewers and placing it all within a narrative structure. For Marvel, the introduction of these elements was as crucial as the introduction of the Spider-Man character himself because now what was being taught was not only how to read words, but *how to read a comic*—how to interpret the particular ways panel sequencing allowed narrative meaning to be made. That is, for viewers familiar with comics, alphabetic literacy could be scaffolded on to yet one more form of multimodal literacy, while for viewers unfamiliar or less familiar with comics, the practice of reading comics could be scaffolded on to the practice of interpreting a television sequence.

As the Spider-Man segment unfolded, the viewer could see the explicit ways that alphabetic literacy was incorporated as an integral part of the narrative and the implicit ways that the importance of panel sequencing in comics narratives was taught. As the camera focused on the drawn panel described above, the audience heard the narrator's voice saying, "Ever alert, the legendary wall-crawler is looking for something." At this point, there was a cut to another panel (clearly indicated as a panel by the portions of other panels that border it) in which a live-action version of Spider-Man sat on a curb, with the narrator saying, "And he's found it." As would be the case in future episodes, the panel framed a short scene in which both narrative and actual movement occurred. Here Spider-Man sat on the curb holding a rubber glove sandwich. There was then a cut to a panel in which Spider-Man discovered a fire hydrant with a sign that read "No Dogs Allowed," followed, after enough pause to allow the viewers to read what it said, by a cut to a panel with a close-up of the sign. At this point the narrator read the words on the sign. The edit was then to a frame with Spider-Man holding the glove sandwich while sitting beside the fire hydrant, as the narrator said, "Who would do anything so cruel?" As Spider-Man shook his head, the narrator continued, "Spoil somebody's lunch by giving him a rubber-glove sandwich and spoil a dog's morning walk by not letting him near a hydrant." With the camera still holding on this panel, a thought balloon with the words "The Spoiler!" popped up over Spider-Man's head as sound effects cued that he had had a brainstorm. Instead of reading what Spider-Man thought, the narrator simply said, "Spidey knows."

In this sequence of panels/shots that open the story, it is readily apparent how the act of reading became an integral part of understanding what was happening in this multimodal narrative. As with the episode title, there was a pause between the appearance of the printed words and the reading of those words by the narrator. In this case, the delay was actually until the next shot/panel, a move that stressed the links between one panel and the next in the sequence. This series of shots, framed as they were within comics panels, emphasized the sequential nature of the narrative, even as action also occurred within each shot so that it represented more than a single moment in time. Of course, each panel of a comic similarly marks a segment of time, but here live-action motion stood in for motion lines, multiple drawings of characters, or other ways used in comics to indicate motion, just as the narrator's voice stood in for the caption boxes that we would normally associate with comics. This mixing of techniques from television and comics media challenged viewers to draw on all of their Available Designs in order to make sense of the text and, as they were doing so, to add additional resources for their next encounter with a multimodal text, whether that be television, comics, or the kind of hybrid seen here. In encountering this kind of text, viewers not only saw the ways in which the written word was integral to the story (as seen when the name of the villain is shown in Spider-Man's thought balloon), but also the way the story was told through sequential shots that equated to the sequential panels that comprise a comic book. In other words, *multiple* literacies were taught and encouraged through this simple narrative sequence.

The story continued with the introduction of The Spoiler in the next panel/shot (accompanied by the narrator saying, "Who else but The Spoiler!?!") in which he was shown doing all he could to spoil various things and activities. As he pranced within the confines of the panel, the audience saw him spoiling such things as cake (the narrator says, "He likes to spoil cake") by hurling it out of the frame. As the viewers watched his antics, it was clear for those in the know that The Spoiler was a villain of a different order than

Spider-Man faced in the pages of his regular comic book; it was also clear that The Spoiler was exactly the kind of villain to be expected on *The Electric Company* in that his villainy was linked to the fact that he was not being very nice to people. The viewer was left to come to this kind of interpretation through visuals (the homemade nature of his costume), gestures (the exaggerated way that he moved and pantomimed his actions, as well as his melodramatic facial expressions), and sound (the mock villainous tone of his voice as he explained his motives and plans). The spatial element was operative in the way that the viewer recognized that this was supposed to represent one panel on a comics page and thus activate and/or teach the ways of interpreting a comics narrative. Finally, the verbal element existed in memory from the previous panel in which Spider-Man was shown to be thinking "The Spoiler!" This panel/shot, then, not only reinforced the alphabetic literacy demonstrated in the previous panel/shot, but it also played on the idea that in comics, information from one panel would be used to build on and create expectations for subsequent panels.

As this first scene with The Spoiler came to an end, he finished throwing cake and moved toward the camera. Picking up on the narrator's words ("He likes to spoil cake"), The Spoiler continued, "And ice cream!" Cut to the panel with a man and a woman sitting on a bench reading comics, a link back to the opening scene in which Crank was shown sitting on a bench reading comics. In this case, the woman was eating ice cream, a connection to The Spoiler's words in the previous panel in the sequence. No one was surprised, then, when the Spoiler snuck up behind the woman and placed his cymbals on either side of the ice cream cone. Rather than showing the results of the cymbals hitting the ice cream, there was a cut to another frame, but this time the frame was not live-action, but instead a drawn comics frame that depicted The Spoiler smashing the cone. Here the viewer was able to interpret the scene not through the movements, expressions, words, and costuming of the actors, but through lines that were used to indicate the movement of the cymbals (usually called motion lines in comics), the visual representation of the ice cream exploding, the expression on The Spoiler's face, the jagged shape surrounding the action, and the aural sound effects that accompanied the crash of the cymbals. In other words, there was an almost complete switch to the medium of comics, with the exception of the substitution of actual sound for visual sound effects. What's more, this panel set up a later sequence in the narrative in which a live-action scene showed The Spoiler ready to crash his cymbals around Spider-Man's head. Since the viewers had seen the previous sequence from live-action to drawn panel, there was an expectation about what would happen to Spider-Man because of the previous panel involving cymbals crashing. However, the edit moved the action to a drawn panel in which Spider-Man grabbed the cymbals away from The Spoiler; as in the previous drawn panel, meaning was created almost exclusively through the comics medium, with the exception again of the sound of the cymbals. The segment ended with Spider-Man defeating The Spoiler as the theme song's refrain played and a hand was shown closing the comic book, thus emphasizing that this was a comics narrative, though one that has been modified for presentation on television. By moving back and forth between the multimodal media, viewers learned how to read comics by starting with an ability to interpret television narratives that was already in place, a strategy similar to what CTW had been using with alphabetic literacy from the beginning of *The Electric Company*.

Easy Reader says, "This comic book is easy to read!": *Spidey Super Stories*

Spider-Man not only appeared on *The Electric Company*, but the cast of the show also appeared in the new *Spidey Super Stories*. As noted earlier, CTW saw this kind of commercial outreach as a way to draw attention to the show, reinforce its lessons, and provide reading practice. For CTW, this material was designed to make reading exciting and to supplement what was happening on the show, always with the explicit goal of having the children move on to ever more complex word-based texts. For Marvel, this material reinforced the lessons about multimodal literacy in general and multimodal comics literacy in particular, while also using Spider-Man as a way to draw new readers into the Marvel Universe.

As would be the case in every issue of *Spidey Super Stories*, the first issue featured a version of a narrative from the television

FIGURE 6.1 *Page from "Spidey Meets the Spoiler, " Spidey Super Stories #1.* © 2012 *Marvel Entertainment, Inc. and its subsidiaries.*

show,[8] in this case "Spidey Meets The Spoiler," which was explicitly marked "as seen on *The Electric Company*" and "based on *The Electric Company* script by Tom Whedon" (*Spidey Super Stories* #1, n.p.). In this retelling of the story, the hybrid television/comics form is replaced by story-telling that happens exclusively in the comics medium (see Figure 6.1). For example, caption boxes are used to contain some of the words spoken by the narrator in the television version of the story, while Spider-Man's dialogue replaces some of the narration. Here the opening full-page panel depicts The Spoiler about to crash his cymbals on Spider-Man's head, a move that both takes the place of the cover in the television version and foreshadows the later panel in which The Spoiler similarly menaces Spider-Man.[9] The second page echoes the opening sequence of the television version, setting up the situation in four simple panels in which the words in the caption boxes reinforce the action that is depicted in the panel, while the words spoken by Spider-Man add significant meaning to what is conveyed by the pictures themselves. This set of panels corresponds roughly to the edited sequence that moves the viewer through the narrative set-up in the television version of the show. The notable exception is the lack of a close-up of the sign with the accompanying voice-over reading it; in the television version, this technique is used to give the viewer a chance to read the sign for themselves, but here the reader must make sense of what is happening without the aid of the narrator's voice, thus relying much more heavily on alphabetic literacy as it is situated within the comics medium.

In the first three panels (see Figure 6.1), Spider-Man is depicted in his search for clues and the caption boxes reinforce this interpretation of the images (Panel one: "Our wall-crawler is looking for clues." Panel two: "And he's found one!" Panel three: "Then he finds another one!"). In panel two, Spider-Man's speech begins to show his interpretation of the clues ("Who would give someone a rubber glove sandwich?") as he think through the case. Panel four utilizes the cartoon icon of a lightbulb to show that Spider-Man has an idea as the text in his speech balloon declares, "I know!" As with the television version, readers must use their multimodal literacies to make sense of the page and the narrative set-up, though in this case those literacies must be geared toward the specific challenges of reading a comics page that uses design elements like layout (spatial), drawing (visual), words (linguistic), character body language (gestural), and visual representations of sound effects and speech volume, intonation, and inflection (audio). In re-telling a story that readers have already encountered on *The Electric Company*, both alphabetic literacy and multimodal literacy can be reinforced. More importantly from Marvel's perspective, the transition from the multimodal literacy needed for television to that needed for comics begun in the television version of "Spidey Meets

The Spoiler" can be completed here as the reader is further taught how to engage and make meaning from comics. To this end, the word "Who?" appears inside an arrow at the bottom right of the fourth panel, pointing the reader to the next page and the reveal of The Spoiler, and adding the additional element of how pagination controls narrative pacing to the developing resources (or Available Designs) that these new readers of comics have at their disposal.

In retelling this narrative in comics form, the aim then is to reinforce and extend the lessons presented in the television program, both in terms of decoding words (CTW) and engaging with comics (Marvel). Moreover, through the addition of material to the story, including a subplot about how Easy Reader is tricked by The Spoiler and a new ending that depends upon this new subplot, the reader is forced to go beyond what he or she already knows from their earlier encounter with the narrative; the reader must interpret both the new words that have been added to the text and the multimodal contexts in which they are embedded. By scaffolding this new material on to an existing narrative, the reader is challenged to practice multiple kinds of literacy in order to understand the ways in which the story has been expanded and altered.

Of course, the new material included in *Spidey Super Stories* went beyond just these alterations in the stories already seen on *The Electric Company*. The first issue, for example, opens with a story entitled "Spider-Man is Born!," a simplified retelling of the Spider-Man origin story that would be familiar to regular readers of the Spider-Man titles, but would serve as an introduction to those unfamiliar with Spider-Man's backstory. In this version, there is no mention of the Uncle Ben character (who, in the original version, is killed during a bank robbery that Peter Parker—i.e. Spider-Man—could have prevented) nor any moral quandary about how Peter Parker should use his new-found powers. In this version, the decision and transformation into Spider-Man happens in a compact two-page spread at the end of the story in which Peter Parker decides to use his power to help others, designs and sews a costume, invents and builds webshooters, and bursts from his bedroom (and the panel) to confront wrong-doing wherever he finds it. As well, the reader is presented with one-page explanations (in comics form) of the secrets of Spider-Man's webs and mask, as well as a two-page story in which Valerie persuades Spider-Man to help fix a faulty power cable on the set and, subsequently, to join the cast of *The Electric Company*. In these features, readers are given backstory on the character of Spider-Man and the reasons that he decided to join the show, material that supplements and extends the experience of the viewers of *The Electric Company* if they are willing and able to engage the comics form in which they are presented.

FIGURE 6.2 *Page from "Help! I'm Spider-Man!," Spidey Super Stories #1.* © 2012 Marvel Entertainment, Inc. and its subsidiaries.

The final story of the first issue, entitled "Help! I'm Spider-Man!," performs a number of functions in that it solidifies the cross-over between the narrative worlds of Spider-Man and *The Electric Company*, gives additional practice in reading and interpreting multimodal texts, and begins to introduce the other characters from the Marvel Universe. The narrative involves Duane, one of the members of *The Electric Company*'s resident band, The Short Circus. Here he attempts to pass some neighborhood toughs on his way to Vi's Diner, only to be unceremoniously dropped on his head by one of them. As seen in Figure 6.2, after a close-up panel in which Duane lies on the ground with stars circling his head (shown by motion lines and indicating that he has been knocked out), the narrative proceeds into a dream sequence, indicated by a change in the outline of the panels from a solid rectangles to rectangles with scalloped corners. In the dream, we see Duane reading a Hulk comic (another Marvel character) in his room (that also features a Thor poster—another Marvel reference), an activity that is interrupted by Spider-Man who asks Duane to take his place. This event precipitates an extended episode in which he fights both Electro and the Vulture, two of Spider-Man's recurring villains. Not only are the two fictional worlds melding here, but Duane, an ordinary kid within the confines of the world of *The Electric Company*, actually becomes one of the superheroes he reads about, just as every reader of this comic can imaginatively become Spider-Man through the act of reading. New readers were thus drawn into the Marvel Universe through both the identification with Spider-Man and the introduction of additional characters from that fictional world. Stories such as this one built on the groundwork that had been laid by Spider-Man's appearances on *The Electric Company* as Marvel tried to create a generation of readers devoted to Marvel comics. For both CTW and Marvel, the material in *Spidey Super Stories* both reinforced and extended the narratives and literate practices embodied by the television program.

Conclusion

As a not-for-profit educational group, CTW worked explicitly through *The Electric Company* to support and augment the educational endeavors (and literacy sponsorship) that was being undertaken by the nation's schools. Like CTW, Marvel also supported the development of literacy, both explicitly in their partnership with CTW, but also more indirectly in the act of publishing comic books to which children would be attracted and which they would then read. However, as a commercial enterprise, Marvel's concern and the advantage they gained through these efforts lay in the development and sustenance of new markets for their comics. Through their cross-media partnership, CTW and Marvel effectively linked content across media even at the earliest stages of the development of children's literacies and in the service of that literacy development. As children moved between the narratives presented in multiple media, they learned the literate behaviors necessary to make meaning from these texts. While CTW wanted to create readers of word-based texts and Marvel wanted to create readers of comics texts, their cross-media partnership sponsored multiple kinds of literacy, including but not limited to the literacies that were most important to them as sponsors. In teaming up for literacy, both parties gained advantage while underwriting literacies in both intended and unintended ways. Despite their differing agendas, Marvel and CTW were able to come together in ways that were beneficial to each of them and to the children whose multimodal literacies they sponsored. Often, however, such disparate interests in the sponsorship of multimodal literacy led to conflicts over the kinds of literacy that should be sponsored and the ends to which those literacies should be used, as seen in earlier chapters. Nowhere is the history of these debates more pronounced than in the response of libraries to the question of comic books from the 1930s to the present, which I will explore in Chapter Seven.

Notes

1 Research had also been an integral part of the planning and execution of *Sesame Street*. For an excellent description of how research was used in the production of *Sesame Street*, see Gerald Lesser's *Children and Television: Lessons from Sesame Street*.
2 For more on Marvel's creation of reader identification, see Chapter One.
3 Another reason that the producers of *The Electric Company* decided that Spider-Man should never speak was that he did not have a visible

mouth and there would thus be no mouth movements to correspond with the words the viewers were hearing.

4   While DC did not engage in the same kind of cross-media partnership, in the early 1970s they did experiment with using comics to teach literacy. In his memoir, *The Boy Who Loved Batman*, Michael Uslan, a writer and teacher associated with DC throughout the 1970s, describes a 1972 conversation with Sol Harrison (then Vice President at DC) about a project called Edu-Graphics that used "Batman, Superman, and Wonder Woman in a series of specifically prepared comic books to motivate students to read and then teach them to read with controlled-vocabulary comic book stories that introduced one new word on each page. The pictures reinforced the text" (110).

5   For a more extended discussion of the ways in which Marvel created a feeling of shared community, see my essay "Marveling at *The Man Called Nova*: Comics as Sponsors of Multimodal Literacy."

6   In keeping with Marvel's practice of releasing comics several months before their cover dates, it is possible that the first issue of *Spidey Super Stories* actually appeared on newsstands in the late summer of that year, before his debut on *The Electric Company*. However, given that Spider-Man's first appearance on *The Electric Company* was slated for late October, the first issue may have been delayed so that the cover date actually matched the date of release.

7   By season four, the number of goals per show had been decreased to three.

8   While it is possible that a reader would encounter the version in *Spidey Super Stories* prior to that in *The Electric Company*, I am operating on the assumption that the television version represents the text that would normally have been seen first since CTW clearly saw the comic book as a supplement. In addition, the way the stories are structured seems to indicate that the television version would more usefully serve as a precursor to the comic book in terms of the ways in which it could teach the multiple kinds of literacy necessary to engage the comic book.

9   The comics reader could, of course, flip back to this panel at any point, unlike the television viewer who had only the memory of the cover.

CHAPTER SEVEN

Libraries and the sponsorship of literacy through comics

Throughout *Graphic Encounters*, I have endeavored to show how various people, corporations, and organizations have used comic books to sponsor literacies—both multimodal and alphabetic—in accordance with their aims and goals and in response to the specific contexts in which they operated. This chapter will continue along these lines, examining how libraries have historically viewed comic books and graphic novels, how they historically have seen their role in using comics to sponsor literacy, how the thinking has changed about the kinds of literacy that are operative in the reading of comics, and how these changes have altered the ways in which libraries approach their sponsorship of literacies through comics. In looking at these questions, I am interested in the role of libraries with respect to comics in the sponsorship of multimodal literacy, especially the ways in which libraries have been important in the conception of whether or not comics are appropriate texts for children in their literacy learning and acquisition.

In order to trace this evolution in librarians' thinking with respect to these questions, it will be useful to examine closely key moments and trends in the professional library literature around comic books and graphic novels.[1] By situating this literature within a framework of multimodal literacy sponsorship, we can contextualize it and connect it with the attitudes toward and uses of comics and comic books that we have seen in the preceding chapters, and in doing so, pull together the various strands of the book. As we shall see, the position of libraries and librarians in the history of comic books is very much tied to the ways in which comic books have been used to sponsor literacy by other people and organizations. In their involvement with literacy sponsorship with respect to comics, however, libraries and librarians have undergone a radical shift in attitude, motives, and goals. Since libraries are autonomous institutions that seek to serve the public good (as librarians perceive it in any particular time period), the evolution of libraries' and librarians' stances toward comics over the past 70 plus years provides a fascinating and instructive case study on multimodal literacy sponsorship.

Each of the organizations that sponsored literacy (and the creators who worked for them) took note of the exigencies of their specific situations and adapted the ways in which they sponsored literacy in order to achieve their specific goals—the benefits derived through this relationship of literacy sponsorship—whether profit, dissemination of specific worldviews and values, or a combination of the two. Like these organizations, libraries have positioned themselves as sponsors of literacy with regard to comic books in response to specific situations and as a result of their shifting goals as institutions. In the 1940s and early 1950s, libraries and librarians acted mainly as agents of the *status quo* (as evidenced by the discussions in their professional journals), opposed to comic books in their role of arbiters of taste and sponsors of sanctioned alphabetic literacies.[2] Here it is important, I think, to reiterate that Brandt defines literacy sponsors as "any agents, local or distant, concrete or abstract, who enable, support, teach, model, as well as recruit, **regulate, suppress, or withhold literacy**" (emphasis added; 166). That is, during this period, the main way that libraries and librarians sponsored literacy with respect to comic books was through their efforts to "regulate, suppress, or withhold" access to these multimodal texts in direct opposition to the efforts of publishers such as DC, Timely, EC, Fawcett, Dell, and even the Parents' Institute and Elliott Publishing. With the advent of the Comics Code and the rise of television as the entertainment medium of choice for most children, through the later 1950s and 1960s there was almost no discussion of comic books in librarians' professional literature, as if the threat had been contained and the situation no longer had any exigence to spur them to action. For almost the first 40 years of the history of comic books, virtually the only active engagement that libraries and librarians had with comic books was in opposition to them.

Beginning in the 1970s, however, some librarians began to see comics as a way to attract children to the library and get them interested in reading. The main thrust of this argument was that the presence of comic books (and later graphic novels) would make the library seem cool and interesting, especially among the so-called reluctant readers, mainly adolescent boys, who seemed to show little interest in reading or in libraries. Comic books were seen as the kind of enticement that could compete with television and movies (and later video games), giving the library the kind of advantage it needed to entice this specifically targeted demographic through the door, getting them first to read those comics, and then building on that scaffold to turn them into lifelong readers. Of course, this way of viewing the use of comics in the library acknowledges only the importance of alphabetic literacy and libraries' roles in the sponsorship of that literacy; the benefit that libraries derive in this relationship is in patronage both now and in the future (as comics readers become book readers), which results in continued funding because they are seen to be fulfilling their mission of promoting (or sponsoring) alphabetic literacy. As can be seen in the professional literature in the last decade, though, librarians have recently begun to reconsider this narrow view of literacy and embrace the kinds of multimodal literacy offered by comics. In doing so, libraries and librarians have done much to lead the way in reconceptualizing the reading of comics as multimodal and important in its own right.

"Thrown like garbage on the beach of our time": Librarians respond to comic books in the 1940s and early 1950s

Although comic books were greeted with almost universal disapproval by librarians during and after 1941, before that almost nothing was said in the professional literature. It is this silence that makes the mention of comics in the 1934 *Library Quarterly* article,

"The Use of the School Library by Teachers and Pupils in Junior and Senior High Schools," so interesting. In language that prefigures many of the arguments posed by public and school librarians in the 1970s, A. Elwood Adams wrote that the library "is an agency of fundamental importance in the organization and administration of public education" and "a dynamic means of instruction," but "its facilities are not adequately used" (414). Here Adams referred not only to school education, but to the education of "the public" writ large, and to the betterment of society as a whole. In thinking through this problem, Adams keyed on the necessity of establishing a free reading program and noted that "newspaper and magazine reading were the most popular forms of recreational reading" and that "sports and comics were the most popular" (417). Not only does this article demonstrate that the issue of how to get patrons into the library (so that the library can fulfill their mission of literacy sponsorship) is not a new one, but it begins to acknowledge the role that comics play in the reading lives of both children and adults and does so without judgment.

Later, in October of 1941, Mary R. Lucas, one of the few librarians to dissent from the scathing critiques of comics and comic books after the appearance of North's "A National Disgrace," extended this idea in a *Library Journal* article entitled "Our Friendly Enemy?: The Library Looks at Comics." In it she argued, "In these days of shrinking juvenile circulation, no children's librarian can afford to ape the ostrich and bury her head in the sand at the first note of the word 'comics.' It behooves us to investigate, to look at all sides of the problem, to experiment, and then to decide fairly how best to meet their tremendous influence" (827). She not only saw possibilities for using comics with reluctant readers—an idea that would not be raised again for thirty years—but she also argued that there was value in striking a partnership between libraries and DC to promote "Good Books Suggested by Superman" (824–5). For DC such a partnership aided in sanitizing their corporate image and reassuring parents and teachers that they could be seen as trusted sponsors of literacy, while for libraries the partnership helped promote their collections of traditional children's literature; like the later cross-media partnership between Marvel and CTW, there was mutual benefit for the way that each party wanted to sponsor literacy. In other words, Lucas saw value in using the multimodal form of comics as a way for the library to draw in patrons and sponsor alphabetic literacy, an idea foreshadowed by Adams in 1934 but left to lie fallow for the next 30 years.

Articles such as these were, however, the exception before the 1970s. More typical were articles such as "On Behalf of Dragons" (1941), "Libraries, to Arms!" (1941), "Youth's Librarians Can Defeat Comics" (1948), and "The Role of the Librarian in the Development of Taste" (1950), all of which decried comic books for a variety of reasons that echo the now familiar concerns raised by critics such as North and Wertham—the content was objectionable; reading comics retarded the ability to read and caused damage to the sight; reading comics caused behavioral problems of all sorts; comic books were poor substitutes for real literature; comics detracted from the imagination and the ability to make aesthetic judgments.[3] Even pieces in which librarians tried to engage with comic books were usually almost wholly negative, as suggested by Lucas, and as evidenced by the 1942 *Library Journal* article "A Public Library Experiments with the Comics" by Ethel C. Wright. In it, she described a six-week experiment in providing non-circulating access to comic books in the reading room of the Toledo Public Library. Their purpose "was to observe how children reacted to Comics when exposed to them in an environment of attractive children's books which equaled in story interest, on the child's own plane of experience, the adult experiences found in the Comics" (833). Although Wright acknowledged that the children were drawn to the comic books and read them avidly, she could not understand why "when one considered the very poor print and confusing sequences" and "wondered what continuity of thought or meaning they could get from the pictures alone" (833). The kind of literacy needed to read these comic books and the pleasures the children derived from them were so far outside Wright's frame of reference as a librarian who promoted alphabetic literacy through the use of children's literature that all she could do was dismiss them. Control over what children should read and why needed, in her estimation, to be left to responsible adults such as librarians and teachers, a familiar theme throughout the period.

As early as March of 1941 (before the publication of "A National Disgrace"), Eva J. Antonnen was sounding the alarm about comic books in "On Behalf of Dragons," issuing "an S.O.S. cry to librarians, as well as to all lovers of literature" (567). She associated comic books not only with the "countless children who seldom come to the library," but also with the children who do patronize the library (567). Of this latter group of children she wrote, "In some strange manner, they know that what they are reading would not be approved by either the school teacher or the librarian" (567). In her eyes, then, the library "becomes antithetical to the desires of the children, the library becomes a vague symbol of the conscience" (567). She further admitted that "the library can offer nothing as stimulating as comics" and that "too many children are bored in the library" (567). Unlike Lucas, however, Antonnen was unequivocal in her opposition to comic books, arguing, "Yet, I see no justification for our surrender to the comic-world. I do see a need for united opinion and action" (567). Rather than seeing comic books as a means to support the mission of the library in terms of literacy sponsorship, Antonnen saw comic books as threatening to that mission, seducing children by conforming to their desires instead of supplying them with what they really needed, as she saw the library doing.

In other words, Antonnen saw no value in the multimodal literacy used in reading comics (and would likely not even have recognized it as literacy) and viewed any sponsorship of literacy that placed comic books rather than approved children's literature in the hands of children as dangerous and misguided. In her suggestion that good books be substituted for the bad comic books that children were reading, Antonnen, like North, advocated a kind of literacy sponsorship that suppressed comic books, regulated children's reading habits, and supplied reading material that supported official forms of literacy like those seen in schools. Antonnen's argument here accords with the summary of the library literature of the period supplied by Nyberg in "How Librarians Learned to Love the Graphic Novel" in which she argued, "comic books represented a challenge to the dominance of adults because they were selected and purchased by children often without any direction from adults" (28). While I agree with Nyberg in general terms, placing such dominance within the context of literacy sponsorship will help to further explain the dynamics of librarians' responses to comic books.

As we have seen in earlier chapters, the sponsorship of literacy (especially when it comes to children) is often about control—what kinds of literacy get sponsored and by whom—and comic books threatened that control because they were inexpensive enough to allow children to make their own decisions with regard to reading. The sense was that adults in official positions, such as teachers and librarians, knew best what children should be reading and, as Allen Ellis and Doug Highsmith wryly note of the period in "About Face: Comic Books in Library Literature," "[t]he consideration that children were human beings with minds of their own was apparently a novel precept" (28). As a sponsor of alphabetic literacy that was squarely within the *status quo*, Antonnen saw comic books as a threat to the control libraries and librarians exerted over children's reading, control that operated in tandem with the official literacy of school. Clearly, she was not alone in her views.

Not only were most librarians opposed to the various genres of comic books issued by the mainstream publishers, but many were also very skeptical of the educational comic books that had been introduced by the Parents' Institute and Elliott Publishing. Such an attitude can be seen in "Libraries, to Arms!" an opinion piece in the "Roving Eye" section of the April, 1941 edition of *Wilson Library Bulletin*. After extensively quoting North's argument, the anonymous author described *True Comics* and the efforts of the Parents' Institute to "attempt to provide an antidote for those objectionable publications" (670). The author went on to describe the project and acknowledged that many educators supported their work. This author, however, was not one of them, later calling comics "garbage on the beach of our time" (671). Her argument is worth quoting in full since it provides a useful summation of many of the attitudes that existed within the library community during the period with regard to comic books and literacy. She wrote,

> For myself, I must confess, despite my sympathetic interest in the experiment, that I am a little skeptical of the ultimate educational value of fighting comics with comics. Although the subject matter of *True Comics* is a vast improvement, the basic crudeness of the medium remains, and what we have is still an aesthetic monstrosity, a monument to bad taste in color and design, a disconcerting surrender to sensationalism. Our problem, as teachers and librarians, is to train children *how to read* and to make them *want to read*, so that they can fall heir to the wealth of the spirit, the line of beauty, the satisfactions of proportion, all the fine values of the imaginative tradition that is

the ennobling work of man and the sign of his civilization. I fail to see how the comics—do with them what you will—can help us achieve this end. Fundamentally there is no relation between the technique of "reading" the comics and reading a book; I am convinced, even, that a child conditioned by the jerky, jiggling, inflamed world of the comics is a damaged child, incapacitated for enjoyment of the more serene pleasures of the imagination. The chances are that a child who likes *True Comics* will be even more delighted with the "false" comics. I doubt that the reverse is true. The reaction of children of my own acquaintance to *True Comics* is that it is a pale imitation of "the real thing." (670)

Even though the content was not deemed objectionable (and presumably not a detrimental influence on behavior), comic books were still seen as entirely problematic. Despite the protestations of Harold C. Field, Editor of *True Comics*, who in a talk to the Institute for New Jersey Librarians in July, 1944 (and later published in *New Jersey Library Bulletin*) called on librarians to "learn to make use of the good comics," opinion was decidedly not on the side of comics. In fact, such was the bias against comics both here and in most of the professional literature of the period that the entire project of trying to substitute good comics for bad comics, as undertaken by the Parents' Institute, Elliott Publishing, and the Catechetical Guild, was seen as counterproductive to what libraries and librarians were attempting to do in their sponsorship of children's literacy.

The argument in "Libraries, to Arms!" contains the familiar complaints about the quality of production, but the focus is sharpened to comics as an "aesthetic monstrosity" that impedes the development of good taste—that is, taste that is in line with the accepted cultural norms of the time (670). In an opinion repeated throughout the period, both in the library literature and by critics such as North, learning to read involved not only the ability to decode written language, but the inculcation of "all the fine values of the imaginative tradition that is the ennobling work of man and the sign of his civilization" ("Libraries, to Arms!" 670). The author is not only clear that this should be the aim for libraries and librarians in their sponsorship of literacy, but that comics could play no part in achieving this goal. In teaching children how to read, the library should be teaching them not only to want to read, but also *what* to read. The fact that "reading" comics is put in scare quotes makes it clear that this author did not see any value in comics in terms of any of these aspects of literacy. In its call to arms, the article emphasized the familiar issue of control—what gets read by children and for what purposes, and who is allowed to make such decisions. Comic books were seen as threatening because they not only represented a different kind of literacy than the sanctioned print literacy, but their existence shifted the balance of control so that who sponsored children's literacy and for what ends was called into question.

Despite the occasional attempt by librarians to quell the panic, such as the effort by Gweneira M. Williams and Jane S. Wilson in their 1942 *Library Journal* article, "They Like it Rough: In Defense of Comics," negative attitudes toward comics and comic books persisted through the rest of the 1940s and into the 1950s, abating only with the advent of the Comics Code.[4] While articles like Antonnen's and "Libraries, to Arms!" were designed to raise awareness of the threat these authors saw in comic books, two notable articles that followed spelled out more forcefully what librarians should do in response and, in effect, how they should be sponsoring literacy. In the provocatively titled 1946 article "Youth's Librarians Can Defeat Comics," Jean Gray Harker acknowledged that comic books are part of the context of reading for children and then rehearsed all of the familiar arguments against comics, keying especially on the perceived link between comic books and juvenile delinquency. However, she did not just raise the alarm, but instead clearly stated the role that she saw for libraries in the face of the threat posed by comics and comic books. She wrote, "The library is the one public agency fully equipped to present children with something better to take the place of the comics. Without the aggressive leadership of children's librarians, the comic book fight has been lost before it has even begun" (1705). Rather than attempting to regulate or suppress the reading of comic books, Harker's vision involved substituting children's literature for comic books (as North had suggested) in a way that would make these books more appealing to children. She was unequivocal in the important place she saw for libraries in promoting reading habits and selecting "good" literature that accorded with officialized/elite norms of taste and value, suggesting that libraries fulfilled perhaps the most important role in the literacy sponsorship of the country's youth. Children's librarians were thus, in her estimation, on the front lines of the battle for control over the sponsorship of children's literacy and their training needed to reflect the importance of this role.

In a similar vein, John Emmett Burke stated his view of the place of libraries in the sponsorship of literacy in the title to his 1950 article "The Role of the Libraries in the Development of Taste." Throughout the piece, Burke emphasized how taste is nurtured through education—or what I have called literacy sponsorship—as it "should bring out, develop in everyone, an appreciative attitude to the world about us, to those things in the world about us which are things of beauty" (279). In order to further this concept of education, librarians should, in his view, see the collection of books as "a dynamic organization whose high function is to render a service of enlightenment. Such a service is rendered by getting more people to read more books and better books" (280). The influence of the librarian in aiding the cultivation of taste and "good manners" "depends only on his salesmanship," especially in connection with young people who must be steered away from reading light fiction or comic books. Burke's program involved the inculcation of a cultural literacy of Great Books that he believed every cultured person should read (he even included several lists of possible texts). Unlike Gaines and his staff at EC who were using comics and comic books to actively push against the *status quo* during this period, Burke's program was specifically intended to support a specific cultural *status quo*.

In working toward this goal, Burke explicitly labeled reading as "a Librarian's Problem," comparing the role of the librarian with respect to books to that of the doctor and dietician with respect to food. Building on this analogy, Burke argued, "This is where some knowledge by the librarian of what the reading process is, how it takes place, why it is so often halting, and how to make it better, may become a vital part of his job and provide the stimulus for better reading and the appreciation of the beautiful" (282). For him, as for virtually all librarians and educators during this period, the reading process involved words and the facilitation of making sense of those words. But more than that, for Burke, the reason for librarians to be involved in that process was inextricably connected to the development of a particular vision of taste. Here, as in much of the professional literature of the period, the benefit derived by libraries and librarians in the relationship of literacy sponsorship was connected to their role as stewards of the dominant culture, acting as public agencies in the maintenance of the *status quo*. Moreover, libraries needed to be visible in this role; as Ellis and Highsmith argue, "By entering the anti-comics fray, librarians were able to publicly reaffirm their position as agents of High Culture, and in justifying their existence, remind the public of just what the library was for" (30). Given this reality, the almost universal negative stance toward comic books is not surprising, working as it did in opposition to comic book publishers who represented commercialized popular culture. Over the coming decades that stance would evolve as both the contexts of literacy sponsorship for children and the role of the library underwent their own changes.

Calling all reluctant readers

After a lengthy silence on the subject of comics, librarians slowly started to consider the possible benefits of including comic books in their collections. A few voices from both school libraries and public libraries began to argue for the power of comics as a tool for drawing young people into the library, getting them first to read those comics, and then building on that scaffold to turn them into lifelong readers of alphabetic literature. One of the first of these articles appeared in the "Magazines" column of *Library Journal* in early January, 1968, a gap of more than ten years since the last serious consideration of the relationship between libraries and comics. In introducing this guest column by Ann Prentice, a professor at the School of Library Science and SUNY Albany, editor Bill Katz (also a professor at SUNY Albany) was equivocal, to say the least, in his description of the topic. He wrote,

> The so-called culturally disadvantaged are of recent concern to librarians but, like any new discovery, they present some horrible problems. The major hurdle is one of identification, getting down (in many cases, "up") to their interest levels.
>
> Comic magazines present one channel. In this column, Professor Ann E. Prentice discusses the contribution of comics to the library scene. She is primarily concerned with children, but the

argument has some cogency for anyone working with those who have yet to discover the joys of print.

The editor of this column would be most interested in reactions, both from those who violently disagree, and from those who go along with Mrs. Prentice's theory. (59)

While Prentice's column itself consisted of a tentative claim that comic books might be useful as an alternative for teenagers reading below grade level and an annotated list of possible titles for the periodical shelves, Katz's introduction seems designed to buffer the expected stream of criticism "from those who violently disagree." Notice, too, that Katz expected no enthusiastic agreement, but only that some readers might "go along with" her suggestions. While he acknowledged the possible efficacy of comic magazines in terms of her argument, his attitude toward both comics and the patrons who might read them was certainly still influenced by the sentiments seen in the last section of this chapter. Not only was Katz dubious about the whole idea of cultural disadvantage, but it is clear that the very existence of a new demographic using the library was very troubling to him because of the "horrific problems" they introduced for libraries and librarians. By printing Prentice's column and offering equivocal support for her ideas, Katz provided the first venue for the coming reconsideration of the place of comic books in the library. However, in his language and the embedded expectation of violent disagreement, we can also see the vestiges of earlier notions of what libraries should be and what roles they should play in the sponsorship of literacy. The internal debate that seems to be taking place here would presage the debate around libraries and their use of comics in the sponsorship of literacy for the coming years.

From this point on, articles supporting the use of comic books in school libraries began to appear every few years in the pages of *School Library Journal*. Meanwhile, between 1975 and 1977, *The U*N*A*S*H*E*D* Librarian* published several articles espousing the value of comics, with titles such as "How I Use Comic Books Good at My Branch," "Chronology of a Comic Book Collection," and "And My Branch: An Experimental Comic Book Collection." Given its much larger readership and influence in the field, however, it is the role of *School Library Journal* in this debate that most interests me, beginning with a 1974 article by Will Eisner entitled "Comic Books in the Library." In it, the comics pioneer gave a short history of comics and the stigma that has surrounded them before moving on to their potential use as teaching tools, a topic with which he was well acquainted through his work in instructional comics such as *P.S. Magazine*, a series of how-to comics about preventative maintenance (for the Department of Defense), and *Job Scene*, a series of comics aimed at disadvantaged job seekers (for the Department of Labor). Citing the earliest educational comic books, Eisner wrote, "By combining words and visual impact, the printed sequential story accomplished what it could do best: teach by conveying ideas quickly" ("Comic Books" 76). In other words, for Eisner, as for the Parents' Institute, the Catechetical Guild, and other educational and religious publishers, one of the benefits derived from sponsorship lay in the way that the comics medium could be used to convey information succinctly and in an understandable form. From there, Eisner went on to argue that comic books were useful in reaching reluctant readers because they were timely and appealed to readers' interests. As well, a sidebar to the article, written by Jan Ballard and Christine Kirby provided a wholly pragmatic view of the situation: "Why comic books? Because the kids are *reading* them. Do we need any other justification?" (77). Here we can see the enormity of the change from librarians as stewards of taste and culture to librarians as responsive to patrons' own wishes/tastes. The article thus acts as both a counter to the earlier arguments by librarians that had opposed even the educational comics of the 1940s and an impetus to the coming arguments about why libraries should embrace comics, as evidenced by how often it was cited by those who made this argument. The door to comics that had been cracked by Katz and Prentice was opened even further by Eisner.

Three years later, *School Library Journal* published Laurel F. Goodgion's "Holy Bookshelves!: Comics in the Children's Room" in which she described her efforts to integrate comic books into the children's collection at the New Britain (CT) Public Library. In the introduction to the article, she wrote, "Inspired by reports of libraries circulating comic books with success, the library's children's department started a comic book collection with the goal of attracting new borrowers to the library by providing this innovative service" (37). This goal was a far cry from Burke's idea that libraries should "provide the stimulus for better reading and the appreciation of the beautiful" (282). Rather than attempting to mold the tastes of the young readers, the goal here was to get more potential readers—especially reluctant readers, as she later explains—into the library so that they would simply begin to read, moving eventually from comic books to strictly alphabetic texts. She argued that "Comics are a great way to begin to convince children that the library *does* have something to offer them" and that after children were enticed into the library, librarians could "encourage the transition from comics to more traditional reading materials" (38). Just as Al Hartley had piggybacked a Christian message on to Archie and the Children's Television Workshop had used Spider-Man to promote reading, librarians began to recognize that the popularity of the comic book medium could be harnessed for their own specific purposes, including getting more children into the library and boosting circulation.

Similarly, in the 1981 article "Spider-Man at the Library," Larry Dorrell and Ed Carroll stressed that comic books should be used in "improving the school library's image" and that their inclusion would result in "unexpected and welcome changes in student attitudes towards the library" (18–19). Of course, not everyone agreed, as evidenced by an anonymous editorial in *School Library Journal* that same issue in which the author wrote, "The real questions are: how much library users must adapt to a user's intent and how much a library's purpose can or should be modified to attract users" ("Answers Urged" 7). At the heart of this resistance is once again the issue of control and the fear that children will have increased say over not only what they will read and why they will read it, but in this case, how the library will figure into those reading practices. Embedded in that response, however, is also the question of what role libraries will play in terms of the larger culture. That is, should a library determine a community's taste or reflect it? This author was clearly wary of the movement toward libraries catering to the tastes of patrons. This opinion, however, was no longer a vocal majority and more voices seemed to be on the side that saw value in comic books in the library. As Dorrell succinctly put it in his 1987 piece "Why Comic Books?" "Children like to read comic books. If school libraries can provide something that children like to read, more reading will occur. As more reading occurs, reading skills will improve" (31). This approach to sponsoring literacy involved the kind of scaffolding described in Chapter 1 in which multimodal literacy is seen to have value, but only as a step toward alphabetic literacy. Still, this marked a significant change from the idea of the library as a gatekeeper to literacy and taste whose function was as much to regulate as it was to provide access to literacy.

What were the effects of such a scaffolding approach and its conception of comics and their relation to developing literate practices in the library? On the one hand, the use of comic books in libraries was seen as one strategy in teaching and encouraging literacy and literate practices; on the other hand, comic books were still regarded as a way station on the road to "higher" forms of literacy and to more challenging and, by implication, worthwhile texts. Such an approach was in keeping with the assumption that in the development of children's and adolescents' literacies, reading comics was a debased form of word-based literacy—albeit an important intermediate step to more advanced forms of textual literacy—rather than as a complex form of multimodal literacy. However, by acknowledging comic books as an important part of the literacy landscapes of children and teenagers, librarians' inclusion of comic books in the library did work toward the legitimation of the medium, within both the library and education communities. As well, despite the intention to use comic books only to attract attention and provide a scaffold for alphabetic literacy, librarians, like CTW in their partnership with Marvel, *were* sponsoring multimodal literacy for their patrons by providing access to material and encouraging the reading of that material. Only later would librarians (and educators) begin to see that they were, in fact, sponsoring literacies beyond the strictly alphabetic, and that doing so was valuable to both them and their patrons.

From comic books to graphic novels

While these forays into bringing comic books into the library in the 1970s laid the groundwork for the current popularity of the comics medium with librarians, perhaps the most important factor in this change in attitude was the change in format from the center-stapled pamphlet to the larger, bound graphic novel. From a material point of view, the graphic novel format was simply easier for libraries to handle since they could be shelved like other books instead of with the magazines. As well, the graphic novel would prove more durable as a circulating item than a comic book and could be rebound rather than simply discarded. More importantly, though, because the graphic novel looked like a physical book and often included subject matter that was not aimed strictly at children, librarians were able to conceptualize it *as a book* and thus worthy of a place in their collections.

The movement toward this reconceptualization was well articulated in Keith R. A. DeCandido's 1990 *Library Journal* article "Picture This: Graphic Novels in Libraries." In it DeCandido asserted that though not many libraries collected graphic novels (defined as "a self-contained story that uses a combination of text and art to articulate the plot"), it was an area that should be developed (50). Readership of the graphic novel, according to DeCandido, consisted of "a higher age group, mid-20s, due to their generally greater sophistication," and the themes covered in them ran the gamut of those seen in other literature (50, 52). In words that both echoed Eisner and presaged the way the comics medium would come to be seen, DeCandido wrote, "It is not simply art conveying a story, nor just words, but the combination that sets the medium apart" (52). Finally, DeCandido addressed some of the practical concerns about starting a graphic novels collection, how to buy books for it, and what to acquire.[5] In pushing librarians to reassess the medium, its readership, and the material form in which it was packaged, DeCandido began to reconcile the conflict between good taste and increased gate counts and circulation statistics. That is, if graphic novels were seen to be good literature, libraries buying them was not simply a capitulation to users' tastes, but a way to build a collection of appropriate literature. In this way, DeCandido began to lay the groundwork for how libraries could rethink the place of comics in the library. The articles that followed over the next 20 years would flesh out these ideas.

In her 1997 *School Library Journal* article entitled "'Zap! Whoosh! Kerplow!': Build High-Quality Graphic Novel Collections with Impact," Lora Bruggeman offered a step-by-step primer in how to build an effective graphic novel collection. The inclusion of such practical advice continued the thinking of DeCandido's article and marked the beginning of an ongoing trend in the literature, as seen most forcefully in a pair of pieces from 2002: Stephen Weiner's *Library Journal* article, "Beyond Superheroes: Comics Get Serious," and Michele Gorman's *School Library Journal* article, "What Teens Want: Thirty Graphic Novels You Can't Live Without."[6] The emphasis in Bruggeman's piece remained on reaching reluctant readers and the development of lifelong readers. However, Bruggeman approached these issues with reference to Scott McCloud's idea of visual literacy since in her view, "graphic novels take advantage of this emerging literacy" (23). Similarly, in his 2002 article Weiner argued that "reading comics is an acquired skill" (56). That same year Evan St Lifer ended his *School Library Journal* editorial ("Graphic Novels, Seriously") by quoting Francisca Goldsmith of the Berkeley Public Library: "Graphic novel readers have learned to understand not only print, but can also decode facial and body expressions, the symbolic meanings of certain images and postures, metaphors, and similes, and other social and literary nuances teenagers are mastering as they move from childhood to maturity" (9). Goldsmith's ideas about the literacy needed to read graphic novels were once more referenced at the end of 2002 in Maureen Mooney's *The Book Report* article, "Graphic Novels: How They Can Work in Libraries." Here Goldsmith was quoted as saying that graphic novels "require active, critical participation by the reader, who must not only be able to decode text, but also follow its flow and grasp essentials of narrative, mood, character, or plot through images" (18). Taken together, it is clear that the literacy being described and embraced by librarians in their descriptions of graphic novels was growing ever closer to the kind of multimodal literacy for which I have been arguing throughout this book. Certainly 2002 marked a watershed year in not only the thinking about the relationship between libraries and graphic novels, but in librarians' overall conception of the literacy that was needed to read those graphic novels and, thus, the type literacy that libraries sponsored in collecting them.

Around this time, ALA was developing a statement that was adopted in 2004 under the title "Core Values of Librarianship." Among these values were ideas such as access, confidentiality, democracy, diversity, education and lifelong learning, intellectual freedom, preservation, the public good, and social responsibility. At the same time, by 2004, the idea that graphic novels could be used as a way for libraries to foster lifelong reading that included not just alphabetic texts, but graphic novels themselves, had become a standard claim. The days of the library as protector of high culture and guardian of taste had, for the most part, ended, and the thrust behind their sponsorship of literacy for children and teenagers (especially reluctant readers) was tied to this idea of creating lifelong readers, whether of alphabetic or multimodal texts. Not only did sponsoring literacy in this way fulfill the library's mandate that was underscored by such values as lifelong learning, diversity (of available texts), and access, but such a strategy also made sense in that creating lifelong readers carried the benefit of creating ongoing library patrons whose usage justified the existence of the library. These ideas can be seen in both Philip Crawford's "A Novel Approach: Using Graphic Novels to Attract Reluctant Readers" and Will Heckman's "Reading Heroes for a New Generation," both of which were published in the spring of 2004. Crawford wrote, "When programs like SSR [Sustained Silent Reading] are combined with a strong school library media program, students obtain the requisite materials, encouragement, and environment to help them develop lifelong reading habits" (26). For Crawford, the key for the library lay in providing diverse reading materials, including a strong graphic novel collection that would act as a scaffold to lifelong reading of both graphic novels and alphabetic texts. Echoing Crawford, Heckman wrote, "School districts and states have mandated how schools teach students to read, but these programs have been found to be extremely lacking when it comes to creating lifelong readers" (3). The relationship between libraries and schools envisioned here by Heckman is consistent with that of Crawford and others of the period: schools sponsor literacy through overt instruction, while libraries sponsor literacy by providing diverse materials that will sustain lifelong reading in a diverse population. As Mary Jane Heaney summarized it in 2007, "The ultimate challenge is developing a population of literate people and finding innovative ways to encourage lifelong reading for all individuals" (72). In this model, literacy sponsorship by the library complements, but does not replicate, that of the school's officialized literacy instruction, leaving room for texts such as graphic novels and literacies other than the alphabetic. Rather than reinforcing standards of taste, libraries were now on the forefront in the expansion of thinking about literacy, the public good, what it meant to be a lifelong reader, and the possibilities of literacy sponsorship within their overarching core values.

As in the articles from 2002 discussed above, Heckman argued that reading graphic novels required a different kind of literacy than that needed in reading strictly alphabetic texts. He wrote, "the reading of Graphic Novels requires the readers to make a connection between graphics and text. This seems to cause an even more complex reading experience and in some cases force the reader to use a higher cognitive skill level" (4). Peg Dombeck, in her 2005 *MEDIUM* article "Graphic Novels—School Library, Public Library," went even further, writing, "Reading Graphic Novels/Comics involves more brain cells than reading regular books, as the reader must integrate the text and the pictures into an understandable whole. Thus, Graphic Novels/Comics are especially appropriate for a population whose frontal lobes are not yet fully developed" (39). In her introduction to *Getting Graphic!: Comics for Kids*, Gorman listed ten reasons for libraries to collect and promote comics for kids. Included in her list was not only the familiar idea that comics could be used as a bridge to alphabetic literacy, but also ideas about visual learning, active participation in reading through interaction with the gutters, the development of strong language art skills, and the development of lifelong readers. Such stances toward reading comics, and thus the potential of integrating comics into both libraries and teaching, could not be farther from those exhibited by librarians in the 1940s and 1950s.

Although the beginnings of such a change in attitude can be traced back to the late 1960s, it was not until the 1990s and the advent of the graphic novel that there was any real traction for the integration of comics into public and school libraries. By 2002, the calls for libraries to include graphic novels in their collections had begun to reach a critical mass. By the time Gorman's *Getting Graphic!: Comics for Kids* was published in 2007, she was able to comment on the changes that had taken place in the perceptions of both the public and librarians with regard to comic books and graphic novels. For her, "the most important change has been at the hands of librarians, who have willingly accepted and embraced books created in a comic format" (ix). By 2012, there was continuous programming at the Graphic Novel Stage at the Exhibition Hall of the American Library Association Conference in Anaheim, featuring presentations such as "Graphic Novels: The New Visual Literacy," "Graphic Novels: The Next Digital Frontier," "Manga—A Must Have Genre in the Library," "Getting Graphic with Kids," "The Future of Graphic Novels," and "Making Comics Come Alive: A Workshop for Your School or Library." As well, at the 2012 ALA conference there was a substantial presence of graphic novel publishers; of the major, mainstream publishers, virtually all of them had at least some graphic novel titles. During the conference, the Will Eisner Graphic Novel Prize for Libraries, an offshoot of the Eisner Awards, one of the major sets of awards in the comics industry, was also announced. According to the promotional brochure, this prize "both highlights Eisner's contributions to the comics industry and recognizes the important role that librarians have played in the phenomenal growth of the graphic novel category" (1). No longer were libraries opposed to the ways that publishers sponsored children's literacy, but were now actively entwined with them in the multimodal sponsorship of literacy through the medium of comics and the material object of the graphic novel.

Coda

Since their inception in the early 1930s, comics have been one of the central kinds of texts in the literate lives of both children and adults. As seen in the examples throughout *Graphic Encounters*, comics have been used by for-profit companies, creators, critics, not-for-profit educational groups, churches, schools, parents' groups, and libraries to sponsor particular kinds of multimodal and alphabetic literacies. Through these examples, I have endeavored to show how the complex relationships of multimodal literacy sponsorship throughout that history offers insights into the varied motivations of sponsors, the ways they responded to the exigencies of their particular contexts, and the benefits, both intended and unintended, derived by those they sponsored. By focusing specifically on comics and the sponsorship of multimodal literacy, I have tried to examine the complexities of these concepts in a way that might also offer possibilities for analysis of how literacy sponsorship operates in other kinds of multimodal texts. The examples on which I have focused are not intended to come together in a neat conclusion, but instead are offered as points of entry that will help us begin to think about comics, multimodality, and literacy sponsorship, the ways these terms have interacted historically, and the ways they might interact today.

Notes

1   In addition to my own search in the Library, Information Science and Technology Archives database, I am indebted to two earlier surveys of the literature, "About Face: Comic Books in the Library Literature" by Allen Ellis and Doug Highsmith and "How Librarians Learned to Love the Graphic Novel" by Amy Kiste Nyberg, both of which also trace the change in attitudes among librarians. While the focus here will be on an examination of the literature itself, I will also at times refer to and examine the conclusions of these two studies.

2   These discussions can be seen in articles published in journals such as *Library Journal* and *Wilson Library Bulletin.*

3   Fredric Wertham himself is represented in the library literature of the period as his September, 1954 talk to the Free Library Festival in Philadelphia was reprinted in the April, 1955 issue of *Wilson Library Bulletin* under the title "Reading for the Innocent."

4   The one notable exception is Grace W. Gilman's "Bread or Stones?" from 1956, in which she made the familiar argument that engagement with any comics actually impeded reading.

5   DeCandido's "must" titles included *Maus, Cerebus: High Society, Cerebus: Church and State* (2 volumes), *Watchmen, Moonshadow, American Splendor, Love and Rockets, The Journey Saga* Volume 1, and *Batman: The Dark Knight Returns.*

6   Weiner and Gorman would publish three important books of practical advice for librarians in setting up graphic novels collections: Weiner's *The 101 Best Graphic Novels*, edited by Keith R. A. DeCandido in 2001, and Gorman's *Getting Graphic!: Using Graphic Novels to Promote Literacy with Preteens and Teens* in 2003 and *Getting Graphic!: Comics for Kids* in 2007.

WORKS CITED

Adams, A. Elwood. "The Use of the School Library by Teachers and Pupils in Junior and Senior High Schools." *Library Quarterly* 4.3 (July 1934): 413–19.

American Library Association. *Core Values of Librarianship*. American Library Association Website. Accessed 28 September 2012.

Andrae, Thomas. *Creators of the Superheroes*. New Castle, PA: Hermes Press, 2011.

"Answers Urged." Editorial. *School Library Journal* 27.10 (August 1981): 7.

Antonnen, Eva J. "On Behalf of Dragons." *Wilson Library Bulletin* 15 (March 1941): 567, 595.

Auerbach, Nina. *Our Vampires, Ourselves*. Chicago, IL: University of Chicago Press, 1995.

Ballard, Jan and Christine Kirby. "Batman? Spiderman? Archie? In the Library????" *School Library Journal* 21.2 (October 1974): 77.

Beaty, Bart. *Fredric Wertham and the Critique of Mass Culture*. Jackson, MS: University of Mississippi Press, 2005.

Bechdel, Alison. *Fun Home*. New York: Houghton Mifflin, 2006.

Benton, Mike. *The Comic Book in America: An Illustrated History*. Dallas, TX: Taylor Publishing, 1989.

Bernowitz, Fred von and Grant Geissman. *Tales of Terror!: The EC Companion*. Timonium, MD and Seattle, WA: Fantagraphic Books and Gemstone Publishing, 2000.

Biro, Charles and Bob Wood, eds. *Crime Does Not Pay* #22 (July 1942), Comic House (Lev Gleason).

Bitz, Michael. *When Commas Meet Kryptonite: Classroom Lessons from the Comic Book Project*. New York: Teachers College Press, 2010.

Bolter, Jay David and Richard Grusin. *Remediation: Understanding New Media*. Cambridge, MA: MIT Press, 1999.

Brandt, Deborah. "Sponsors of Literacy." *College Composition and Communication* 49.2 (May 1998): 165–85.

Brother, Andrew with John Sherill and Elizabeth Sherill. *God's Smuggler*. New York: Signet Books, 1968.

Bruggeman, Lora. "'Zap! Whoosh! Kerpow!': Build High-Quality Graphic Novel Collections with Impact." *School Library Journal* 43.1 (January 1997): 22–7.

Burke, John Emmett. "The Role of the Librarian in the Development of Taste." *Peabody Journal of Education* 27.5 (March 1950): 277–83.

Butler, Nate. "Christian Comics Pioneers: Al Hartley." *Christian Comics International*. Comix 35, n.d. Accessed 10 August 2012.

Carlson, Johanna Draper. "Archie's Christian Comics." *Hogan's Alley* 16 (March 2009). Rpt. in *Comics Worth Reading*. Comics Worth Reading, 14 May 2010. Accessed 10 August 2012.

Carlson, Mark. "Hey! That Ain't Funny (Part 2): Religious Comic Books in the Forties." *The Nostalgia Zine* 2.2 (2006): n.p. Accessed 10 August 2012.

The Carnegie Commission on Educational Television. *Public Television: A Program for Action*. New York: Bantam Books, 1967.

Carter, James Bucky, ed. *Building Literacy Connections with Graphic Novels: Pages by Page, Panel by Panel*. Urbana, IL: National Council of Teachers of English, 2007.

Cary, Stephen. *Going Graphic: Comics at Work in the Multilingual Classroom*. Portsmouth, NH: Heinemann, 2004.

Children's Television Workshop. *The Electric Company: An Introduction to the New Television Program Designed to Help Teach Reading to Children*. New York: Children's Television Workshop, 1971.

— "*The Electric Company* Final Report." New York: Children's Television Workshop, 1978.

Classic Comics #1 (October 1941), Elliott Publishing Company.

"Comic Book Sales by Month." *The Comics Chronicles: A Resource for Comics Research*, n.d. Accessed 7 August, 2012.

"Comics and Comic Books are No Longer Comical." *The New World* (20 November 1942): 548–56.

Coogan, Peter. *Superhero: The Secret Origin of a Genre*. Austin, TX: Monkeybrain Books, 2006.

Cooney, Joan Ganz. "It Was Early 1970." *The Best of The Electric Company* Box Set Liner Notes. Los Angeles: Shout! Factory, 2006. 4–5.

"Television and the Teaching of Reading." Children's Television Workshop. *The Electric Company: An Introduction to the New Television Program Designed to Help Teach Reading to Children*. New York: Children's Television Workshop, 1971.

Cope, Bill and Mary Kalantzis. "Multiliteracies: The Beginnings of an Idea." *Multiliteracies: Literacy Learning and the Design of Social Futures*. Ed. Bill Cope and Mary Kalantzis. New York: Routledge, 2000: 3–8.

Crawford, Philip. "A Novel Approach: Using Graphic Novels to Attract Reluctant Readers." *Library Media Connection* 22.5 (February 2004): 26–8.

Crist, Judith. "Horror in the Nursery." *Collier's* (29 March 1948): 22–3, 95–7.

Daly, John. "Frontier Fighters." *True Comics* #1 (April 1941), Parents' Magazine Press: n.p.

Daniels, Les. *Comix: A History of Comic Books in America.* New York: Random House, 1988.

David, B. *Epileptic.* New York: Pantheon, 2005.

Davison, Carol Margaret. "Introduction." *Bram Stoker's Dracula: Sucking through the Century, 1897–1997.* Ed. Carol Margaret Davison. Toronto: Dundurn Press, 1997: 19–40.

DeCandido, Keith R. A. "Picture This: Graphic Novels in Libraries." *Library Journal* 115.5 (March 1990): 50–5.

Denny, George V. Jr., Al Capp, George Hecht, John Mason Brown, and Marya Mannes. "What's Wrong with the Comics?" *Town Meeting* 13.45 (March 1948): 3–23.

Dombeck, Peg. "Graphic Novels—School Library, Public Library." *MEDIUM* 29.3 (Spring 2005): 13, 39.

Dorrell, Larry D. "Why Comic Books?" *School Library Journal* 34.3 (November 1987): 30–2.

Dorrell, Larry and Ed Carroll. "Spider-Man at the Library." *School Library Journal* 27.10 (August 1981): 17–19.

Doyle, Thomas F. "What's Wrong with the Comics?" *Catholic World* 156 (February 1943): 549, 551.

Eco, Umberto. "The Myth of Superman." Trans. Natalie Chilton. *Diacritics* 2.1 (Spring 1972): 14–22.

Editorial. *New York Daily Mirror* 6 January 1941: n.p.

Edwards, Janis L. "Echoes of Camelot: How Images Construct Cultural Memory through Rhetorical Framing." *Defining Visual Rhetorics.* Ed. Charles A. Hill and Marguerite Helmers. Mahwah, NJ: Lawrence Earlbaum Associates, 2004: 179–94.

Eisner, Will. *Comics and Sequential Art: Principles and Practices from the Legendary Cartoonist.* New York: W. W. Norton, 2008.

— "Comic Books in the Library." *School Library Journal* 21.2 (October 1974): 75–9.

— *PS Magazine: The Best of Preventative Maintenance Monthly.* New York: Abrams Comic Arts, 2011.

The Electric Company Episode 371. Prod. Children's Television Workshop. PBS. 21 October 1974.

Ellis, Allen and Doug Highsmith. "About Face: Comic Books in Library Literature." *Serials Review* 26.2 (2000): 21–43.

Feldman, Michael. "Men of Tomorrow." *Comix Scholars Discussion List.* University of Florida, 10 September 2012.

Feldstein, Al (w) and George Evans (a/i). "Clot's My Line." *Tales from the Crypt* #43 (August–September 1954), EC: n.p.

Feldstein, Al (w) and Jack Kamen (a/i). "By Dawn's Early Light." *Tales from the Crypt* #42 (June–July 1954), EC: n.p.

Field, Harold C. "Are the Comic Books a Problem?" *New Jersey Library Bulletin* 13 (1945): 75–83.

Frey, Nancy and Douglas Fisher. *Teaching Visual Literacy: Using Comic Books, Graphic Novels, Anime, Cartoons, and More to Develop Comprehension and Thinking Skills.* Thousand Oaks, CA: Corwin Press, 2008.

Funnies on Parade (1933), Eastern Color Printing Company.

Gabilliet, Jean-Paul. *Of Comics and Men: A Cultural History of American Comic Books.* Trans. Bart Beaty and Nick Nguyen. Jackson, MS: University of Mississippi Press, 2009.

Gaines, M. C. *Narrative Illustration: The Story of the Comics.* N.P.: n.p., 1942.

Garrett-Petts, W.F. and Donald Lawrence, eds. *Integrating Visual and Verbal Literacies.* Winnipeg, MB: Inkshed Press, 1996.

Gauger, Lucia. "How I Use Comic Books Good at My Branch." *The U*N*A*S*H*E*D* Librarian* 18 (Winter 1976): 3.

Gee, James Paul. "What is Literacy?" *Journal of Education* 178.1 (March 1989): 18–25.

Genette, Gerard. *Paratexts: Thresholds of Interpretation.* Trans. Jane E. Lewin. Cambridge: Cambridge University Press, 1987.

Gilman, Grace W. "Bread or Stones?" *ALA Bulletin* (January 1956): 17–18.

Gleason, Lev. "Crime Does Not Pay: A Completely New Kind of Magazine." *Crime Does Not Pay* #22 (July 1942), Comic House (Lev Gleason): n.p.

Goldwater, John. *Americana in Four Colors: A Decade of Self Regulation by the Comics Magazine Industry.* New York: Comics Magazine Association of America, 1964.

— *Americana in Four Colors: Twenty Years of Self Regulation by the Comics Magazine Industry.* New York: Comics Magazine Association of America, 1974.

Goodgion, Laurel F. "Holy Bookshelves!: Comics in the Children's Room." *School Library Journal* 23 (January 1977): 37–9.

Gordon, Ian. *Comic Strips and Consumer Culture.* Washington, DC: Smithsonian Institute Press, 2002.

Gorgias. *Encomium of Helen. The Older Sophists.* 1972. Trans. George Kennedy. Ed. Rosamund Kent Sprague. Indianapolis, IN: Hackett Publishing, 2001: 50–4.

Gorman, Michele. *Getting Graphic!: Comics for Kids.* Santa Barbara, CA: Linworth Books, 2007.

— *Getting Graphic!: Using Graphic Novels to Promote Literacy with Preteens and Teens.* Santa Barbara, CA: Linworth Books, 2003.

— "What Teens Want: Thirty Graphic Novels You Can't Live Without." *School Library Journal* 48 (August 2002): 42–5.

Gray, Kathleen. "Chronology of a Comic Book Collection." *The U*N*A*S*H*E*D* Librarian* 15 (Spring 1975): 4.

Groensteen, Thierry. *The System of Comics.* Trans. Bart Beaty and Nick Nguyen. Jackson, MS: University of Mississippi Press, 2009.

Hajdu, David. *The Ten-Cent Plague: The Great Comic-Book Scare and How It Changed America.* New York: Farrar, Straus and Giroux, 2008.

Handa, Carolyn, ed. *Visual Rhetoric in a Digital World: A Critical Sourcebook.* New York: Bedford/St. Martin's, 2004.

Happiness and Healing for You (1955), Commercial Comics.

Harker, Jean Gray. "Youth's Librarians Can Defeat Comics." *Library Journal* 73 (December 1948): 1705–7, 1720.

Harrell, David Edwin. *Oral Roberts: An American Life.* Bloomington, IN: Indiana University Press, 1985.

Harrison, George and August M. Froehlich. "World Hero No. 1." *True Comics* #1 (April 1941), The Parents' Magazine Press: n.p.

Hartley, Al. *Archie's Clean Slate* (1973), Spire Christian Comics.

— *Archie's Love Scene* (1973), Spire Christian Comics.

— *Archie's One Way* (1973), Spire Christian Comics.

— *Come Meet My Friend!* Old Tappan, NJ: Fleming H. Revell Company, 1977.

— *The Cross and the Switchblade* (1972), Spire Christian Comics.

— "Foreword." *Proverbs and Parables.* Kevin Young, ed. Temple City, CA: New Creation Publications, 1998: VI.

— *God's Smuggler* (1972), Spire Christian Comics.

— "Nostalgia Gets Ya!" *Life with Archie* #129 (January 1973), Archie Comics: 1–20.

— "Solomon's Child." *Archie Giant Series Magazine* #205 (January 1973): n.p.

— "When You Witch Upon a Star." *Sabrina The Teen-age Witch* #7 (August 1972), Archie Comics: 1–8.

Harvey, Robert C. "Comedy at the Juncture of Word and Image." *The Language of Comics: Word and Image.* Ed. Robin Varnum and Christine T. Gibbons. Jackson, MS: University of Mississippi Press, 2002: 75–96.

Hatfield, Charles. *Alternative Comics: An Emerging Literature.* Jackson, MS: University of Mississippi Press, 2005.

— "Defining Comics in the Classroom." *Teaching the Graphic Novel.* Ed. Stephen Tabachnik. New York: Modern Language Association, 2009: 19–27.

Heaney, Mary Jane. "Graphic Novels: A Sure Bet for Your Library." *Collection Building* 26.3 (2007): 72–6.

Hecht, George. "A New and Different Comic Magazine" [column]. *True Comics* 1 (April 1941), New York: Parents' Magazine Press.

Hecht, George Joseph. *A Lifelong Commitment to Children*. New York: Parents' Magazine Press, 1975.

Heckman, Will. "Reading Heroes for a New Generation." *Florida Media Quarterly* 29.3 (Spring 2004): 3–4.

Hill, Charles A. and Marguerite Helmers, eds. *Defining Visual Rhetorics*. Mahwah, NJ: Lawrence Earlbaum Associates, 2004.

Hirsch, E. D., Joseph F. Kett, and James Trefil. *The New Dictionary of Cultural Literacy: What Every American Needs to Know*. 3rd edn. New York: Houghton Mifflin Harcourt, 2002.

Horrocks, Dylan. "Inventing Comics: Scott McCloud Defines the Form in *Understanding Comics*." *The Comics Journal* 234 (June 2001): 29–52.

Jacobs, Dale. "Marveling at *The Man Called Nova*: Comics as Sponsors of Multimodal Literacy." *College Composition and Communication* 59.2 (2007): 180–205.

Jacquet, Lloyd, ed. *New Fun* 1 (February 1935), National Allied Publications.

Jenkins, Henry. *Convergence Culture: Where Old and New Media Collide*. New York: NYU Press, 2008.

Johns, Geoff (w), Jim Lee (a), and Scott Williams (i). *Justice League* v2 1 (October 2011), DC Comics.

Johnson, Scott "New Superman Costume Revealed." *Comicbook.com*, 11 June 2011. Accessed 7 August 2012.

Jones, Gerard. *Men of Tomorrow: Geeks, Gangsters, and the Birth of the Comic Book*. New York: Basic Books, 2005.

Jones, William B. *Classics Illustrated: A Cultural History*. 2nd edn Jefferson, NC: McFarland, 2011.

Katz, Bill. "Magazines." *Library Journal* 93 (January 1968): 59.

Kist, William. *New Literacies in Action: Teaching and Learning in Multiple Media*. New York: Teachers College Press, 2005.

Kitchen, Denis. "Biro & Wood: Partners in Crime." *Blackjacked and Pistol-Whipped: A Crime Does Not Pay Primer*. Portland, OR: Dark Horse Comics, 2011.

Kostelnick, Charles and Michael Hassett. *Shaping Information: The Rhetoric of Visual Conventions*. Carbondale, IL: Southern Illinois University Press, 2003.

Kress, Gunther. "Design and Transformation: New Theories of Meaning." *Multiliteracies: Literacy Learning and the Design of Social Futures*. Ed. Bill Cope and Mary Kalantzis. New York: Routledge, 2000: 153–61.

Kunzle, David. *The Early Comic Strip*, Vol. 1. Berkeley, CA: University of California Press, 1973.

— *The Early Comic Strip*, Vol. 2. Berkeley, CA: University of California Press, 1990.

Lee, Stan. *Origins of Marvel Comics*. New York: Simon and Schuster, 1974.

Lenroot, Katherine F. "Our Children's Heritage." *Parents' Magazine* (March 1941): 15.

Lesser, Gerald. *Children and Television: Lessons from Sesame Street.* 1974. New York: Vintage Books, 1975.

Lethem, Jonathan. "The Return of the King, or, Identifying with Your Parents." *Give Our Regards to the Atomsmashers!: Writers on Comics.* Ed. Sean Howe. New York: Pantheon, 2004: 2–22.

"Libraries, to Arms!" *Wilson Library Bulletin* 15.8 (April 1941): 670–1.

Littledale, Clara Savage. "What to Do about the 'Comics'?" *Parents' Magazine* (March 1941): 26–7, 93.

Lopes, Paul. *Demanding Respect: The Evolution of the American Comic Book.* Philadelphia, PA: Temple University Press, 2009.

Lucas, Mary R. "Our Friendly Enemy?: The Library Looks at Comics." *Library Journal* 66 (October 1941): 824–7.

Mannes, Marya. "Junior Has a Craving." *The New Republic* (17 February 1947): 20–3.

Marke, David T., ed. *True Comics* 1 (April 1941), Parents' Magazine Press.

Mayo, John. "DC Comics Dominates September's Sales." *Comic Book Resources*, 11 October 2011. Accessed 7 August 2012.

Mazzucchelli, David. *Asterios Polyp.* New York: Pantheon, 2009.

McCloud, Scott. *Understanding Comics.* New York: Harper Perennial, 1994.

"Message to Our Readers: Introducing the Editorial Advisory Board" [column]. *More Fun Comics* #72 (October 1941), DC Comics: n.p.

Minick, Evelyn and Judy Kurman. "And My Branch: An Experimental Comic Book Collection." *The U*N*A*S*H*E*D* Librarian* (Winter 1976): 3.

Monnin, Katie. *Teaching Graphic Novels: Practical Strategies for the Secondary ELA Classroom.* Gainesville, FL: Maupin House, 2010.

Mooney, Maureen. "Graphic Novels: How They Can Work in Libraries." *The Book Report* 21.3 (November/December 2002): 18–19.

Moore, Harold A. and Stephen A. Douglas, eds. *Famous Funnies* #1 (July 1934), Eastern Color Printing Company.

Morrison, Grant and Rags Morales. "Inside the Action" [column]. *Action Comics* v2 #2 (December 2011), DC Comics: n.p.

— *Supergods: What Masked Vigilantes, Miraculous Mutants, and a Sun God from Smallville Can Teach Us About Being Human.* New York: Spiegel & Grau, 2011.

Morrison, Grant (w), Rags Morales (a), and Rick Bryant (i). *Action Comics* v2 #1 (November 2011), DC Comics.

Mulford, Montgomery, ed. *Picture Stories from the Bible* #1 (Fall 1942), DC Comics.

Mulford, Montgomery (w) and Don Cameron (a). "Noah and His Ark." *Picture Stories from the Bible* #1 (Fall 1942), DC Comics: n.p.

— "The Story of Moses and His Struggle for Israel." *Picture Stories from the Bible* #1 (Fall 1942), DC Comics: n.p.

Murray, Don, dir. *The Cross and the Switchblade*. Gateway Productions, 1970.

Naifeh, Ted. *Polly and the Pirates* #1 (September, 2005), Oni Press: 1–2.

New London Group. "A Pedagogy of Multiliteracies: Designing Social Futures." *Multiliteracies: Literacy Learning and the Design of Social Futures*. Ed. Bill Cope and Mary Kalantzis. New York: Routledge, 2000: 9–37.

Normanjon, Peter. "The Dark Age of Comics." *The Mammoth Book of Best Horror Comics*. Ed. Peter Normanjon. Philadelphia, PA: Running Press, 2008: 9–13.

North, Sterling. "A National Disgrace (And a Challenge to American Parents)." Reprinted in *Childhood Education* 17.1 (October 1940): 56.

— "The Antidote for Comics." *National Parent-Teacher* (March 1941): 16–17.

Norton, Bonny. "The Motivating Power of Comic Books: Insights from Archie Comic Readers." *The Reading Teacher* 57.2 (October 2003): 140–7.

Nyberg, Amy Kiste. "How Librarians Learned to Love the Graphic Novel." *Graphic Novels and Comics in Libraries and Archives: Essays on Readers, Research, History, and Cataloging*. Ed. Robert G. Weiner. Jefferson, NC: McFarland, 2010: 26–40.

— *Seal of Approval: The History of the Comics Code*. Jackson, MS: University of Mississippi Press, 1998.

"The Oral Roberts Comics." *Christian Comics International*. Comix 35, n.d. Accessed 10 August 2012.

Oral Roberts' True Stories (The Miracle Worker) #1 (1956), Oral Roberts Evangelical Association.

Oral Roberts' True Stories (Released!) #104 (1956), Oral Roberts Evangelical Association.

Plato. *Phaedrus. Plato: Complete Works*. Trans. Alexander Nehamus and Paul Woodruff. Ed. John M. Cooper. Indianapolis, IN: Hackett Publishing, 1997: 506–56.

Podrazik, Walter J. "It Was 1971." *The Best of The Electric Company* Box Set Liner Notes. Los Angeles, CA: Shout! Factory, 2006: 9–17.

Prentice, Ann E. "The Comics Scene." *Library Journal* 93 (January 1968): 59.

Prior, Paul A. and Julie A. Hengst. "Introduction: Exploring Semiotic Remediation." *Exploring Semiotic Remediation as Discourse Practice*. Ed. Paul A. Prior and Julie A. Hengst. Houndsmills, UK: Palgrave Macmillan, 2010.

Reed, Christopher. "Oral Roberts Obituary." *The Guardian*. The Guardian, 15 December 2009. Accessed 10 August 2012.

Roberts, Oral. "Christian Adventure Club." *Oral Roberts' True Stories* #1 (1956), Oral Roberts Evangelical Association: n.p.

— *Oral Roberts' True Stories (Released!)* #104 (1956), Oral Roberts Evangelical Association: n.p.

Robinson, Jerry. *The Comics: An Illustrated History of Comic Strip Art.* Portland, OR: Dark Horse Comics, 2011.

Roy, Michael. "Simón Bolivar." *True Comics* #1 (April 1941), Parents' Magazine Press: 56–4.

Sabin, Roger. *Comics, Comix, and Graphic Novels: A History of Comic Art.* London: Phaidon Press, 2001.

Satrapi, Marjane. *Persepolis.* New York: Pantheon, 2003.

Schwarz, Gretchen E. "Expanding Literacies Through Graphic Novels." *English Journal* 95.6 (July 2006): 58–64.

— "Graphic Novels for Multiple Literacies." *Journal of Adolescent and Adult Literacy* 46.3 (2002): 262–5.

Siegel, Jerry (w) and Joe Shuster (a). "Superman." *Action Comics* v1 #1 (June 1938), National Allied Publications [DC Comics]: 1–13.

Smith, Jeff. *Bone: Out from Boneville.* New York: Scholastic, 2005.

Spurgeon, Tom. "Obituary: Al Hartley, 1922–2003." *The Comics Journal* 254 (July 2003). Rpt. in *The Comics Reporter.* The Comics Reporter, 30 June 2003. Accessed 10 August 2012.

St. Lifer, Evan. "Graphic Novels, Seriously." *School Library Journal* 48 (August 2002): 9.

"Supermen of America" [column]. *Superman* v1 #12 (September–October 1941), DC Comics: n.p.Thomas, Jean (w), Bill Effros (w), Tom Whedon (w), Byron Preiss (w), Winslow Mortimer (a), and Mike Esposito (a). *Spidey Super Stories* #1 (October 1974), Marvel Comics.

True Comics. Advertisement. *Parents' Magazine* September 1941: 38.

True Comics. Advertisement. *New York Times Magazine* 14 December 1941: 32.

Tuska, George (p/i) and [Uncredited] (a)/ "The Short But Furious Crime Career of Irene Dague and Her Yes-Man Husband." *Crime Does Not Pay* #57 (November 1947), Comic House (Lev Gleason): n.p.

Tye, Larry. *Superman: The High-Flying History of America's Most Enduring Superhero.* New York: Random House, 2012.

Uslan, Michael. *The Boy Who Loved Batman.* San Francisco, CA: Chronicle Books, 2011.

Vaughn, Brian K. (w), Adrian Alphonsa (p), and Takeshi Miyazawa (i). *Runaways,* Vol. 1. 2003–2004. New York: Marvel Comics, 2005.

Versaci, Rocco. "How Comic Books Can Change the Way Our Students See Literature: One Teacher's Perspective." *The English Journal* 91.2 (November 2001): 61–7.

Volp, Frank (p) and [Uncredited] (a). "Officer Edward Maher and the Mad Dog Killers of Fifth Avenue." *Crime Does Not Pay* #22 (July 1942), Comic House (Lev Gleason): n.p.

Waugh, Coulton. *The Comics*. Oxford, MS: University Press of Mississippi, 1991.

Weiner, Stephen. *The 101 Best Graphic Novels*. Ed. Keith R. A. DeCandido. New York: NBM, 2001.

— "Beyond Superheroes: Comics Get Serious." *Library Journal* 127 (February 2002): 55–8.

Wertham, Frederic. "Reading for the Innocent." *Wilson Library Bulletin* 29 (April 1955): 610–3.

— *Seduction of the Innocent*. New York: Rinehart, 1953.

— "The Comics . . . Very Funny!" *Saturday Review of Literature* (29 May 1948): 6–7, 27–9.

Wessler, Karl (w) and Jack Kamen (a/i). "The Proposal." *Tales from the Crypt* #44 (October–November 1954), EC: n.p.

Wilkerson, David with Elizabeth Sherill, and John Sherill. *The Cross and the Switchblade*. New York: Random House, 1963.

Williams, Gweneira M., and Jane S. Wilson. "They Like it Rough: In Defense of Comics." *Library Journal* 67 (March 1942): 204–6.

Witek, Joseph. *Comic Books as History: The Narrative Art of Jack Jackson, Art Spiegelman, and Harvey Pekar*. Jackson, MS: University of Mississippi Press, 1989.

Wolfman, Marv (w), John Buscema (p), and Joe Sinnott (i). *The Man Called Nova*, Vol. 1 #1 (September 1976), Marvel Comics.

Wolfman, Marv. "Letters. We've Got Letters!" *marvwolfman.com*. Accessed 7 August, 2012.

Wright, Bradford K. *Comic Book Nation: The Transformation of Youth Culture in America*. Baltimore, MD: Johns Hopkins University Press, 2001.

— "Tales from the American Crypt: EC and the Culture of the Cold War, 1950–1954." *Inside the World of Comic Books*. Ed. J. Klaehn. Montreal, QC: Black Rose Books, 2007: 3–26.

Wright, Ethel C. "A Public Library Experiments with the Comics." *Library Journal* 68 (October 1943): 832–5.

"Zatara." *The Grand Comics Database*, n.d. Accessed August 7, 2012.

INDEX